G U I D E

Service Organizations

Applying SSAE No. 16, *Reporting on Controls at a Service Organization* (SOC 1)

MAY 1, 2011

Copyright © 2011 by
American Institute of Certified Public Accountants, Inc.
New York, NY 10036-8775

All rights reserved. For information about the procedure for requesting permission to make copies of any part of this work, please visit www.copyright.com or call (978) 750-8400.

2 3 4 5 6 7 8 9 0 AAP 1 9 8 7 6 5 4 3 2 1

ISBN 978-0-87051-971-0

Preface

Purpose and Applicability

This guide, *Service Organizations—Applying Statement on Standards for Attestation Engagements No. 16*, Reporting on Controls at a Service Organization *(SOC 1)*, provides guidance to practitioners engaged to examine and report on a service organization's controls over the services it provides to user entities when those controls are likely to be relevant to user entities' internal control over financial reporting. Statement on Standards for Attestation Engagements (SSAE) No. 16, *Reporting on Controls at a Service Organization* (AICPA, *Professional Standards*, AT sec. 801),[1] establishes the requirements and guidance for reporting on controls at a service organization relevant to user entities' internal control over financial reporting. The controls addressed in SSAE No. 16 are those that a service organization implements to prevent, or detect and correct, errors or omissions in the information it provides to user entities. A service organization's controls are relevant to a user entity's internal control over financial reporting when they are part of the user entity's information and communication system maintained by the service organization.[2] In the attestation standards, a CPA performing an attestation engagement ordinarily is referred to as a *practitioner*. In SSAE No. 16, a CPA who reports on controls at a service organization is known as a *service auditor*.

The SSAEs are also known as the attestation standards. The attestation standards enable a practitioner to report on subject matter other than financial statements. In the case of SSAE No. 16, the subject matter is the fairness of the presentation of management's description of the service organization's system, the suitability of the design of its controls relevant to user entities' internal control over financial reporting, and in a type 2 engagement, the operating effectiveness of those controls.

This guide also assists service auditors in understanding the kinds of information auditors of the financial statements of user entities (user auditors) need from a service auditor's report. Currently, AU section 324, *Service Organizations* (AICPA, *Professional Standards*), addresses the user auditor's responsibility for obtaining sufficient appropriate audit evidence in an audit of the financial statements of a user entity.

Changes From Statement on Auditing Standards No. 70

Prior to the issuance of SSAE No. 16, the requirements and guidance for both service auditors reporting on controls at a service organization and user auditors auditing the financial statements of a user entity were contained in AU section 324 (Statement on Auditing Standards [SAS] No. 70, *Service Organizations* [AICPA, *Professional Standards*]).

---

[1] Statement on Standards for Attestation Engagements No. 16, *Reporting on Controls at a Service Organization* (AICPA, *Professional Standards*, AT sec. 801), is effective for service auditor's reports for periods ending on or after June 15, 2011.

[2] Controls also may be relevant when they are part of one or more of the other components of a user entity's internal control over financial reporting. The components of an entity's internal control over financial reporting are described in detail in appendix B of Statement on Auditing Standards (SAS) No. 109, *Understanding the Entity and Its Environment and Assessing the Risks of Material Misstatement* (AICPA, *Professional Standards*, AU sec. 314).

The requirements and guidance for service auditors have been moved to SSAE No. 16, which is an attestation standard. The requirements and guidance for user auditors has been retained in AU section 324. When the new clarified SAS *Audit Considerations Relating to an Entity Using a Service Organization* becomes effective,[3] it will replace the guidance for user auditors currently located in AU section 324.

An important objective of this guide is to assist CPAs in transitioning from performing a service auditor's engagement under SAS No. 70 to doing so under SSAE No. 16. The following are some changes in the requirements for a service auditor's engagement introduced by SSAE No. 16:

- The service auditor is required to obtain a written assertion from management of the service organization about the subject matter of the engagement. For example, in a type 2 engagement, the service auditor would obtain a written assertion from management about whether, in all material respects and based on suitable criteria,

    — management's description of the service organization's system fairly presents the service organization's system that was designed and implemented throughout the specified period;

    — the controls related to the control objectives stated in management's description of the service organization's system were suitably designed throughout the specified period to achieve those control objectives; and

    — the controls related to the control objectives stated in management's description of the service organization's system were operating effectively throughout the specified period to achieve those control objectives.

- Suitable criteria are used by management to measure and present the subject matter and by the service auditor to evaluate the subject matter. Paragraphs 14–16 of SSAE No. 16 provide suitable criteria for the fairness of the presentation of a service organization's description of its system and the suitability of the design and operating effectiveness of its controls. (Criteria are the standards or benchmarks used to measure and present the subject matter and against which the service auditor evaluates the subject matter).

- The service auditor's examination report contains the report elements identified in paragraph .85 of AT section 101, *Attest Engagements* (AICPA, *Professional Standards*). Paragraphs 52–53 of SSAE No. 16 tailor these report elements to a service auditor's engagement.

- The service auditor may not use evidence obtained in prior engagements about the satisfactory operation of controls in prior periods to provide a basis for a reduction in testing in the current period, even if it is supplemented with evidence obtained during the current period.

---

[3] The new clarified SAS *Audit Considerations Relating to an Entity Using a Service Organization* is effective for audits of financial statements for periods ending on or after December 15, 2012.

- The service auditor is required to identify, in the description of tests of controls, any tests of controls performed by the internal audit function (other than those performed in a direct assistance capacity) and the service auditor's procedures with respect to that work. (Tests of controls are procedures designed to evaluate the operating effectiveness of controls in achieving the control objectives stated in management's description of the service organization's system.)
- In a type 2 report, the description of the service organization's system covers a period—the same period as the period covered by the service auditor's tests of the operating effectiveness of controls. In SAS No. 70, the description of the service organization's system in a type 2 report is as of a specified date.
- The SSAE specifically states that SSAE No. 16 is not applicable when the service auditor is reporting on controls at a service organization other than controls that are relevant to user entities' internal control over financial reporting (such as controls related to regulatory compliance or privacy).

Convergence

The AICPA's Auditing Standards Board is converging its audit, attest, and quality control standards with those of the International Auditing and Assurance Standards Board (IAASB). SSAE No. 16 is based on the IAASB's International Standard on Assurance Engagements (ISAE) 3402, *Assurance Reports on Controls at a Service Organization*. Differences between SSAE No. 16 and ISAE 3402 in objectives, definitions, or requirements are identified in exhibit B of SSAE No. 16, "Comparison of Requirements of Section 801, *Reporting On Controls at a Service Organization*, With Requirements of International Standard on Assurance Engagements 3402, *Assurance Reports on Controls at a Service Organization*." The clarified SAS *Audit Considerations Relating to an Entity Using a Service Organization* is based on the IAASB's International Standard on Auditing 402, which bears the same title as the clarified SAS.

Service Organization Controls Reports That Are Relevant to Subject Matter Other Than Internal Control Over Financial Reporting

Some service organizations provide services that are relevant to subject matter other than user entities' internal control over financial reporting, for example, controls relevant to the security of a system or to the privacy of information processed by a system for user entities. The standard for performing and reporting on such engagements is provided in AT section 101. The AICPA Guide *Reporting on Controls at a Service Organization Relevant to Security, Availability, Processing Integrity, Confidentiality, or Privacy (SOC 2)* is an interpretation of AT section 101 that assists CPAs in reporting on the security, availability, or processing integrity of a system or the confidentiality or privacy of the information processed by the system. To make practitioners aware of the various professional standards and guides available to them for examining and reporting on controls at a service organization that address various subject matter and to help practitioners select the appropriate standard or guide for a particular engagement, the AICPA has introduced the term *service organization controls (SOC) reports*. Appendix E, "Comparison of SOC 1, SOC 2, and SOC 3 Engagements and Related Reports," of this guide contains a table that identifies features of three SOC engagements and related reports, including an SSAE No. 16 engagement and report.

Authority of This Guide

This AICPA guide was prepared by the Service Organizations Guide Task Force of the AICPA's Auditing Standards Board (ASB) to assist CPAs in examining and reporting under SSAE No. 16 on a service organization's controls over the services it provides to user entities when those controls are likely to be relevant to user entities' internal control over financial reporting. The ASB has found the descriptions of attestation standards, procedures, and practices in this guide to be consistent with existing standards covered by Rule 202, *Compliance With Standards* (AICPA, *Professional Standards*, ET sec. 202 par. .01), and Rule 203, *Accounting Principles* (AICPA, *Professional Standards*, ET sec. 203 par. .01).

Attestation guidance included in an AICPA guide is an interpretive publication pursuant to AT section 50, *SSAE Hierarchy* (AICPA, *Professional Standards*). *Interpretive publications* are recommendations on the application of the SSAEs in specific circumstances, including engagements performed for entities in specialized industries. An interpretive publication is issued under the authority of the ASB after all ASB members have been provided with an opportunity to consider and comment on whether the proposed interpretive publication is consistent with the SSAEs. The members of the ASB have found this guide to be consistent with existing SSAEs.

A practitioner should be aware of and consider interpretive publications applicable to his or her examination. If a practitioner does not apply the attestation guidance included in an applicable interpretive publication, the practitioner should be prepared to explain how he or she complied with the SSAE provisions addressed by such attestation guidance.

Auditing Standards Board (2010–2011)

Darrel R. Schubert, *Chair*	Edwin G. Jolicoeur	Mark H. Taylor
Ernest F. Baugh, Jr.	David M. Morris	Kim L. Tredinnick
Brian R. Bluhm	Kenneth R. Odom	H. Steven Vogel
Robert E. Chevalier	Thomas A. Ratcliffe	Phil D. Wedemeyer
Samuel K. Cotterell	Brian R. Richson	Kurtis Wolff
James R. Dalkin	Thomas M. Stemlar	Megan F. Zietsman
David D. Duree		

Service Organizations Guide Task Force

Joseph G. Griffin, Chair	Suzanne K. Nersessian	Thomas Wallace
Robert F. Dacey	David L. Palmer	David E. Weiskittel
Susan E. Kenney	Sheryl K. Skolnik	Richard L. Wood
James R. Merrill		

AICPA Staff

Charles E. Landes
Vice President
Professional Standards

Judith Sherinsky
Senior Technical Manager
Audit and Attest Standards

TABLE OF CONTENTS

Chapter		Paragraph
1	Introduction and Background	.01-.10
	Other Types of Internal Control Engagements	.10
2	Understanding How a User Auditor Uses a Type 1 or Type 2 Report	.01-.19
	Services Provided by a Service Organization That Are Part of a User Entity's Information System	.01-.02
	Service Organization Services to Which AU Section 324 Does Not Apply	.03
	Understanding Whether Controls at a Service Organization Affect a User Entity's Internal Control	.04-.10
	Types of Service Auditor's Reports	.11-.12
	Obtaining Evidence of the Operating Effectiveness of Controls at a Service Organization	.13-.17
	Information That Assists User Auditors in Evaluating the Effect of a Service Organization on a User Entity's Internal Control	.18-.19
3	Planning a Service Auditor's Engagement	.01-.106
	Responsibilities of Management of the Service Organization	.01-.106
	Defining the Scope of the Engagement	.02
	Determining the Type of Engagement to Be Performed	.03-.06
	Determining the Period to Be Covered by the Report	.07-.08
	Determining Whether a Subservice Organization Will Be Included in the Description	.09-.25
	Selecting the Criteria for the Description of the System	.26
	Preparing the Description	.27-.53
	Specifying the Control Objectives	.54-.73
	Preparing Management's Written Assertion	.74-.92
	Assessing the Suitability of Criteria	.93-.94
	Planning to Use the Work of the Internal Audit Function	.95-.102
	Coordinating Procedures With the Internal Audit Function	.103-.106
4	Performing an Engagement Under Statement on Standards for Attestation Engagements No. 16	.01-.132
	Obtaining and Evaluating Evidence About Whether the Description of the Service Organization's System Is Fairly Presented	.01-.14
	Other Information in the Description That Is Not Covered by the Service Auditor's Report	.11-.12
	Materiality Relating to the Fair Presentation of the Description of the Service Organization's System	.13-.14

Chapter		Paragraph
4	**Performing an Engagement Under Statement on Standards for Attestation Engagements No. 16—continued**	
	Evaluating Whether Control Objectives Relate to Internal Control Over Financial Reporting	.15-.41
	Implementation of Service Organization Controls	.18-.23
	Changes to the Scope of the Engagement	.24-.27
	Complementary User Entity Controls	.28-.31
	Subservice Organizations	.32-.40
	Other Matters Relating to Fair Presentation	.41
	Obtaining and Evaluating Evidence Regarding the Suitability of the Design of Controls	.42-.63
	Obtaining and Evaluating Evidence Regarding the Operating Effectiveness of Controls in a Type 2 Engagement	.64-.65
	Determining Which Controls to Test	.66-.71
	Designing and Performing Tests of Controls	.72-.91
	Nature of Tests of Controls	.77-.82
	Timing of Tests of Controls	.83-.84
	Extent of Tests of Controls	.85-.91
	Selecting Items to Be Tested	.92-.95
	Using the Work of the Internal Audit Function	.96-.107
	Direct Assistance	.106-.107
	Evaluating the Results of Tests of Controls	.108-.113
	Documentation	.112-.113
	Extending or Modifying the Period	.114-.132
	Management's Written Representations for the Extended or Modified Period	.124
	Reports of Deficiencies	.125-.128
	Examination Quality Control	.129-.132
5	**Reporting and Completing the Engagement**	.01-.96
	Responsibilities of the Service Auditor	.01-.12
	Describing Tests of Controls and the Results of Tests	.02-.07
	Describing Tests of Controls and Results of Tests When Using the Internal Audit Function	.08-.12
	Elements of the Service Auditor's Report	.13-.67
	Information Not Covered by the Service Auditor's Report	.15-.21
	Modifications to the Service Auditor's Report	.22-.32
	Illustrative Explanatory Paragraphs: Description Is Not Fairly Presented	.33-.51
	Illustrative Explanatory Paragraphs: Controls Are Not Suitably Designed	.52-.55
	Illustrative Explanatory Paragraphs: Controls Were Not Operating Effectively	.56-.58
	Illustrative Explanatory Paragraphs: Disclaimer of Opinion	.59-.62

Chapter		Paragraph
5	Reporting and Completing the Engagement—continued	
	Illustrative Explanatory Paragraph: Management's Assertion Does Not Reflect Deviations Identified in Service Auditor's Report	.63
	Intended Users of the Report	.64-.66
	Report Date	.67
	Completing the Engagement	.68-.86
	Obtaining Written Representations	.69-.80
	Subsequent Events	.81-.86
	Service Auditor's Recommendations for Improving Controls	.87
	Management's Responsibilities During Engagement Completion	.88-.96
	Modifying Management's Written Assertion	.89-.93
	Distribution of the Report by Management	.94-.96

Appendix	
A	Statement on Standards for Attestation Engagements No. 16, *Reporting on Controls at a Service Organization*
B	Illustrative Type 2 Reports
C	Illustrative Management Representation Letters
D	Illustrative Control Objectives for Various Types of Service Organizations
E	Comparison of SOC 1, SOC 2, and SOC 3 Engagements and Related Reports
F	Other Referenced Authoritative Standards

Chapter 1

Introduction and Background

This chapter provides examples of service organizations, describes how a service organization's controls may affect a user entity's internal control over financial reporting, and identifies other engagements performed under Statements on Standards for Attestation Engagements that involve reporting on controls.

1.01 Many entities outsource aspects of their business activities to organizations that provide services ranging from performing a specific task under the direction of the entity to replacing entire business units or functions of the entity. Many of the services provided by such organizations are integral to their customers' business operations. However, not all of those services are relevant to their customers' internal control over financial reporting and, therefore, to an audit of financial statements.

1.02 Statement on Standards for Attestation Engagements (SSAE) No. 16, *Reporting on Controls at a Service Organization* (AICPA, *Professional Standards*, AT sec. 801), uses the term *service organization* to refer to an entity to which services are outsourced. SSAE No. 16 defines a *service organization* as an organization or segment of an organization that provides services to user entities that are likely to be relevant to those user entities' internal control over financial reporting. The entities that use the services of a service organization are termed *user entities*.

1.03 Services performed by service organizations and controls related to these services may affect a user entity's internal control over financial reporting. When this situation occurs, an auditor performing an audit of a user entity's financial statements (a user auditor) is required to perform risk assessment procedures to obtain an understanding of how the user entity uses the services of a service organization.

1.04 Risk assessment procedures are described in paragraph 6 of Statement on Auditing Standards (SAS) No. 109, *Understanding the Entity and Its Environment and Assessing the Risks of Material Misstatement* (AICPA, *Professional Standards*, AU sec. 314), and are designed to provide a user auditor with a basis for identifying and assessing the risks of material misstatement at the financial statement and assertion levels related to the services provided by the service organization. Paragraphs .09–.10 of AU section 324, *Service Organizations* (AICPA, *Professional Standards*), identify sources of information about the nature of the services provided by a service organization and the service organization's controls over those services. A number of sections of the SASs are referred to in SSAE No. 16 and in this guide. Familiarity with those sections is integral to understanding and implementing SSAE No. 16.

1.05 An example of the service organizations addressed by SSAE No. 16 and this guide is a health insurance company that processes medical claims for other companies that have self-insured health plans. When the medical claims processing function is outsourced, the participants in the self-insured health plan are instructed to submit their claims directly to the medical claims processor. The medical claims processor processes the claims for the self-insured health plans based on rules established by the companies with the self-insured health plans, for example, rules related to eligibility and the amount to be paid for each service. The medical claims processor provides claims data to the companies that have self-insured health plans, such as the cost of claims paid during the period under examination and the cost of claims incurred during the examination period but not recorded until after the examination period. The self-insured companies use this data to record their claims expense and the related liability. That information flows through to the self-insured company's financial statements. Controls at the claims processor will affect the quality of the data provided to the self-insured health plans. Therefore, controls at the service organization (medical claims processor) are relevant to user entities' (companies with a self-insured health plan) internal control over financial reporting.

1.06 Following are some additional examples of service organizations that perform functions that are relevant to user entities' internal control over financial reporting:

- *Trust departments of banks and insurance companies.* The trust department of a bank or an insurance company may serve as custodian of an employee benefit plan's assets, maintain records of each participant's account, allocate investment income to the participants based on a formula in the trust agreement, and make payments to the participants. If an employee benefit plan engages a service organization to perform some or all of these tasks, the services provided by the service organization generate information that is included in the plan's financial statements.

- *Custodians for investment companies.* Custodians for investment companies are responsible for the receipt, delivery, and safekeeping of an investment company's portfolio securities; the receipt and disbursement of cash resulting from transactions in these securities; and the maintenance of records of the securities held for the investment company. The custodian also may perform other services for the investment company, such as collecting dividend and interest income and distributing that income to the investment company. The custodian is a service organization to the investment company.

- *Mortgage servicers or depository institutions that service loans for others.* Investor entities may purchase mortgage loans or participation interests in such loans from thrifts, banks, or mortgage companies. These loans become assets of the investor entities, and the sellers may continue to service the loans. Mortgage servicing activities generally include collecting mortgage payments from borrowers, conducting collection and foreclosure activities, maintaining escrow accounts for the payment of property taxes and insurance, paying taxing authorities and insurance companies as payments become due, remitting monies to investors (user entities), and reporting data concerning the mortgage to user entities. The user entities may have little or no contact with the mortgage servicer other than receiving the monthly payments and reports from the mortgage servicer. The user entities record transactions related to the underlying mortgage loans based on data provided by the mortgage servicer.

- *Application service providers (ASPs).* ASPs provide packaged software applications and a technology environment that enables customers to process financial and operational transactions. An ASP

Introduction and Background 3

may specialize in providing a particular software package solution to its users, may provide services similar to traditional mainframe data center service bureaus, may perform business processes for user entities that they traditionally had performed themselves, or may provide some combination of these services. As such, an ASP may be a service organization if it provides services that are part of the user entity's information system.

- *Internet service providers (ISPs) and Web hosting service providers.* ISPs enable user entities to connect to the Internet. Web hosting service providers generally develop, maintain, and operate websites for user entities. The services provided by such entities may be part of a user entity's information system if the user entity is using the Internet or a website to process transactions. If so, the user entity's information system may be affected by certain controls maintained by the ISP or Web hosting service provider, such as controls over the completeness and accuracy of the recording of transactions and controls over access to the system. For example, if a user entity takes orders and accepts payments through a website, certain controls maintained by the Web hosting service provider, such as controls over security access and controls that address the completeness and accuracy of the recording of transactions, may affect the user's information system.

- *Regional transmission organizations (RTOs).* These are entities in the electric utility industry (also referred to as independent system operators) that are responsible for the operation of a centrally dispatched electric system or wholesale electric market. They also are responsible for initiating, recording, billing, settling, and reporting transactions, as well as collecting and remitting cash from participants based on the transmission tariff or other governing rules. These services may be part of a participant's information system therefore making the RTO a service organization.

1.07 Some service organizations provide services and implement controls that are relevant to subject matter other than user entities' internal control over financial reporting, for example, controls at a service organization relevant to the privacy of user entities' information or to user entities' compliance with the requirements of laws or regulations. SSAE No. 16 and this guide do not apply to engagements to report on such controls. Management of a service organization may wish to engage a practitioner to report on such controls under other AICPA professional standards such as the following:

- AT section 101, *Attest Engagements* (AICPA, *Professional Standards*), which provides a framework for reporting on subject matter other than financial statements. The AICPA Audit Guide *Reporting on Controls at a Service Organization Relevant to Security, Availability, Processing Integrity, Confidentiality, or Privacy (SOC 2)* is an application of AT section 101 and is intended to assist practitioners in reporting on the security, availability, or processing integrity of a system or the confidentiality or privacy of the information processed.

- AT section 601, *Compliance Attestation* (AICPA, *Professional Standards*).

AAG-ASO 1.07

Paragraph 1.10 of this guide contains a table that provides examples of engagements to report on controls other than those relevant to user entities' internal control over financial reporting and the professional standard or interpretive guidance that addresses or provides a framework for the engagement.

1.08 As stated in the preface of this guide, prior to the issuance of SSAE No. 16, the applicable requirements and guidance for both service auditors reporting on controls at a service organization and user auditors auditing the financial statements of a user entity were contained in AU section 324. Paragraph .03 of that section indicates that AU section 324 does not apply

- when the services performed by the service organization are limited to processing an entity's transactions that are specifically authorized by the entity, such as the processing of checking account transactions by a bank or the processing of securities transactions by a broker in situations in which the user entity retains responsibility for authorizing the transactions and maintaining the related accountability, or
- to an audit of the financial statements of an entity that holds a proprietary financial interest in another entity, such as a partnership, corporation, or joint venture, if the partnership, corporation, or joint venture performs no processing on behalf of the entity.

1.09 In addition to controls that affect user entity's internal control over financial reporting, a service organization implements controls that are relevant to its own internal control over financial reporting, not to the services it provides to user entities. This guide focuses only on those controls at service organizations that are likely to be relevant to user entities' internal control over financial reporting, whether or not they may be relevant to the service organization's own financial reporting objectives.

Other Types of Internal Control Engagements

1.10 Many attest engagements that involve reporting on controls or internal control are not performed under SSAE No. 16. The following table is intended to assist practitioners in determining the appropriate attestation standard or interpretive guidance to be used when reporting on controls in a variety of circumstances.

Engagement	Professional Standard or Other Guidance	Restrictions on the Use of the Report
Reporting on Controls at a Service Organization Relevant to User Entities' Internal Control Over Financial Reporting: Controls Were Not Designed by the Service Organization		

Introduction and Background

Engagement	Professional Standard or Other Guidance	Restrictions on the Use of the Report
Management of the Service Organization Will Not Provide an Assertion Regarding the Suitability of the Design of the Controls		
Reporting on • the fairness of the presentation of management's description of the service organization's system and	Report on the fairness of the presentation of the description under AT section 101, *Attest Engagements* (AICPA, *Professional Standards*), using the description criteria in paragraph 14 of Statement on Standards for Attestation Engagements (SSAE) No. 16, *Reporting on Controls at a Service Organization* (AICPA, *Professional Standards*), and adapting the relevant requirements and guidance therein	Management of the service organization, user entities, and the auditors of the user entities' financial statements.
• the operating effectiveness of the service organization's controls relevant to user entities internal control over financial reporting. Such a report may include a description of tests of the operating effectiveness of the controls and the results of the tests.	Report on the operating effectiveness of controls under AT section 101 or AT section 201, *Agreed-Upon Procedures Engagements* (AICPA, *Professional Standards*)	The specified parties that agreed upon the sufficiency of the procedures for their purposes

(continued)

AAG-ASO 1.10

Service Organizations: Applying SSAE No. 16 (SOC 1)

Engagement	Professional Standard or Other Guidance	Restrictions on the Use of the Report
Reporting on Controls at a Service Organization Relevant to User Entities' Internal Control Over Financial Reporting: Controls Were Not Designed by the Service Organization Management of the Service Organization Provides an Assertion Regarding the Suitability of Design of Controls	SSAE No. 16	Management of the service organization, user entities, and the auditors of the user entities' financial statements
Reporting on Controls at a Service Organization Relevant to Security Availability, Processing Integrity, Confidentiality, or Privacy—Includes Description of Tests and Results		
Reporting on the fairness of the presentation of management's description of a service organization's system; the suitability of the design of controls at a service organization relevant to security, availability, processing integrity, confidentiality, or privacy; and in a type 2 report, the operating effectiveness of those controls A type 2 report includes a description of tests of the operating effectiveness of controls performed by the service	AT section 101 AICPA Guide *Reporting on Controls at a Service Organization Relevant to Security, Availability, Processing Integrity, Confidentiality, or Privacy (SOC 2)*	Parties that are knowledgeable about • the nature of the service provided by the service organization. • how the service organization's system interacts with user entities, subservice organizations, and other parties. • internal control and its limitations. • the criteria and how controls address those criteria.

AAG-ASO 1.10

Introduction and Background

Engagement	Professional Standard or Other Guidance	Restrictions on the Use of the Report
auditor and the results of those tests.		• complementary user entity controls and how they interact with related controls at the service organization.
Reporting on Controls at a Service Organization Relevant to Security Availability, Processing Integrity, Confidentiality, or Privacy—No Description of Tests and Results		
Reporting on whether an entity has maintained effective controls over its system with respect to security, availability, processing integrity, confidentiality, or privacy If the report addresses the privacy principle, the report also contains an opinion on the service organization's compliance with the commitments in its privacy notice. This report does not contain a description of the service auditor's tests performed and the results of those tests.	AT section 101 AICPA/CICA Trust Services Principles, Criteria, and Illustrations (TSP section 100, "Trust Services Principles, Criteria, and Illustrations for Security, Availability, Processing Integrity, Confidentiality, and Privacy" [AICPA, *Technical Practice Aids*])	This is a general-use report.[1]

(continued)

---

[1] The term *general use* refers to reports for which use is not restricted to specified parties.

AAG-ASO 1.10

Engagement	Professional Standard or Other Guidance	Restrictions on the Use of the Report
Reporting on a Service Provider's Controls to Achieve Compliance Control Objectives Relevant to SEC Rules 38a-1 and 206(4)-7		
Reporting on the suitability of the design and operating effectiveness of a service provider's controls over compliance that may affect user entities' compliance This report does not contain a description of the practitioner's tests performed and the results of those tests.	AT section 101 Statement of Position (SOP) 07-2, *Attestation Engagements That Address Specified Compliance Control Objectives and Related Controls at Entities that Provide Services to Investment Companies, Investment Advisers, or Other Service Providers* (AICPA, *Technical Practice Aids*, AUD sec. 14,430)	Chief compliance officers, management, boards of directors, and independent auditors of the service provider and of the entities that use the services of the service provider
Performing the Agreed-Upon Procedures Referred to in Paragraph 3 of SSAE No. 16		
Performing and reporting on the results of agreed-upon procedures related to the controls of a service organization or to transactions or balances of a user entity maintained by a service organization This report contains a description of the procedures performed by the practitioner and the results of those procedures.	AT section 201	The specified parties that agreed upon the sufficiency of the procedures for their purposes

AAG-ASO 1.10

Engagement	Professional Standard or Other Guidance	Restrictions on the Use of the Report
Reporting on Controls Over Compliance With Laws and Regulations		
Reporting on the effectiveness of an entity's internal control over compliance with the requirements of specified laws, regulations, rules, contracts, or grants	AT section 601, *Compliance Attestation* (AICPA, *Professional Standards*)	Use is restricted if the criteria are • appropriate for only a limited number of parties who established the criteria or can be presumed to understand the criteria. • available only to specified parties.
Reporting on Internal Control in an Integrated Audit		
Reporting on the design and operating effectiveness of an entity's internal control over financial reporting that is integrated with an audit of financial statements	AT section 501, *An Examination of an Entity's Internal Control Over Financial Reporting That Is Integrated With an Audit of Its Financial Statements* (AICPA, *Professional Standards*)	This is a general-use report.

AAG-ASO 1.10

Chapter 2

Understanding How a User Auditor Uses a Type 1 or Type 2 Report

This chapter is intended to provide service auditors with an understanding of how a user auditor uses a type 1 or type 2 report in auditing the financial statements of a user entity. Knowing how a user auditor uses such reports helps the service auditor in evaluating management's description of the service organization's system and in determining whether the service organization's control objectives are reasonable in the circumstances. In addition, this chapter may be useful to user auditors in understanding how to use a given type 1 or type 2 report in an audit of a user entity's financial statements.[1]

Services Provided by a Service Organization That Are Part of a User Entity's Information System

2.01 Paragraph .03 of AU section 324, *Service Organizations* (AICPA, *Professional Standards*), indicates that the guidance for user auditors in AU section 324 is applicable to the audit of a user entity's[2] financial statements if the services provided by the service organization are part of the user entity's information system. A service organization's services are part of a user entity's information system if these services affect any of the following:[3]

a. The classes of transactions in the user entity's operations that are significant to the user entity's financial statements

b. The procedures, both automated and manual, by which the user entity's transactions are initiated, authorized, recorded, processed (including transactions being corrected as necessary and transferred to the general ledger), and reported in the financial statements

c. The related accounting records, whether electronic or manual, supporting information, and specific accounts in the user entity's financial statements involved in initiating, authorizing, recording, processing, and reporting the user entity's transactions

d. How the user entity's information system captures other events and conditions that are significant to the financial statements

---

[1] The clarified Statement on Auditing Standards (SAS) *Audit Considerations Relating to an Entity Using a Service Organization*, which addresses the user auditor's responsibilities when a user entity uses one or more service organizations that affect the user entity's internal control over financial reporting, has been approved and is effective for audits of financial statements for periods ending on or after December 15, 2012. This chapter refers to the requirements in AU section 324, *Service Organizations* (AICPA, *Professional Standards*), which were in effect for user auditors at the time this guide was published.

[2] AU section 324 uses the term *user organization* when referring to a customer of a service organization; whereas, Statement on Standards for Attestation Engagements No. 16, *Reporting on Controls at a Service Organization* (AICPA, *Professional Standards*, AT sec. 801), uses the term *user entity*. These terms are interchangeable; for simplicity the term *user entity* is used throughout this guide.

[3] In the clarified SAS *Audit Considerations Relating to an Entity Using a Service Organization*, a service organization's services are also part of a user entity's information system if these services affect controls related to journal entries, including nonstandard journal entries used to record nonrecurring, unusual transactions or adjustments.

AAG-ASO 2.01

e. The financial reporting process used to prepare the user entity's financial statements, including significant accounting estimates and disclosures

2.02 Other controls at the service organization may be relevant to the audit, such as controls over the safeguarding of assets. However, services that do not affect the items described in paragraph 2.01 are not part of a user entity's information system and service providers that provide such services would not be considered service organizations for the purpose of Statement on Standards for Attestation Engagements (SSAE) No. 16, *Reporting on Controls at a Service Organization* (AICPA, *Professional Standards*, AT sec. 801).

Service Organization Services to Which AU Section 324 Does Not Apply

2.03 As stated in the preface of this guide, prior to the issuance of SSAE No. 16, the applicable requirements and guidance for both service auditors reporting on controls at a service organization and user auditors auditing the financial statements of a user entity were contained in AU section 324. Paragraph .03 of that section indicates that AU section 324 does not apply to

- services provided by a service organization that are limited to executing client organization transactions that are specifically authorized by the client, such as the processing of checking account transactions by a bank or the execution of securities trades by a broker (for example, when the user entity retains responsibility for authorizing the transactions and maintaining the related accountability), or
- the audit of transactions arising from financial interests in partnerships, corporations, or joint ventures when proprietary interests are accounted for and reported to interest holders (for example, when the partnership, corporation, or joint venture performs no processing on behalf of the user entity).

Understanding Whether Controls at a Service Organization Affect a User Entity's Internal Control

2.04 Paragraph .06 of AU section 324 indicates that when a user entity uses a service organization, transactions that affect the user entity are subjected to controls that are, at least in part, physically and operationally separate from the user entity. Paragraph .07 of AU section 324 indicates that the user auditor may need to understand controls at the service organization to understand each of the five components of the user entity's internal control, which consist of the control environment, risk assessment process, information and communication systems (including the related business processes), control activities, and monitoring controls.

2.05 Paragraph 40 of Statement on Auditing Standards (SAS) No. 109, *Understanding the Entity and Its Environment and Assessing the Risks of Material Misstatement* (AICPA, *Professional Standards*, AU sec. 314), states that in an audit, the auditor should obtain an understanding of each of the five components of the entity's internal control sufficient to assess the risks of material misstatements, whether due to error or fraud, and to design the

Understanding How a User Auditor Uses a Type 1 or Type 2 Report

nature, timing, and extent of further audit procedures.[4] This understanding may encompass controls placed in operation by the entity as well as controls placed in operation by service organizations whose services are part of the user entity's information system. It also states that the auditor's understanding should be sufficient to evaluate the design of controls relevant to an audit of financial statements and to determine whether they have been implemented.

2.06 Paragraph .06 of AU section 324 indicates that the significance of controls at a service organization to those of the user entities depends on the nature of the services provided by the service organization, primarily the nature and materiality of the transactions it processes for the user entities and the degree of interaction between its activities and those of the user entity.

2.07 Interaction between a service organization and a user entity relates to the extent to which a user entity is able to monitor the activities of the service organization and implement controls over those activities. For example, when a user entity initiates transactions and the service organization executes, processes, and records those transactions, a high degree of interaction exists between the activities at the user entity and those at the service organization. In these circumstances, the user entity could implement effective controls over those transactions. To elaborate further, an entity that uses a payroll processing service organization could implement its own controls over those transactions, for example, by recalculating a sample of payroll amounts. In contrast, when a service organization initiates, executes, and does the processing and recording of the user entity's transactions, a lower degree of interaction exists, and it may not be practicable for the user entity to implement effective controls for those transactions. If the user auditor determines that the service organization's controls are significant, the user auditor should gain a sufficient understanding of those controls to assess the risks of material misstatement.

2.08 Paragraph .09 of AU section 324 identifies sources of information for obtaining an understanding of the services provided by a service organization, and the service organization's controls over those services, such as user manuals, system overviews, technical manuals, the contract between the user entity and the service organization, and reports by service auditors, internal auditors, or regulatory authorities on the service organization's controls. Understanding the objectives of user auditors and the procedures they perform helps management of the service organization to anticipate the information and assurance needs of user auditors.

2.09 Paragraphs .11–.16 of AU section 324 describe how the user auditor assesses control risk at the user entity. If the user auditor determines that appropriate controls implemented at the user entity are designed to prevent,

---

[4] The clarified SAS *Audit Considerations Relating to an Entity Using a Service Organization* requires the auditor to obtain an understanding of how the user entity uses the services of a service organization in the user entity's operations, including the
    a. nature of the services provided by the service organization and the significance of those services to the user entity, including their effect on the user entity's internal control;
    b. nature and materiality of the transactions processed or accounts or financial reporting processes affected by the service organization;
    c. degree of interaction between the activities of the service organization and those of the user entity; and
    d. nature of the relationship between the user entity and the service organization, including the relevant contractual terms for the activities undertaken by the service organization.

or detect and correct, material misstatements in the user entity's financial statements, the user auditor's risk assessment may include an expectation of the operating effectiveness of user entity controls for particular assertions affected by the service organization, without identifying and testing controls at the service organization. In these situations, the user auditor is not likely to ask the service organization for a service auditor's report or other information.

2.10 On the other hand, obtaining an understanding of controls implemented at the service organization, either by themselves or in concert with controls at the user entity, may be necessary to assess the risk of material misstatement for relevant financial statement assertions affected by those controls. In these situations, the user auditor generally will ask the service organization, through the user entity, for a service auditor's report on controls at the service organization.

Types of Service Auditor's Reports

2.11 Paragraph 7 of SSAE No. 16 defines the two following types of reports:

- *Report on management's description of a service organization's system and the suitability of design of controls* (a type 1 report), which encompasses management's description of the service organization's system, management's written assertion, and the service auditor's report[5] in which the service auditor expresses an opinion on the fairness of the presentation of management's description of the service organization's system and the suitability of the design of the controls to achieve the related control objectives included in the description as of a specified date. (Control objectives are the aim or purpose of specified controls at the service organization and address the risks that controls are intended to mitigate.)

- *Report on management's description of a service organization's system and the suitability of the design and operating effectiveness of controls* (a type 2 report), which includes management's description of the service organization's system, management's written assertion, and the service auditor's report in which the service auditor expresses an opinion on the fairness of the presentation of management's description of the service organization's system and the suitability of the design and operating effectiveness of the controls to achieve the related control objectives included in the description throughout a specified period.

2.12 If the user auditor concludes that information is not available to obtain a sufficient understanding to assess the risks of material misstatement of the user entity's financial statements (the service organization does not provide a type 1 or type 2 report or the available report does not meet the user auditor's needs), the user auditor will need to do the following:

- Contact the service organization, through the user entity, to obtain specific information

---

[5] The term *service auditor's report* in this guide means the service auditor's letter in which he or she expresses an opinion on management's description of the service organization's system, the suitability of the design of the controls included in the description, and in a type 2 report, the operating effectiveness of the controls.

Understanding How a User Auditor Uses a Type 1 or Type 2 Report

- Request that a service auditor be engaged to perform procedures that will supply the necessary information
- Visit the service organization and perform such procedures

Generally a service organization will want to minimize the number of user auditors or other auditors performing their own tests of controls at the service organization. However, this may be a practical option if the service organization has few user entities or conducts a number of specific procedures and controls for each user entity.

Obtaining Evidence of the Operating Effectiveness of Controls at a Service Organization

2.13 The user auditor may determine that it is necessary to test controls at the service organization, either because the auditor's risk assessment includes an expectation of the operating effectiveness of such controls at the service organization or because substantive procedures alone do not provide sufficient appropriate audit evidence. In these circumstances, the user auditor generally will ask the service organization, through the user entity, for a type 2 report that provides audit evidence to support the user auditor's risk assessment. Because a type 1 report does not include tests of the operating effectiveness of controls, a type 1 report would not meet the user auditor's needs. In practice, most user auditors will need evidence of the operating effectiveness of controls at the service organization. Accordingly, to minimize the number of visits by user auditors, especially if the service organization has a large number of user entities, a service organization would provide a type 2 report.

2.14 The user auditor evaluates whether the period covered by a given type 2 report is appropriate for the user auditor's purposes. To provide evidence in support of the user auditor's risk assessment, the period covered by the type 2 report would need to overlap (typically at least six months) the user entity's audit period.

2.15 In evaluating the appropriateness of the period covered by of the tests of controls, the user auditor keeps in mind that the shorter the period covered by a specific test and the longer the time elapsed since the performance of the test, the less evidence the test may provide. For example, a report on a six-month testing period that covers only one or two months of the user entity's financial reporting period offers less support than a report in which the testing covers six months of the user entity's financial reporting period. If the service auditor's testing period is completely outside the user entity's financial reporting period, the user auditor is unable to rely on such tests to conclude that the user entity's controls are operating effectively because the tests do not provide current audit period evidence of the effectiveness of the controls, unless other procedures are performed such as those described in paragraphs .40–.45 of AU section 318, *Performing Audit Procedures in Response to Assessed Risks and Evaluating the Audit Evidence Obtained* (AICPA, *Professional Standards*). Considering this, the service organization may choose to provide type 2 reports with sufficient frequency and covering sufficient periods to meet user auditor needs.

2.16 The service organization may consider the following examples when determining an appropriate test period for a type 2 report.

- *Example 1.* The majority of user entities have calendar year ends. The service organization may want to provide a type 2 report for the period November 1, 20X0, to October 31, 20X1, to maximize the usefulness of the report to user entities and their auditors.

- *Example 2.* User entities have year ends that span all months of the year. The service organization determines that issuing a report each quarter (or more often than annually) with tests of operating effectiveness that cover twelve months is most likely to maximize the usefulness of the report to user entities and their auditors.

2.17 If there have been significant changes to the system or controls during the period covered by the service auditor's report, the service organization's description would be expected to include relevant details of changes to the service organization's system before and after the change, and in the case of a type 2 report, the service auditor's description of tests of controls and results would describe tests of the controls and results of the tests for the period before the change and for the period after the change.

Information That Assists User Auditors in Evaluating the Effect of a Service Organization on a User Entity's Internal Control

2.18 In performing a service auditor's engagement, a service auditor should consider that the following additional information may assist user auditors in evaluating the effect of the service organization on the user entities' internal control:

- Information about controls at user entities that management of the service organization assumes, in the design of the service provided by the service organization, will be implemented by user entities (complementary user entity controls). If such controls are necessary to achieve the control objectives stated in management's description of the service organization's system, they should be identified as such in the description. The user auditor determines whether complementary user entity controls identified by the service organization are relevant and whether the user entity has designed and implemented such controls. Providing a long list of general complementary user entity controls is likely to be less helpful to user auditors than providing specific complementary user entity controls that relate to the services provided by the service organization.

- The cause of deviations[6] underlying modifications to the service auditor's report, if known

- Situations at the service organization that may constitute significant deficiencies or material weaknesses[7] for user entities

---

[6] In this guide, the term *exceptions* is used interchangeably with the term *deviations*.

[7] Significant deficiencies and material weaknesses are control deficiencies that come to the auditor's attention during a financial statement audit and must be communicated to management and those charged with governance in accordance with paragraph .20 of AU section 325, *Communicating*

(*continued*)

- Incidents of noncompliance with laws and regulations, fraud, or uncorrected errors attributable to management or other service organization personnel that are not clearly trivial and that may affect one or more user entities. If the service auditor becomes aware of such incidents, the service auditor should determine their effect on management's description of the service organization's system, the achievement of the control objectives, and the service auditor's report. Additionally, the service auditor should determine whether this information has been communicated appropriately to affected user entities. If the information has not been so communicated and management of the service organization is unwilling to do so, the service auditor should take appropriate action which may include

    — obtaining legal advice about the consequences of different courses of action;

    — communicating with those charged with governance of the service organization;

    — disclaiming an opinion, modifying the service auditor's opinion, or adding an emphasis paragraph;

    — communicating with third parties, for example, a regulator, when required to do so; or

    — withdrawing from the engagement.

2.19 If a user auditor is unable to obtain sufficient appropriate evidence to achieve the audit objectives, the user auditor should qualify the opinion or disclaim an opinion on the financial statements because of a scope limitation.

(footnote continued)

Internal Control Related Matters Identified in an Audit (AICPA, *Professional Standards*). Paragraph .05 of AU section 325 states that a *control deficiency* exists when the design or operation of a control does not allow management or employees, in the normal course of performing their assigned functions, to prevent or detect misstatements on a timely basis. Paragraph .07 of AU section 325 defines a *significant deficiency* as a deficiency, or combination of deficiencies, in internal control, that is less severe than a material weakness, yet important enough to merit attention by those charged with governance. A *material weakness* is a deficiency or combination of deficiencies, in internal control, such that there is a reasonable possibility that a material misstatement of the entity's financial statements will not be prevented or detected and corrected on a timely basis. The user auditor considers the guidance in AU section 325.

Chapter 3

Planning a Service Auditor's Engagement

This chapter identifies the responsibilities of management of the service organization and the service auditor and the matters to be considered and procedures to be performed in planning a service auditor's engagement. It also identifies the required elements of management's description of a service organization's system and written assertion.

Responsibilities of Management of the Service Organization

3.01 During planning, management of the service organization is responsible for

- defining the scope of the service auditor's engagement;
- determining the type of engagement to be performed (a type 1 or type 2 engagement);
- determining the period to be covered by the report or, in the case of a type 1 report, the specified "as of" date of the report;
- determining whether any subservice organizations will be included in or carved out of the description;
- selecting the criteria to be used;
- preparing the description of the service organization's system;
- specifying the control objectives;
- identifying the risks that threaten the achievement of the control objectives; and
- preparing management's written assertion.

Defining the Scope of the Engagement

3.02 In defining the scope of a service auditor's engagement, management of the service organization considers which services, business units, functional areas, or applications are likely to be relevant to its user entities' internal control over financial reporting. Management also considers whether the service organization has any contractual obligations to provide a service auditor's report to one or more of its user entities, including the frequency with which the report is to be issued and the period that will be covered by the report. In the case of a recurring or existing engagement, the prior report provides a useful starting point for defining the scope of the engagement.

Determining the Type of Engagement to Be Performed

3.03 Management of a service organization is responsible for determining whether the service auditor will perform a type 1 or type 2 engagement and the period to be covered by the report (or in the case of a type 1 report, the specified as of date). To provide a report that is likely to be useful to user entities and their auditors, management of the service organization may find the guidance for user auditors in AU section 324, *Service Organizations* (AICPA, *Professional Standards*), helpful. Chapter 2, "Understanding How a User Auditor Uses a

AAG-ASO 3.03

Type 1 or Type 2 Report," of this guide presents information to assist service auditors in understanding how a user auditor uses a type 1 or type 2 report in auditing the financial statements of a user entity.

3.04 Because user auditors may need evidence of the operating effectiveness of controls at a service organization, the service organization generally will choose to provide a type 2 report rather than a type 1 report. If a type 2 report is not available, user auditors may need to obtain evidence about the operating effectiveness of controls by visiting the service organization and performing tests there or requesting that another practitioner perform such tests. When a service auditor's report is not available, a greater likelihood exists that user auditors will visit the service organization to perform their own tests or will request that another practitioner perform such tests, increasing the level of disruption at the service organization.

3.05 Typically, a type 1 engagement may be appropriate in either of the following instances:

- User entities are able to exercise effective user entity controls over the functions performed by the service organization.
- The service organization is issuing a report on controls at the service organization for the first time.

Focus on Type 2 Reports

3.06 A type 1 engagement enables the service organization to provide user auditors with a report on the fairness of the presentation of the description of the service organization's system and the suitability of the design of controls. Such a report is designed to meet the user auditor's needs for planning an audit of the user entity's financial statements. However a type 1 report does not provide any assurance that the control objectives stated in management's description of the service organization's system were achieved because the service auditor's objective in a type 1 engagement does not include obtaining evidence about the operating effectiveness of controls. The discussion in this guide focuses on type 2 reports, given their predominance in practice. However, except for performing and reporting on tests of the operating effectiveness of controls, the information in this guide may be useful in performing and reporting on a type 1 engagement.

Determining the Period to Be Covered by the Report

3.07 Paragraph A42 of Statement on Standards for Attestation Engagements (SSAE) No. 16, *Reporting on Controls at a Service Organization* (AICPA, *Professional Standards*, AT sec. 801), states that a type 2 report that covers a period of less than six months is unlikely to be useful to user entities and their auditors. However, certain circumstances, such as the following, may prevent a service organization from providing a description of its system, or a service auditor from providing a type 2 report, that covers a period of at least six months:

- The service auditor is engaged close to the date by which the report is needed and evidence of the operating effectiveness of controls cannot be obtained retroactively.
- For example, testing the control requires that the service auditor observe the control being performed.

Planning a Service Auditor's Engagement

- The service organization's system or controls have been in operation for less than six months.
- Significant changes have been made to the controls and it is not practical to (a) wait six months to issue a report or (b) issue a report that covers the system before and after the changes.
- The service organization is issuing a report on controls at the service organization for the first time.
- A new or modified law or regulation has an effective date that results in a report that covers a period of less than six months in the first year of the law or regulation's enactment.

3.08 To increase the likelihood that the service auditor will provide a report that is useful to user entities and their auditors, if circumstances permit, management of the service organization may wish to discuss with user entities the scope of the engagement, including the type of engagement to be performed, and the period, business units, functional areas, business processes, classes of transactions, or applications to be covered by the service auditor's report.

Determining Whether a Subservice Organization Will Be Included in the Description

3.09 Paragraph 7 of SSAE No. 16 defines a *subservice organization* as a service organization used by another service organization to perform some of the services provided to user entities that are likely to be relevant to those user entities' internal control over financial reporting. An example of a subservice organization is a company that records transactions and maintains the related accountability for customers (user entities) of a broker dealer (service organization), including preparing monthly statements for the customers.

3.10 Subservice organizations may be separate entities from the service organization or may be entities related to the service organization, for example, a subservice organization that is a subsidiary of the same company that owns the service organization.

3.11 During planning, management of the service organization determines whether it uses any subservice organizations, as that term is defined in paragraph 7 of SSAE No. 16. For the purpose of applying SSAE No. 16, the service organization does not need to further consider any service organizations it uses that do not meet the definition of a subservice organization.

3.12 A service organization that uses a subservice organization may use the *carve-out method* or the *inclusive method* to present information about the services provided by the subservice organization in its description of the service organization's system. SSAE No. 16 contains the following definitions of the terms *carve-out method* and *inclusive method*:

Carve-out method. Method of addressing the services provided by a subservice organization whereby management's description of the service organization's system identifies the nature of the services performed by the subservice organization and excludes from the description and from the scope of the service auditor's engagement, the subservice organization's relevant control objectives and related controls. Management's description of the service organization's system and the scope of the service auditor's engagement include controls at the service organization that monitor the effectiveness of controls at the subservice organization, which may include

AAG-ASO 3.12

review by management of the service organization of a service auditor's report on controls at the subservice organization.

Inclusive method. Method of addressing the services provided by a subservice organization whereby management's description of the service organization's system includes a description of the nature of the services provided by the subservice organization as well as the subservice organization's relevant control objectives and related controls.

3.13 The term *controls at a subservice organization* is defined in paragraph 7 of SSAE No. 16 as the policies and procedures at a subservice organization likely to be relevant to internal control over financial reporting of user entities of the service organization. These policies and procedures are designed, implemented, and documented by the subservice organization to provide reasonable assurance about the achievement of control objectives that are relevant to the services covered by the service auditor's report.

3.14 Paragraph A9 of SSAE No. 16 indicates that instances may exist in which the service organization's controls, such as its monitoring controls, enable the service organization to include in its assertion the relevant aspects of the subservice organization's system, including relevant control objectives and related controls at the subservice organization. In such instances, the service organization bases its assertion solely on controls at the service organization; hence, neither the inclusive method nor the carve-out method is applicable. The following are three examples of situations in which a service organization uses the services of another service organization and is determining whether to treat that service organization as a subservice organization

Example 1. A bank trust department uses three pricing vendors to determine the price of listed securities included in statements prepared for user entities. The bank trust department uses a program to compare the prices provided by each pricing vendor, and it generates a report that identifies outliers, which are reviewed. A manager reviews that report on a daily basis and investigates outliers. Although the functions performed by the pricing vendors may affect the user entities' internal control over financial reporting, the bank trust department has implemented controls over that function to identify prices that may be incorrect. In this situation, the bank trust department will not employ the carve-out method or the inclusive method of presentation for the pricing service vendors.

Example 2. XYZ Service Organization operates its savings application at a data processing service organization. Although XYZ Service Organization implements certain controls over the functions performed by the data processing service organization, XYZ Service Organization relies on certain controls at the data processing service organization, specifically, the general computer controls. The data processing service organization meets the definition of a subservice organization provided in paragraph 7 of SSAE No. 16, and the service organization would determine whether to use the carve-out or inclusive method of presentation.

Example 3. A bank trust department uses ABC Investment Advisers to provide investment recommendations to its user entities and DEF Broker Dealer to execute, record, and process investment transactions for user entities. The functions performed by the bank trust

Planning a Service Auditor's Engagement

department are limited to establishing and maintaining account relationships with the user entities. The functions performed by the bank trust department alone may not likely be relevant to user entities' internal control over financial reporting. However, the functions performed by ABC Investment Advisers and DEF Broker Dealers are highly likely to be relevant to user entities' internal control over financial reporting. Either a service auditor's report on the controls at ABC Investment Advisers and DEF Broker Dealer or a service auditor's report on the bank trust department using the inclusive method for ABC Investment Advisers and DEF Broker Dealer would be useful to user entities.

3.15 Although the inclusive method provides more information for user auditors than the carve-out method does, it may not be appropriate or feasible in all circumstances. Factors that are relevant in determining which approach to use include (1) the nature and extent of the information about the subservice organization that user auditors may need and (2) the challenges entailed in implementing the inclusive method, which are described in paragraphs 3.20 and 3.22 of this guide.

3.16 SSAE No. 16 does not provide for the option of having a service auditor make reference to or rely on a service auditor's report on a subservice organization as the basis, even in part, for the service auditor's opinion.

3.17 A description prepared using the carve-out method generally is most useful in the following circumstances:

- The services provided by the subservice organization are not extensive.

- A type 1 or type 2 report that meets the needs of user entities and their auditors is available from the subservice organization.[1]

3.18 If the service organization is using the carve-out method and obtains a type 1 or type 2 report on the subservice organization that identifies the need for complementary user entity controls, management of the service organization, during planning, considers how to address that information in its description of the service organization's system. For example, a service organization that outsources aspects of its technology infrastructure to a subservice organization finds that the subservice organization's description of its systems includes the following complementary user entity control:

> User entities should have controls in place to provide reasonable assurance that access to system resources and applications is restricted to appropriate user entity personnel.

To address the complementary user entity control included in the subservice organization's description, the service organization would include a control

---

[1] Paragraph A64 of Statement on Standards for Attestation Engagements (SSAE) No. 16, *Reporting on Controls at a Service Organization* (AICPA, *Professional Standards*, AT sec. 801), indicates that a user entity is also considered a user entity of the service organization's subservice organizations if controls at subservice organizations are relevant to internal control over financial reporting of the user entity. In that case, the user entity is referred to as an indirect or downstream user entity of the subservice organization. Consequently, an indirect or downstream user entity may be included in the group to whom use of the service auditor's report is restricted if controls at the service organization are relevant to internal control over financial reporting of the indirect or downstream user entity.

AAG-ASO 3.18

objective, such as the following, in its description of the service organization's system:

> Controls provide reasonable assurance that access to system resources and applications is restricted to appropriate service organization personnel.

3.19 An inclusive report generally is most useful in the following circumstances:

- The services provided by the subservice organization are extensive.
- A type 1 or type 2 report that meets the needs of user entities and their auditors is not available from the subservice organization.
- Information from other sources is not readily available.

3.20 The inclusive method is frequently difficult to implement and, for a number of reasons, may not be feasible in certain circumstances. The approach entails extensive planning and communication between the service auditor, the service organization, and the subservice organization. Both the service organization and the subservice organization need to agree on the inclusive approach before it is adopted. The service auditor needs to be independent of both the service organization and the subservice organization in an inclusive method engagement, because the service auditor's report covers both entities.

3.21 As indicated in paragraph A7 of SSAE No. 16, when the inclusive method is used, both the service organization and the subservice organization acknowledge and accept responsibility for the matters described in paragraph 9(c) of SSAE No. 16, which includes providing a written assertion. The service organization generally coordinates the use of the inclusive method with the subservice organization.

3.22 If the inclusive method is used, the following are other matters that would need to be agreed upon or coordinated, preferably in advance, by all of the parties involved:

- The scope of the examination and the period to be covered by the report
- Acknowledgement from management of the subservice organization that it will provide the service auditor with a written assertion and representation letter (Both management of the service organization and management of the subservice organization are responsible for providing the service auditor with a written assertion and a representation letter.)
- The planned content and format of the inclusive description
- The representatives of the subservice organization and the service organization who will be responsible for
    — providing the initial draft of each entity's description
    — integrating the two descriptions
- For a type 2 report, the timing of the tests of controls
- Other logistic and administrative matters, such as

- providing the service auditor with access to the subservice organization's premises, personnel, and documents and records
- agreeing on how periodic communications and status updates will be provided to the parties involved

3.23 As indicated in paragraph 3.21 of this guide, management of the subservice organization is required to provide a written assertion if the service organization uses the inclusive method of presentation. This assertion ordinarily would be expected to address all three elements (that is, fairness of presentation, suitability of the design of controls, and operating effectiveness of controls). However, in some circumstances the achievement of a control objective may be dependent on a combination of the service organization's controls and the subservice organization's controls. In such circumstances, if the service organization designed the controls for the subservice organization, it may be possible when using the inclusive method, for the service organization to take responsibility for the fair presentation of the description and for the suitability of the design of its own controls and the subservice organization's controls. If the service organization includes an assertion about the fair presentation of the description and suitability of the design of the subservice organization's controls in its assertion, the subservice organization's assertion may be limited to the operating effectiveness of its controls.

3.24 The inclusive method is facilitated if the service organization and the subservice organization are related parties or if the contract between the service organization and the subservice organization provides for inclusive descriptions and reports by the service auditor.

3.25 Using the inclusive method becomes more complex when the service organization uses multiple subservice organizations. When the services of more than one subservice organization are likely to be relevant to user entities' internal control over financial reporting, management of the service organization may use the inclusive method for one or more subservice organizations and the carve-out method for other subservice organizations. In these instances, management's description needs to clearly communicate which subservice organizations and related functions are included in the description and which are carved out.

Selecting the Criteria for the Description of the System

3.26 Management of the service organization is responsible for preparing the description of the service organization's system, including the completeness, accuracy, and method of presentation of the description. During planning, management of the service organization is responsible for selecting the criteria to be used in preparing the description of the service organization's system. Minimum criteria for the description are specified in paragraph 14 of SSAE No. 16. When the inclusive method is used, these requirements also apply to the subservice organization.

Preparing the Description

3.27 The description of the service organization's system is intended to provide user auditors and user entities with information about the service organization's system that may be relevant to the user entities internal control over financial reporting. Aspects of a service organization's system are considered

AAG-ASO 3.27

relevant to user entities' internal control over financial reporting if they affect any of the items discussed in paragraphs 2.01–.02 of this guide.

3.28 Management is responsible for determining how the description of the service organization's system will be documented. Paragraph A16 of SSAE No. 16 indicates that no one particular form of documenting the service organization's system is prescribed and that the extent of the documentation may vary depending on the size and complexity of the service organization and its monitoring activities. The description of the service organization's system is intended to

- provide sufficient information for user auditors to understand how the service organization's processing (or the function the service organization performs) affects user entities' financial statements and
- enable user auditors to assess the risks of material misstatements in the user entities' financial statements.

3.29 Management is also responsible for the completeness and accuracy of the description. A complete and accurate description does not omit or distort information relevant to the service organization's system, understanding that management's description of the service organization's system is prepared to meet the common needs of a broad range of user entities and their user auditors, and may not, therefore, include every aspect of the service organization's system that each individual user entity and its user auditor may consider important in its own particular environment.

3.30 Paragraph A32 of SSAE No. 16 states, in part, that the description need not address every aspect of the service organization's processing or the services provided to user entities. Certain aspects of the processing or of the services provided may not be relevant to user entities' internal control over financial reporting or may be beyond the scope of the engagement. For example, a service organization that provides five different applications to user entities may engage a service auditor to report on only three of those applications. Similarly, a trust department that has separate organizational units providing personal trust services and institutional trust services may engage a service auditor to report on only the institutional trust services. In these situations, the service organization's description would address only the controls pertaining to those applications or organizational units included in the scope of the engagement.

3.31 The degree of detail included in the description generally is equivalent to the degree of detail a user auditor would need if the user entity were performing the outsourced service itself. However, the description need not be so detailed that it would allow a reader to compromise the service organization's security or other controls. The description may be presented using various formats such as narratives, flowcharts, tables, or graphics, or a combination thereof.

3.32 The service auditor or another party may assist management of the service organization in preparing the description of the service organization's system. However, the representations in the description of the service organization's system are the responsibility of management of the service organization. Management of the service organization acknowledges its responsibility (typically in its assertion), and the service auditor needs to maintain his or her

AAG-ASO 3.28

independence from the service organization to meet the fourth general standard of AT section 101, *Attest Engagements* (AICPA, *Professional Standards*), which states, "The practitioner must maintain independence in mental attitude in all matters relating to the engagement."

Content of the Description

3.33 Paragraph 14 of SSAE No. 16 instructs the service auditor to determine whether the criteria used by management to prepare its description include the matters listed in paragraph 14. All of the criteria in paragraph 14 are to be used for all descriptions, unless specified criteria are not applicable. Additional criteria may be needed, for example, to meet a regulatory requirement. Paragraphs 3.27–.71 of this guide provide additional clarification of the requirements in paragraph 14 of SSAE No. 16.

3.34 Paragraph 14(*a*)(i) of SSAE No. 16 requires the description to include the types of services provided, including, as appropriate, the classes of transactions processed. The description need not necessarily describe every individual transaction type, but rather those classes of transactions that are relevant to user entities' financial statements.

3.35 Identifying the business units, functional areas, business processes, and applications covered by the description clarifies what is covered by the description.

3.36 Paragraph 14(*a*)(ii) of SSAE No. 16 requires that the description include the procedures, within both manual and automated systems, by which services are provided, including procedures by which transactions are initiated, authorized, recorded, processed, corrected as necessary, and transferred to the reports and other information prepared for user entities. The description need not necessarily include every step in the processing of the transactions.

3.37 Deficiencies in certain general computer controls can affect both the proper operation of programmed procedures as well as the effectiveness of certain manual controls. If such deficiencies exist, the service organization would ordinarily identify those deficiencies in the description as well as their effect on key programmed procedures and manual controls performed by service organization personnel or manual controls that user entities would be expected to perform (complementary user entity controls).

3.38 Paragraph 14(*a*)(iii)–(v) of SSAE No. 16 requires that the description of the service organization's system include the following:

- The related accounting records, whether electronic or manual, and supporting information involved in initiating, authorizing, recording, processing, and reporting transactions, including the correction of incorrect information and how information is transferred to the reports and other information prepared for user entities
- How the system captures and addresses significant events and conditions other than transactions (Such events and conditions may include how changes to standing data, such as rates, are applied, or how changes to programmed calculations or other programmed procedures are applied.)
- The process used to prepare reports and other information for user entities

AAG-ASO 3.38

3.39 A description of a service organization's controls should include information about the frequency with which a control is performed or the timing of its occurrence, the person or parties responsible for performing the control, the activity being performed, and the source of the information to which the control is applied. The following control description is an example that includes all of these elements:

> The Cash Reconciliation Group (*responsible party*) reconciles (*activity performed*) money movement reflected in the ABC application output report (*source of the information*) to the fund's custodian bank report (*source of the information*) monthly (*frequency*).

Complementary User Entity Controls

3.40 Paragraph 14(*a*)(vi) of SSAE No. 16 requires that the description include the specified control objectives and controls designed to achieve the control objectives, including, as applicable, complementary user entity controls contemplated in the design of the service organization's controls. A service organization may design its service with the assumption that certain controls will be implemented by the user entities. If such complementary user entity controls are necessary to achieve certain control objectives, the description of the service organization's system should describe the user entities' responsibilities for implementing those complementary user entity controls. To be meaningful to user entities and their auditors, complementary user entity controls should be specific to the services provided. Providing a long list of generic "good practice" controls generally is not helpful to user entities and their auditors.

3.41 Some examples of typical complementary user entity controls are controls at user entities over

- logical access to the service organization's application by user entity personnel.
- the completeness and accuracy of input submitted to the service organization.
- the completeness, accuracy, and authorization of output received by the user entity, for example, reconciling input reports to output reports.

Other Aspects of the Service Organization's Internal Control Components

3.42 Paragraph 14(*a*)(vii) of SSAE No. 16 requires the service organization to include in the description any other aspects of the service organization's internal control components (control environment, risk assessment process, information and communication systems [including the related business processes], control activities, and monitoring controls) that are relevant to the services provided.

3.43 Aspects of a service organization's control environment, risk assessment process, information and communication systems, and monitoring components of internal control may affect the achievement of specific control objectives. If these aspects of the entity's internal control relate to the achievement of a specific control objective, they generally would be included in the description of the controls designed to achieve that control objective. A service organization may decide to present these components of its internal control as separate control objectives. A service organization may decide to present these components of its internal control as separate control objectives. However, doing so would require management to include in its description all the controls that address the particular control objective. For a pervasive control component, such as the control environment, the list of controls would be too granular to be useful to users of the report.

3.44 The following is a brief description of the components of a service organization's internal control, other than its control activities, that may be relevant to user entities' internal control over financial reporting and necessary for the achievement of specified control objectives.

- *Control environment.* The control environment sets the tone of an organization, influencing the control consciousness of its people. It is the foundation for all the other components of internal control, providing discipline and structure. Aspects of a service organization's control environment may affect the services provided to user entities. For example, management's hiring and training practices generally would be considered an aspect of the control environment that may affect the services provided to user entities because those practices affect the ability of service organization personnel to provide services to user entities. Paragraph .69 of AU section 314, *Understanding the Entity and Its Environment and Assessing the Risks of Material Misstatement* (AICPA, *Professional Standards*), provides the following examples of control environment factors:

    — Communication and enforcement of integrity and ethical values

    — Commitment to competence

    — Participation of those charged with governance

    — Management's philosophy and operating style

    — Organizational structure

    — Assignment of authority and responsibility

    — Human resource policies and practices

- *Risk assessment.* Aspects of a service organization's risk assessment process may affect the services provided to user entities. How management of a service organization addresses identified risks could affect its own financial reporting process as well as the financial reporting process of user entities. The following is a list of risk assessment factors and examples of how they might relate to a service organization:

    — *Changes in the operating environment.* If a service organization provides services to user entities in a regulated industry, a change in regulations may necessitate a revision to existing processing. Revisions to existing processing may create the need for additional or revised controls.

    — *New personnel.* New personnel who are responsible for executing manual controls that affect user entities may increase the risk that controls will not operate effectively.

AAG-ASO 3.44

- *New or revamped information systems.* A service organization may incorporate new functions into its system that could affect user entities.
- *Rapid growth.* If a service organization gains a substantial number of new customers, the operating effectiveness of certain controls could be affected.
- *New technology.* A service organization may implement a client–server version of its software that was previously run on a mainframe. Although the new software may perform similar functions, it may operate so differently that it affects user entities.
- *New business models, products, or activities.* The diversion of resources to new activities from existing activities could affect certain controls at a service organization.
- *Corporate restructurings.* A change in ownership or internal reorganization could affect reporting responsibilities or the resources available for services to user entities.
- *Expanded foreign operations.* A service organization that uses personnel in foreign locations to maintain programs used by domestic user entities may have difficulty responding to changes in user requirements.
- *New accounting pronouncements.* The implementation of relevant accounting pronouncements in a service organization's software and controls could affect user entities.

- *Information and Communication.* Activities of a service organization that may represent a user entity's information and communication component of internal control include the following:
  - The information system relevant to financial reporting objectives, consisting of the procedures whether automated or manual, and records established by the service organization to initiate, authorize, record, process and report a user entity's transactions (as well as events and conditions) and maintain accountability for the related assets, liabilities, and equity
  - Communication, which involves how the entity communicates financial reporting roles and responsibilities and significant matters relating to financial reporting, including communications between management and those charged with governance and external communications, such as those with regulatory authorities. This may include the extent to which service organization personnel understand how their activities relate to the work of others (including user entities) and the means for reporting exceptions to an appropriate higher level within the service organization and to user entities.

- *Monitoring.* Many aspects of monitoring may be relevant to the services provided to user entities. For example, a service organization may employ internal auditors or other personnel to evaluate the effectiveness of controls over time, either by ongoing activities, periodic evaluations, or various combinations of the two. The service organization's monitoring of the subservice organization's activities that affect user entities' internal control over financial reporting is another example of monitoring. This form of monitoring may be accomplished through visits to the subservice organization or, alternatively, by obtaining and reading a type 1 or type 2 report on the subservice organization. Monitoring external communications, such as customer complaints and communications from regulators, generally would be relevant to the services provided to user entities. Often times, these monitoring activities are included as control activities for achieving a specific control objective.

Changes to the System

3.45 Paragraph 14(*b*) of SSAE No. 16 requires that the description in a type 2 engagement include relevant details of changes to the service organization's system during the period covered by the description. Changes would be included in the description if they are likely to be relevant to a user entity's internal control over financial reporting, for example, the implementation of a new application during the period covered by the report to replace an existing application.

Content of the Description When the Service Organization Uses a Subservice Organization

3.46 In evaluating whether the description of the service organization's system is fairly presented, paragraph 19 of SSAE No. 16 requires the service auditor to evaluate whether services performed by a subservice organization, if any, are adequately described. In making this evaluation, the service auditor determines whether the description identifies the nature of the services performed by the subservice organization, including whether the carve-out or inclusive method of presentation is used. The service auditor also determines whether the description provides sufficient detail to enable user entities and their auditors to understand the significance and relevance of the subservice organization's services to user entities' internal control over financial reporting. When the carve-out method is used, disclosure of the identity of the subservice organization is not required. However, typically that information would be needed by user auditors in order to obtain information and perform procedures related to the subservice organization.

3.47 The purpose of the description of the services provided by the subservice organization is to

- alert user entities and their auditors to the fact that another entity (the subservice organization) is involved in the processing of the user entities' transactions and that such services may affect the user entities' internal control over financial reporting and

- identify the services the subservice organization provides.

3.48 The description of the services provided by a subservice organization should be sufficiently specific to enable user entities and their auditors to assess whether the services provided by a subservice organization are relevant and significant to their internal control over financial reporting. The following are some examples of such descriptions and how they can be revised to make them more useful.

Scenario 1. Trust Group Service Organization uses XYZ Pricing Subservice Organization to obtain market values for all exchange traded securities. The description of the service organization's system states:

> Trust Group uses XYZ Pricing Subservice Organization to obtain market values of securities.

Because the description does not identify which securities the subservice organization prices, user entities and their auditors may be unable to determine the significance of the service provided by the subservice organization. A better description would be:

> Trust Group uses XYZ Pricing Subservice Organization to obtain market values for all exchange traded securities.

Scenario 2. Trust Group Service Organization hosts its Trust System at Computer Outsourcing Subservice Organization, which provides the computer processing infrastructure. The description of the service organization's system states:

> Trust Group Service Organization outsources aspects of its computer processing to Computer Outsourcing Subservice Organization.

This description is not specific enough to enable user entities and their auditors to determine the significance of the services provided by the subservice organization. The following is a more detailed description that provides the necessary information:

> Trust Group Service Organization hosts its Trust System at Computer Outsourcing Subservice Organization. Trust Group maintains responsibility for application changes and user access, and Computer Outsourcing Subservice Organization provides the computer processing infrastructure and changes thereto.

3.49 If the inclusive method is used, the description includes the nature of the services provided by the subservice organization and the relevant control objectives and related controls performed by the subservice organization. Relevant controls at the subservice organization may also include aspects of the subservice organization's control environment, risk assessment, monitoring controls, and information and communication. The description would present the controls at the subservice organization separately from the controls at the service organization. No prescribed format exists for differentiating between controls at the service organization and controls at the subservice organization.

3.50 If the carve-out method is used, the description should include the nature of the services performed by the subservice organization, but it would not describe the detailed processing or controls at the subservice organization. The description of the service organization's system carves out those control objectives for which related controls operate only or primarily at the subservice organization. However, the description would contain sufficient information concerning the carved-out services to enable the user auditor to understand what additional information the service auditor needs to obtain from the subservice organization to assess the risk of material misstatement of the user entity's financial statements.

3.51 Management's description of the service organization's system when using the carve-out or the inclusive method generally includes controls at the service organization designed to monitor services provided by the subservice organization, such as testing by service organization internal auditors of controls at the subservice organization, reviewing output reports from the subservice organization, holding periodic discussions with management of the subservice organization, visiting the subservice organization and performing procedures there, and obtaining and reading a type 1 or type 2 report on the subservice organization, as well as other reports. Management's description of the service organization's system would include a clear delineation of the design of such controls and the persons responsible for performing them.

3.52 Certain control objectives of the service organization may only be achieved if controls are implemented and operating effectively at the subservice organization. When this is the case and the carve-out method is used, management of the service organization would modify the description of the service organization's system and its written assertion to indicate that the achievement of those control objectives depends on whether controls at the subservice organization anticipated in the design of the service organization's system were implemented and operating effectively. Paragraph 5.55 of this guide provides an example of how the scope paragraph and opinion paragraph of a type 2 service auditor's report would be modified if the description refers to the need for controls at the subservice organization.

3.53 A service organization may obtain a copy of a type 1 or type 2 report from the subservice organization, if one is available. If the subservice organization's type 1 or type 2 report identifies the need for complementary user entity controls at the service organization, the service organization's description would describe the processes and controls the service organization has implemented to address the complementary user entity controls identified in the subservice organization's description of its system. The service organization may include in its description of the system factual information included in the subservice organization's type 1 or type 2 report. Such information may include whether the report is a type 1 or type 2 report, the period covered by the report, and the services covered by the report. In example 3 of appendix B, "Illustrative Service Auditor's Reports," the service organization includes that information in the description of its system, identifies the subservice organization's complementary user entity control, and describes the control objective and related controls the service organization implemented to address the subservice organization's requirement for a complementary user entity control.

Specifying the Control Objectives

3.54 Paragraph 14(*a*)(vi) of SSAE No. 16 requires that the description of the service organization's system include the specified control objectives and controls designed to achieve those objectives, including as applicable, complementary user entity controls contemplated in the design of the service organization's controls. Control objectives assist the user auditor in determining how the service organization's controls affect the user entity's financial statement assertions. In determining the control objectives to be included in the description, management of the service organization selects control objectives that relate to the types of assertions commonly embodied in the broad range of user entities' financial statements.

AAG-ASO 3.54

3.55 To evaluate whether the control objectives relate to the types of assertions commonly embodied in the broad range of user entities' financial statements, the service auditor obtains an understanding of the services provided by the service organization in combination with a high-level understanding of the components of the financial statements of user entities.

3.56 For example, consider a service organization that provides investment advisory and processing services to mutual funds. The service auditor could obtain and review a set of mutual fund financial statements and the contract between a mutual fund and the service organization to understand the processing performed by the service organization. In evaluating whether the control objectives relate to the assertions in the user entities' financial statements, the service auditor compares the control objectives included in the description of the system to the assertions embedded in the financial statements of the mutual fund user entity.

3.57 The following is an example of a description of the services that an illustrative service organization provides to its customers, followed by examples of control objectives specified by the service organization and the types of assertions in the user entities' financial statements to which they relate:

> *Example*: Example Trust Organization provides fiduciary services to institutional, corporate, and personal trust customers. Example Trust Organization has engaged a service auditor to report on a description of its system related to the processing of transactions for user entities of the institutional trust division. Example Trust Organization has discretionary authority over investment activities, maintains the detailed records of investment transactions, and it records investment income and expense. Reports are provided to user entities for use in preparing their financial statements. The service organization has specified control objectives that it believes relate to assertions in the user entities' financial statements and that are consistent with its contractual obligations. Table 3-1, "Examples of Assertions in User Entities' Financial Statements and Related Service Organization Control Objectives," identifies some of the control objectives specified by the service organization and the types of assertions in the user entities' financial statements to which they relate.

Table 3-1

Examples of Assertions in User Entities' Financial Statements and Related Service Organization Control Objectives

Assertions in User Entities' Financial Statements	*Control Objectives of the Service Organization Controls provide reasonable assurance that—*
Completeness	Investment purchases and sales are recorded completely, accurately, and on a timely basis.
Valuation or allocation	Investment income is recorded accurately and timely.
Rights and obligations	The entity's records accurately reflect securities held by third parties, for example, depositories or subcustodians.

Planning a Service Auditor's Engagement

3.58 In evaluating whether a service organization's control objectives address the common financial statement assertions in user entities' financial statements, the service auditor may refer to appendix D, "Illustrative Control Objectives for Various Types of Service Organizations," in this guide and other sources, such as AICPA Audit and Accounting Guides, for specialized industries, industry audit guides, and industry standards.

3.59 Paragraph 19(a) of SSAE No. 16 requires the service auditor to determine whether the control objectives stated in management's description of the service organization's system are reasonable in the circumstances. Paragraph 2 of SSAE No. 16 states that the focus of SSAE No. 16 is on controls that are likely to be relevant to user entities' internal control over financial reporting. Accordingly, control objectives that are reasonable in the circumstances should relate to controls that are likely to be relevant to user entities' internal control over financial reporting.

3.60 Paragraph A34 of SSAE No. 16 discusses several points that the service auditor may consider in determining whether the service organization's control objectives are reasonable in the circumstances, including whether the control objectives

- have been specified by the service organization or by outside parties, such as regulatory authorities, a user group, a professional body, or others.

- relate to the types of assertions commonly embodied in the broad range of user entities' financial statements to which controls at the service organization could reasonably be expected to relate (for example, assertions about existence and accuracy that are affected by controls that prevent, or detect and correct, unauthorized access to the system). Although the service auditor ordinarily will not be able to determine how controls at a service organization specifically relate to the assertions embodied in individual user entities' financial statements, the service auditor's understanding of the nature of the service organization's system, including controls, and the services being provided to user entities is used to identify the types of assertions to which those controls are likely to relate.

- are complete. Although a complete set of control objectives can provide a broad range of user auditors with a framework to assess the effect of controls at the service organization on assertions commonly embodied in user entities' financial statements, the service auditor ordinarily will not be able to determine how controls at a service organization specifically relate to the assertions embodied in individual user entities' financial statements and cannot, therefore, determine whether control objectives are complete from the viewpoint of individual user entities or user auditors.

3.61 Appendix B in this guide contains illustrative type 2 reports. The report in example 1 of appendix B is for a service organization that provides computer services primarily to user entities in the financial services industry. Its application software enables user entities to process savings, mortgage loan, consumer loan, commercial loan, and general ledger transactions. The following are illustrations of how the service auditor evaluates the completeness of the control objectives for the service organization described in example 1 of appendix B:

- *Example 1.* Example Service Organization has provided its user entities with a type 2 report that addresses the savings application and the related underlying general computer controls, but the report does not address any of the other applications provided by Example Service Organization. In evaluating whether the control objectives are complete, the service auditor determines that most user entities only use the savings application. As such, the report contains a complete set of control objectives for user entities that use only the savings application.

- *Example 2.* Example Service Organization includes only control objectives related to the savings application and excludes control objectives and controls that address the underlying general computer controls. These control objectives should be included because of their relevance to user entities' internal control over financial reporting. The service auditor would conclude that the control objectives are not complete because general computer controls and the related control objectives are critical to the achievement of the savings application control objectives and would be relevant to user entities that use the savings application. (See paragraph 5.36 for an illustrative explanatory paragraph that would be added to the service auditor's report when the description omits control objectives and related controls required for other controls to be suitably designed and operating effectively.)

- *Example 3.* If control objective 10 stated "Controls provide reasonable assurance that savings and withdrawal transactions received from user entities are recorded completely and accurately" and did not address timeliness in another control objective, the service auditor would conclude that the control objectives were incomplete because the timeliness with which transactions are recorded would be likely to be relevant to user entities' internal control over financial reporting. (See paragraph 5.46 for an illustrative explanatory paragraph that would be added to the service auditor's report when the service organization's description of its system includes an incomplete control objective.)

3.62 Paragraph A34 of SSAE No. 16 points out that ultimately the user entity and the user auditor are responsible for determining whether the control objectives are complete from the perspective of the individual user entities and user auditors.

3.63 Another important attribute of a service organization's control objectives is that they be objectively stated so that individuals having competence in and using the same or similar measurement criteria arrive at similar conclusions about whether the controls are suitably designed and operating effectively to achieve the related control objectives. For example, the following control objective would be too subjective for appropriate evaluation:

> Controls provide reasonable assurance that physical access to computer equipment, storage media, and program documentation is adequate.

This objective could be reworded as follows to meet the objectivity attribute of suitable criteria:

> Controls provide reasonable assurance that physical access to computer equipment, storage media, and program documentation is limited to authorized personnel.

Another example of a control objective that is not sufficiently objective is the following:

> Controls provide reasonable assurance that logical security policies and procedures adhere to management's intentions.

User entities would have no way of knowing what management's intentions are, and the service auditor would have no basis for determining whether the control objective had been achieved. The service auditor would conclude that this control objective is worded in a manner that would not enable user entities, user auditors, or the service auditor to arrive at reasonably similar conclusions about the achievement of the control objective and would ask the service organization to modify the wording of the control objective. Paragraph 5.43 of this guide presents an illustrative explanatory paragraph that would be added to the service auditor's report when the description includes a control objective that is not objectively stated.

Control Objectives Specified by Law, Regulation, or an Outside Party

3.64 Although control objectives usually are specified by the service organization, they may be specified by law or regulation or by an outside party, such as a user entity or a user group. If the control objectives are specified by the service organization, the service auditor considers whether they are reasonable in the circumstances. If the control objectives are specified by an outside party, the outside party is responsible for their completeness and reasonableness.

3.65 Although the service auditor's responsibility is more limited when the control objectives are specified by an outside party, the service auditor will still need to exercise professional judgment in evaluating the control objectives. For example, if an outside party specifies control objectives that only address application controls when the proper functioning of general computer controls is necessary for the application controls to operate effectively, the service organization would be expected to include the relevant general computer controls in its description of the system as they relate to the specified control objectives. Paragraph 5.45 of this guide presents an example of an explanatory paragraph that would be added to the service auditor's report when the set of control objectives established by an outside party omits control objectives that the service auditor believes are necessary for the specified control objectives to be achieved.

Control Objectives When Using the Carve-Out Method

3.66 When using the carve-out method, management of the service organization would carve out those control objectives for which related controls operate only or mostly at the subservice organization. For example, a service organization that maintains responsibility for restricting logical access to its system to properly authorized individuals may adopt the carve-out method for a computer processing subservice organization that hosts the user entity's applications and computers. In this situation, the service organization would include a control objective that addresses restricting logical access to the system to properly authorized individuals, but it would not include a control objective related to physical security. To provide useful information to users of a type 1 or type 2 report, the service organization may wish to identify in its description the control objectives related to the service performed by the service organization for which the carved-out subservice organization is responsible.

3.67 When using the carve-out method, instances may exist in which the achievement of one or more control objectives is dependent upon one or more controls at the subservice organization. In such a situation, management's description of the service organization's system would identify the controls performed at the subservice organization and indicate that the related control objectives would be achieved only if the subservice organization's controls were suitably designed and operating effectively throughout the period. The service organization may wish to include a table in its description that identifies those instances in which control objectives are met solely by the service organization and those in which controls at the service organization and at the subservice organization are needed to meet the control objective.

3.68 Alternatively, the service organization may be able to exclude from the descriptions the elements of the control objectives that are achieved through controls at a subservice organization and include in the description only those elements of the control objectives that are achieved by controls at the service organization. In this circumstance, the description would include the nature of the services provided by the subservice organization and exclude from the description and from the scope of the service auditor's engagement, the subservice organization's relevant control objectives, and related controls. If a type 2 report on the subservice organization's controls exists, the user entity may obtain a copy of the service auditor's report as an indirect or downstream user as outlined in paragraph A64 of SSAE No. 16.

3.69 As indicated in paragraph A1 of SSAE No. 16, controls related to a service organization's operations and compliance objectives may be relevant to a user entity's internal control over financial reporting. Such controls may pertain to assertions about presentation and disclosure relating to account balances, classes of transactions or disclosures, or may pertain to evidence that the user auditor evaluates or uses in applying auditing procedures. For example, a payroll processing service organization's controls related to the timely remittance of payroll deductions to government authorities may be relevant to a user entity because late remittances could incur interest and penalties that would result in a liability for the user entity. Similarly, a service organization's controls over the acceptability of investment transactions from a regulatory perspective may be considered relevant to a user entity's presentation and disclosure of transactions and account balances in its financial statements.

Control Objectives Not Relevant to User Entities' Internal Control

3.70 If the service organization wishes to include control objectives in the description that are not relevant to user entities' internal control over financial reporting, such as control objectives that address the privacy or confidentiality of information processed by a system, the availability or security of a system, the service organization's compliance with specified requirements of laws or regulations, or the efficiency of the service organization's operations, the service auditor should ask the service organization to remove these control objectives from the description and may suggest that management of the service organization engage a practitioner to separately report on those control objectives under AT section 101.

Planning a Service Auditor's Engagement

3.71 Alternatively, control objectives that are not likely to be relevant to user entities' internal control over financial reporting may be included in a separate section of the description that is not covered by the service auditor's report such as a section entitled "Other Information Provided by the Service Organization." An example of such a control objective is one that addresses the service organization's business continuity and contingency planning. Such information generally is of interest to management of the user entities. However, because plans are not controls, a service organization would not ordinarily include in its description a unique control objective that addresses the adequacy of business continuity or contingency planning. Including such information in a separate section of the description provides the means for service organization management to communicate its plans related to business continuity and contingency planning. Reporting guidance for such situations is presented in paragraph 5.41 of this guide.

Identifying Risks That Threaten the Achievement of the Control Objectives

3.72 Control objectives relate to the risks that controls are intended to mitigate. Paragraph 15(a) of SSAE No. 16 indicates that one of the criteria for evaluating whether controls included in management's description of the service organization's system are suitably designed is whether management has identified the risks that threaten the achievement of those control objectives. For example, the risk that a transaction is recorded at the wrong amount or in the wrong period can be expressed in the following control objective:

> Controls provide reasonable assurance that contribution and withdrawal transactions received from user entities are initially recorded completely and accurately.

3.73 Paragraph A18 of SSAE No. 16 discusses various approaches that management of the service organization may employ to identify relevant risks. Management may have a formal or informal process for identifying relevant risks that threaten the achievement of the control objectives. A formal process may include estimating the significance of identified risks, assessing the likelihood of their occurrence, and developing action plans to address them. Because the control objectives relate to the risks that controls seek to mitigate, careful consideration by management of the service organization when designing, implementing, and documenting the service organization's system may represent an informal but effective process for identifying the relevant risks.

Preparing Management's Written Assertion

3.74 Paragraph 9(c)(vii) of SSAE No. 16 indicates that in order for a service auditor to accept or continue an engagement to report on controls at a service organization, management of the service organization must agree to provide the service auditor with a written assertion,[2] and must actually provide such an assertion, to be included in, or attached to, management's description of the service organization's system. If management's assertion is included in the description it should be clearly segregated from the description, for example, through the use of headings, because it is not a part of the description and the service auditor is not reporting on management's assertion. Exhibit A of SSAE

---

[2] SSAE No. 16 does not require that management's assertion be signed.

No. 16 includes illustrative management assertions for a type 1 and type 2 report.

3.75 Management's assertion would be expected to disclose any deviations in the subject matter (that is, the fairness of the presentation of the description, the suitability of the design of the controls, and the operating effectiveness of the controls). During the planning phase of the engagement, the service auditor determines whether management's proposed assertion is appropriate and informs management that the assertion may need to be revised to reflect deviations in the subject matter. Paragraph 5.63 of this guide provides reporting guidance for situations in which management is unwilling to revise its assertion to reflect the deviations in the subject matter identified in the service auditor's report.

3.76 Paragraph 9(c)(ii) of SSAE No. 16 states that a service auditor should accept or continue an engagement only if, among other things, management of the service organization has a reasonable basis for its written assertion. The work performed by the service auditor as part of a type 1 or type 2 engagement would not be considered a basis for management's assertion because the service auditor is not part of the service organization's internal control. SSAE No. 16 does not include requirements for the auditor to perform procedures to determine if management has a reasonable basis for its assertion. However, paragraph A17 of SSAE No. 16 states:

> **A17.** Management's monitoring activities may provide evidence of the design and operating effectiveness of controls in support of management's assertion. Monitoring of controls is a process to assess the effectiveness of internal control performance over time. It involves assessing the effectiveness of controls on a timely basis, identifying and reporting deficiencies to appropriate individuals within the service organization, and taking necessary corrective actions. Management accomplishes monitoring of controls through ongoing activities, separate evaluations, or a combination of the two. Ongoing monitoring activities are often built into the normal recurring activities of an entity and include regular management and supervisory activities. Internal auditors or personnel performing similar functions may contribute to the monitoring of a service organization's activities. Monitoring activities may also include using information communicated by external parties, such as customer complaints and regulator comments, which may indicate problems or highlight areas in need of improvement. The greater the degree and effectiveness of ongoing monitoring, the less need for separate evaluations. Usually, some combination of ongoing monitoring and separate evaluations will ensure that internal control maintains its effectiveness over time. The service auditor's report on controls is not a substitute for the service organization's own processes to provide a reasonable basis for its assertion.

3.77 Monitoring activities need not be separate activities specifically performed by management of the service organization in preparation for the service auditor's engagement.

3.78 When a subservice organization is used, management of the service organization modifies its assertion depending on whether the carve-out or inclusive method is used. The following is an example of the modifications that would be made to the illustrative assertion by management of the service organization shown in example 1 of exhibit A, "Illustrative Assertions by

Planning a Service Auditor's Engagement

Management of a Service Organization," of SSAE No. 16, when the carve-out method is used. New language is shown in boldface italics.

    a. the description fairly presents the [*type or name of*] system made available to user entities of the system during some or all of the period [*date*] to [*date*] for processing their transactions [*or identification of the function performed by the system*]. ***XYZ Service Organization uses a computer processing service organization for all of its computerized application processing. The description in section 3 of this type 2 report includes only the controls and related control objectives of XYZ Service Organization and excludes the control objectives and related controls of the computer processing service organization.*** The criteria we used in making this assertion were that the description. . . .

    c. the controls related to the control objectives stated in the description were suitably designed and operated effectively throughout the period [*date*] to [*date*] to achieve those control objectives ***[and subservice organizations applied the controls contemplated in the design of XYZ Service Organization's controls]***. The criteria we used in making this assertion were that . . .

3.79 Paragraph A7 of SSAE No. 16 states that when the service organization uses a subservice organization and the inclusive method is used, the requirements of SSAE No. 16 also apply to the services provided by the subservice organization, including acknowledging and accepting responsibility for the matters in paragraph 9(*c*)(i)–(vii) of SSAE No. 16. As such, a written assertion covering the services performed by the subservice organization is provided by the subservice organization and included in, or attached to, management's description of the service organization's system, and provided to user entities by the subservice organization. Service organization management includes the assertion in, or attaches it to, the description of the service organization's system. The following is an example of the modifications that would be made to the illustrative assertion by management of the service organization shown in example 1 of exhibit A of SSAE No. 16, when the inclusive method is used. New language is shown in boldface italics.

    a. the description fairly presents the [*type or name of*] system made available to user entities of the system during some or all of the period [*date*] to [*date*] for processing their transactions [*or identification of the function performed by the system*]. ***XYZ Service Organization uses a computer processing service organization for all of its computerized application processing. The description in pages [bb–cc] includes both the control objectives and related controls of XYZ Service Organization and the control objectives and related controls of the computer processing service organization.*** The criteria we used in making this assertion were that the description . . .

Example 2 in appendix B of this guide includes an illustrative assertion by management of a subservice organization when the inclusive method is used.

3.80 In some cases, management of a service organization is asked to implement controls relevant to user entities' internal control over financial reporting that have been designed by another party, for example, controls designed by a user entity or by the former management of a recently acquired

AAG-ASO 3.80

entity. The members of management who would ordinarily provide the assertion (typically those directly responsible for the day to day operations of the service organization) may elect not to provide an assertion covering the design of controls. If these members of management will not provide an assertion with respect to the suitability of the design of the controls, other members of management, for example, members of corporate management, may be in a position to, and may agree to, provide such an assertion. Otherwise, the service auditor may not perform a type 1 or type 2 engagement under SSAE No. 16. In these circumstances, management of the service organization may engage the service auditor or another practitioner to perform tests of the operating effectiveness of controls in either an agreed-upon procedures engagement under AT section 201, *Agreed-Upon Procedures Engagements* (AICPA, *Professional Standards*), or in an examination engagement under AT section 101.

3.81 Management's refusal to provide a written assertion after the engagement has begun represents a scope limitation, and, consequently, the service auditor should withdraw from the engagement. If law or regulation does not allow the service auditor to withdraw from the engagement, the service auditor should disclaim an opinion.

3.82 If management of the service organization wishes to use the inclusive method of presentation, but management of the subservice organization is unwilling to or unable to provide a written assertion, the service organization may not use the inclusive method, but it may instead be able to use the carve-out method.

Additional Responsibilities of Management of the Service Organization

3.83 The planning phase of the engagement is an appropriate time for the service auditor to communicate to management of the service organization its responsibilities throughout the engagement, as provided in the subsequent list:

- Preparing a description of the service organization's system, including the completeness, accuracy, and method of presentation of the description
- Providing a written assertion and having a reasonable basis for that assertion (The assertion will be included in, or attached to, management's description of the service organization's system and provided to user entities. If management's assertion is included in the description, it should be clearly segregated from the description, for example, through the use of headings, because it is not a part of the description and the service auditor is not reporting on management's assertion.)
- Selecting the criteria to be used and stating them in the assertion
- Specifying the control objectives, stating them in the description of the service organization's system, and, if the control objectives are specified by law, regulation, or another party, identifying in the description the party specifying the control objectives
- Identifying the risks that threaten the achievement of the control objectives stated in the description and designing, implementing, and documenting controls that are suitably designed and operating effectively to provide reasonable assurance that the control

Planning a Service Auditor's Engagement

objectives stated in the description of the service organization's system will be achieved

- Providing the service auditor with access to all information, such as records, documentation, service level agreements, and internal audit or other reports, that management is aware of and are relevant to the description of the service organization's system and the assertion
- Providing the service auditor with additional information that the service auditor may request from management for the purpose of the examination engagement
- Providing the service auditor with unrestricted access to personnel within the service organization from whom the service auditor determines it is necessary to obtain evidence relevant to the service auditor's engagement
- Providing the service auditor with written representations at the conclusion of the engagement. When the inclusive method is used, management of the service organization and management of the subservice organization agree to provide and do provide such representations
- Disclosing to the service auditor incidents of noncompliance with laws and regulations, fraud, or uncorrected errors attributable to management or other service organization personnel that are clearly not trivial and that may affect one or more user entities and whether such incidents have been communicated appropriately to affected user entities
- Disclosing to the service auditor knowledge of any actual, suspected, or alleged intentional acts by management or the service organization's employees that could adversely affect the fairness of the presentation of management's description of the service organization's system or the completeness or achievement of the control objectives stated in the description
- Disclosing to the service auditor any deficiencies in the design of controls of which it is aware
- Disclosing to the service auditor all instances in which controls have not operated as described
- Disclosing to the service auditor any events subsequent to the period covered by management's description of the service organization's system up to the date of the service auditor's report that could have a significant effect on management's assertion

Responsibilities of the Service Auditor

3.84 During planning, the service auditor is responsible for

- determining whether to accept or continue an engagement for a particular client,
- assessing the suitability and availability of the criteria management has used in preparing the description,
- reading the description of the service organization's system and obtaining an understanding of the system, and

- establishing an understanding with management of the service organization regarding the services to be performed and the responsibilities of management and the service auditor, which ordinarily is documented in an engagement letter.

Client Acceptance and Continuance

3.85 As a precursor to accepting or continuing an engagement to report on controls at a service organization, the service auditor undergoes a process designed to mitigate relevant risks. One such risk is *association risk*, which is the risk that the service auditor will be associated with management of a service organization that does not possess the appropriate ethical and moral character, thereby damaging the service auditor's professional reputation.

3.86 Generally, a service auditor will accept or continue an engagement for a client only if certain conditions are met, including the following:

- Management of the service organization and significant shareholders or principal owners are regarded as possessing integrity and good repute.

- It is unlikely that association with the client will expose the service auditor to undue risk of damage to his or her professional reputation or financial loss.

- The service auditor is appropriately independent of the service organization and its affiliates pursuant to an independence assessment process.

Independence, as defined by the AICPA Code of Professional Conduct, is required for examination level engagements to report on controls at a service organization. The independence assessment process may address matters such as scope of services, fee arrangements, firm and individual financial relationships, firm business relationships, and alumni and familial relationships.

3.87 When the inclusive method is used, the service auditor should be independent of both the service organization and the subservice organization. In performing an engagement to report on controls at a service organization, the service auditor need not be independent of the individual user entities of the service organization. Likewise, when the inclusive method is used, the service auditor need not be independent of the individual entities that use the subservice organization.

Engagement Acceptance and Continuance

3.88 Paragraphs 9–11 of SSAE No. 16 identify the following conditions as those that should exist in order for a service auditor to accept or continue an engagement to report on controls at a service organization.

- The service auditor has the capabilities and competence to perform the engagement. Having relevant capabilities and competence to perform the engagement includes having

    — adequate technical training and proficiency to perform an attestation engagement,

    — knowledge of the subject matter,

Planning a Service Auditor's Engagement

- reason to believe that the subject matter is capable of evaluation against criteria that are suitable and available to users,
- knowledge of the service organization's industry and business,
- knowledge of the industries of the user entities,
- appropriate knowledge of systems and technology,
- experience evaluating risks related to the suitability of the design of controls, and
- experience designing and performing tests of controls and evaluating their results.

• The service auditor must maintain independence in mental attitude in all matters relating to the engagement and exercise due professional care in the planning and performance of the engagement and the preparation of the report.[3]

• The service auditor's preliminary knowledge of the engagement circumstances indicates that

- the criteria to be used will be suitable and available to the intended user entities and their auditors,
- the service auditor will have access to sufficient appropriate evidence to the extent necessary to conduct the engagement, and
- the scope of the engagement and management's description of the service organization's system will not be so limited that they are unlikely to be useful to user entities and their auditors. If the inclusive method is used, these conditions also apply with respect to the subservice organization.

3.89 Some of the matters the service auditor considers in determining whether to accept or continue an engagement include the scope of the description, the nature of the user entities, how subservice organizations are used, how information about subservice organizations will be presented, the control objectives, the risks that threaten the achievement of the control objectives, and the period covered by the report. The following are examples of the service auditor's consideration of matters that might affect the decision to accept or continue an engagement:

Example 1. The service organization has requested a type 2 report for a period of less than six months because the service organization or the system has been in operation for less than six months and it is not feasible to wait six months to issue a report or to issue a report covering both systems. The service auditor may determine that the request to undertake an engagement with a specified period of less than six months has an appropriate basis.

Example 2. The service organization has requested a type 2 report for the five month period February 1, 20X1–June 30, 20X1, because

---

[3] Introduction to the Attestation Standards (AICPA, *Professional Standards*).

a significant design or operating effectiveness matter, which has not been communicated to the user entities, occurred in January 20X1. The service auditor may question accepting this engagement.

3.90 A service auditor may question accepting an engagement in which a service organization functions primarily as an intermediary between the user entities and the subservice organization and performs few or no functions that affect transaction processing for user entities (the subservice organization performs these functions). If a service organization's controls do not contribute to the achievement of any control objectives, a report that covers only controls at the service organization would not be useful to user entities and their auditors in assessing the risks of material misstatement. In these circumstances, an inclusive report covering the service organization and subservice organization would be appropriate.

3.91 Another condition for engagement acceptance or continuance is that management of the service organization acknowledges and accepts its specified responsibilities. During planning, the service auditor determines the appropriate person(s) within management of the service organization with whom to interact, by considering whether such person(s) have the appropriate responsibility for and knowledge of the relevant matters. Management agrees to provide a written assertion that will be included in, or attached to, the description of the service organization's system. Management's refusal to provide a written assertion represents a scope limitation, and in those circumstances, the service auditor withdraws from the engagement. If the service auditor is required by law or regulation to accept or continue an engagement to report on controls at a service organization and these conditions are not met, the service auditor may conduct the engagement and, ultimately, disclaim an opinion.

3.92 Paragraph A7 of SSAE No. 16 states that when the inclusive method is used, the requirements of SSAE No. 16 also apply with respect to the subservice organization. However, because the service organization is the client rather than the subservice organization, during planning, the service auditor determines whether it will be possible to obtain a written assertion and evidence that supports the portion of the opinion covering the subservice organization and whether it will be possible to obtain an appropriate letter of representation from the subservice organization regarding the subservice organization's controls.

Assessing the Suitability of Criteria

3.93 During planning, the service auditor assesses whether management has used suitable criteria in preparing the description of the service organization's system, and in evaluating whether the controls were suitably designed and operating effectively throughout the specified period to achieve the control objectives stated in the description. The service auditor assesses the suitability of criteria by determining whether the criteria listed in paragraphs 14–16 of SSAE No. 16 have been used.

3.94 If the service auditor determines that suitable criteria were not used, the service auditor typically works with management of the service organization during the planning process to make the appropriate corrections. If management of the service organization refuses to amend the criteria, the service auditor considers whether to withdraw from the engagement or modify the service auditor's report.

Planning to Use the Work of the Internal Audit Function

3.95 The phrase "using the work of the internal audit function" is derived from AU section 322, *The Auditor's Consideration of the Internal Audit Function in an Audit of Financial Statements* (AICPA, *Professional Standards*), and refers to work designed and performed by the internal audit function. This includes tests of controls (and the results of those tests) designed and performed by the internal audit function during the period covered by the type 2 report and the results of those tests. This differs from work the internal audit function performs to provide direct assistance to the service auditor, including assistance in performing tests of controls that are designed by the service auditor and performed by members of the internal audit function, under the direction, supervision, and review of the service auditor. When members of the internal audit function provide direct assistance, their work undergoes a level of direction, review, and supervision that is similar to that of work performed by the service auditor's staff.

3.96 Paragraph 7 of SSAE No. 16 defines the term *internal audit function* as the service organization's internal auditors and others, for example, members of a compliance or risk department, who perform activities similar to those performed by internal auditors. Paragraph 28 of SSAE No. 16 states that if the service organization has an internal audit function, the service auditor should obtain an understanding of the nature of the internal audit function's responsibilities and activities to determine whether the internal audit function is likely to be relevant to the engagement. Examples of matters that may be important to this understanding are the internal audit function's

- organizational status within the service organization,
- application of and adherence to professional standards,
- audit plan (including the nature, timing, and extent of audit procedures), and
- access to records and whether limitations exist on the scope of the function's activities.

3.97 Internal audit activities that are relevant to a service auditor's engagement are those that provide information or evidence about the services provided to user entities, the fair presentation of management's description of the service organization's system, or the suitability of the design or operating effectiveness of the service organization's controls that are likely to be relevant to user entities' internal control over financial reporting. Certain internal audit activities may not be relevant to a service auditor's engagement, for example, the internal audit function's procedures to evaluate the efficiency of certain management decision making processes.

3.98 As part of the process of obtaining an understanding of the internal audit function's responsibilities and activities, the service auditor reads information about the internal audit function included in the description of the service organization's system and ordinarily requests and reads any relevant internal audit reports related to the period covered by the service auditor's report. Such reports may identify risk factors, control deficiencies, or other matters that may alter the nature, timing, or extent of the service auditor's procedures or affect the service auditor's overall assessment of engagement risk.

AAG-ASO 3.98

3.99 If, after obtaining an understanding of the internal audit function, the service auditor concludes that (*a*) the activities of the internal audit function are not relevant to a service auditor's engagement or (*b*) it may not be efficient to consider the work of the internal audit function, the service auditor does not need to give further consideration to the work of the internal audit function.

3.100 If the service auditor determines that the work of the internal audit function is relevant to the service auditor's engagement and intends to use the work of the internal audit function, the service auditor should determine whether the work of the internal audit function is likely to be adequate for the purposes of the engagement by evaluating (1) the objectivity and technical competence of members of the internal audit function, (2) whether the internal audit function is carried out with due professional care, and (3) whether there is likely to be effective communication between the internal audit function and the service auditor, including the effect of any constraints or restrictions placed on the internal audit function by management of the service organization or those charged with governance.

3.101 The extent to which the service auditor uses the work of the internal audit function is a matter of professional judgment. Typically the service auditor does not solely use tests performed by members of the internal audit function to support the service auditor's opinion on the operating effectiveness of controls. If the service auditor determines that the work of the internal audit function is likely to be adequate for the purposes of the engagement, the service auditor should evaluate the following factors in determining the planned effect that the work of the internal audit function will have on the nature, timing, and extent of the service auditor's procedures.

- The nature and scope of specific work performed, or to be performed, by the internal audit function
- The significance of that work to the service auditor's conclusions
- The degree of subjectivity involved in the evaluation of the evidence gathered in support of those conclusions

3.102 The service auditor's use of the work of the internal audit function in a type 1 engagement generally would be more limited than it would be in a type 2 engagement, because a type 1 engagement does not include tests of the operating effectiveness of controls.

Coordinating Procedures With the Internal Audit Function

3.103 If the service auditor has determined that the work of the internal audit function is likely to be adequate for the purposes of the engagement, the service auditor may find it helpful to review the internal audit function's audit plan as a basis for determining whether the internal audit function's procedures may be coordinated with the service auditor's procedures. The audit plan provides information about the nature, timing, extent, and scope of the work performed by the internal audit function, as well as the work to be performed. Such information may be helpful to the service auditor in determining and scheduling the procedures to be performed. For example, if the service auditor determines that the internal audit function will be testing a particular control during the month of April, the service auditor may decide to test that control during a different month to increase the coverage of the testing. If the internal audit function has not yet completed its work for the period covered by the service auditor's report, the service auditor may consider coordinating certain work with the internal audit function for the remainder of the period.

3.104 Meeting with the internal audit function may assist the service auditor in understanding the role of the internal audit function at the service organization, management's directives to the internal audit function, and any significant issues that have arisen and how they were resolved. In addition, the service auditor will be able to discuss administrative matters such as the organization of the internal audit function's working papers and reports and how the service auditor can access paper and electronic files.

Engagement Letter

3.105 AT section 101, which provides a framework for all attestation engagements, states in paragraph .46 that the practitioner should establish an understanding with the client regarding the services to be performed. That understanding should be documented in the working papers preferably through a written communication with the client. Typically, this understanding is documented in an engagement letter. A documented understanding reduces the risk that either the service auditor or the management of the service organization may misinterpret the needs or expectations of the other party. For example, it reduces the risk that management of the service organization may rely on the service auditor to protect the service organization against certain risks or to perform certain management functions. The engagement letter documents the services to be provided during the engagement.

3.106 The engagement letter typically includes the objectives of the engagement, a description of the services to be provided, the responsibilities of management of the service organization, responsibilities of the service auditor, and the limitations of the engagement, including the restricted use of the service auditor's report. Such matters as fees and timing may also be addressed in the engagement letter. If the service auditor believes an understanding has not been established with management of the service organization, the service auditor would typically decline to accept or perform the engagement.

Chapter 4

Performing an Engagement Under Statement on Standards for Attestation Engagements No. 16

In performing a service auditor's engagement, both the service organization and the service auditor have specific responsibilities. This chapter describes those responsibilities and identifies matters the service auditor considers and the procedures the service auditor performs to test the fair presentation of management's description of the service organization's system and the suitability of the design and operating effectiveness of the controls included in management's description of the service organization's system.

Obtaining and Evaluating Evidence About Whether the Description of the Service Organization's System Is Fairly Presented

4.01 Paragraph 19 of Statement on Standards for Attestation Engagements (SSAE) No. 16, *Reporting on Controls at a Service Organization* (AICPA, *Professional Standards*, AT sec. 801), requires the service auditor to obtain and read management's description of the service organization's system and to evaluate whether those aspects of the description that are included in the scope of the engagement are presented fairly, including whether

 a. the control objectives stated in management's description of the service organization's system are reasonable in the circumstances.

 b. the controls identified in management's description of the service organization's system were implemented (that is, actually placed in operation).

 c. complementary user entity controls, if any, are adequately described.

 d. the services performed by a subservice organization, if any, are adequately described, including whether the inclusive method or the carve-out method was used in relation to them.

4.02 Paragraph A32 of SSAE No. 16 states that considering the following questions may assist the service auditor in determining whether management's description of the service organization's system is fairly presented, in all material respects:

- Does management's description address the major aspects of the service provided and included in the scope of the engagement that could reasonably be expected to be relevant to the common needs of a broad range of user auditors in planning their audits of user entities' financial statements?

- Is the description prepared at a level of detail that could reasonably be expected to provide a broad range of user auditors with sufficient information to obtain an understanding of internal control in accordance with AU section 314, *Understanding the Entity*

AAG-ASO 4.02

and Its Environment and Assessing the Risks of Material Misstatement, (AICPA, *Professional Standards*)? The description need not address every aspect of the service organization's processing or the services provided to user entities and need not be so detailed that it would potentially enable a reader to compromise security or other controls at the service organization.

- Is the description prepared in a manner that does not omit or distort information that might affect the decisions of a broad range of user auditors; for example, does the description contain any significant omissions or inaccuracies regarding processing of which the service auditor is aware?
- When the description covers a period of time, does the description include relevant details of changes to the service organization's system during the period covered by the description?
- Have the controls identified in the description actually been implemented?
- Are complementary user entity controls, if any, adequately described? In most cases, the control objectives stated in the description are worded so that they are capable of being achieved through the effective operation of controls implemented by the service organization alone. In some cases, however, the control objectives stated in the description cannot be achieved by the service organization alone because their achievement requires particular controls to be implemented by user entities. This may be the case when, for example, the control objectives are specified by a regulatory authority. When the description does include complementary user entity controls, the description separately identifies those controls along with the specific control objectives that cannot be achieved by the service organization alone.
- If the inclusive method has been used, does the description separately identify controls at the service organization and controls at the subservice organization? If the carve-out method is used, does the description identify the functions that are performed by the subservice organization? When the carve-out method is used, the description need not describe the detailed processing or controls at the subservice organization.

4.03 Procedures the service auditor may perform to evaluate whether the description of the service organization's system is fairly presented typically include a combination of the following:

- Obtaining a list of user entities and determining how the services provided by the service organization are likely to affect the user entities; for example, determining the predominant businesses of the user entities, the common types of services they provide, and whether they are regulated.
- Reading contracts with user entities to understand the nature and scope of the services provided by the service organization as well as the service organization's contractual obligations to user entities.
- Observing the procedures performed by service organization personnel.

Performing an Engagement Under SSAE No. 16 53

- Reading service organization policy and procedure manuals and other documentation of the system; for example, flowcharts and narratives.
- Performing walkthroughs of transactions and identifying controls.
- Discussing the contents of the assertion and the description with management and other service organization personnel.

4.04 The service auditor compares his or her understanding of the services included in the scope of the engagement to the description of the service organization's system to determine if it is fairly presented. The items in paragraph 14 of SSAE No. 16, at a minimum, provide criteria for evaluating whether management's description of the service organization system is fairly presented. Paragraphs A31–A35 of SSAE No. 16 provide guidance concerning the service auditor's determination of the fair presentation of the description of the service organization's system, some of which is discussed in more detail in paragraphs 4.05–.42 of this guide.

4.05 SSAE No. 16 indicates that management's description of the service organization's system is fairly presented if it

    a. presents how the service organization's system was designed and implemented including, if applicable, the matters identified in paragraph 14(*a*) and, in the case of a type 2 report, includes relevant details of changes to the service organization's system during the period covered by the description.

    b. does not omit or distort information relevant to the service organization's system, while acknowledging that management's description of the service organization's system is prepared to meet the common needs of a broad range of user entities and may not, therefore, include every aspect of the service organization's system that each individual user entity may consider important in its own particular environment.

4.06 The description is not fairly presented if it states or implies that controls are being performed when they are not being performed or if it inadvertently or intentionally omits relevant controls performed by the service organization that are not suitably designed or operating effectively. Paragraph 5.34 of this guide presents an illustrative explanatory paragraph that would be added to the service auditor's report when the description includes controls that have not been implemented.

4.07 Additionally, a description that is fairly presented does not contain subjective statements that cannot be objectively evaluated. For example, describing a service organization as being "the world's best" or "the most respected in the industry" is subjective and, therefore, would not be appropriate for inclusion in the description of the service organization's system. Paragraph 5.35 describes reporting implications when the description contains subjective information and management will not revise the description.

4.08 As part of the service auditor's evaluation of whether the description omits information that may affect user entities' internal control over financial reporting and the needs of user auditors, the service auditor determines whether the description addresses all of the major aspects of the processing within the scope of the engagement that may be relevant to user auditors in

AAG-ASO 4.08

assessing the risks of material misstatement as they relate to user entities' internal control over financial reporting and whether it objectively describes what occurs at the service organization. Paragraph 5.37 of this guide presents an illustrative explanatory paragraph that would be added to the service auditor's report when the description omits information that may be relevant to user entities' internal control over financial reporting.

4.09 A service organization may have controls that it considers to be outside the boundaries of the system, such as controls related to the conversion of new user entities to the service organization's systems. To avoid misunderstanding by readers of the description, the service auditor considers whether the description clearly delineates the boundaries of the system that is included in the scope of the engagement.

4.10 Paragraph 23 of SSAE No. 16 states that in a type 2 engagement, the service auditor should inquire about changes to the service organization's controls that were implemented during the period covered by the service auditor's report. In addition, the service auditor may become aware of changes during the performance of the engagement. If the service auditor believes the changes would be considered significant by user entities and their auditors, the service auditor should determine whether the changes have been described in the description of the service organization's system at an appropriate level of detail, for example, including a description of the controls before and after the change and an indication of when the control changed. If management has not included such changes in the description of the service organization's system, the service auditor generally requests that management amend the description to include this information. If management will not include this information in the description, the service auditor would describe the changes in the service auditor's report. Paragraph 5.39 of this guide presents an illustrative explanatory paragraph that would be added to the service auditor's report when the description fails to identify changes to the service organization's controls.

Other Information in the Description That Is Not Covered by the Service Auditor's Report

4.11 A service organization may wish to provide report users with other information in its description that does not relate to user entities' internal control over financial reporting. In those circumstances, the service auditor discusses those aspects of the description with management of the service organization to determine whether such information will be deleted, placed in a separate section of the description, included in an attachment to the description, or included in a document that also contains management's description of the service organization's system and the service auditor's report. If the other information is included in a separate section of the description, in an attachment to the description, or in a document that also contains management's description of the service organization's system and the service auditor's report, the other information should be distinguished from the service organization's description of its system, for example, through the use of a title such as "Other Information Provided by Example Service Organization." Paragraph 5.40 of this guide presents an illustrative explanatory paragraph that would be added to the service auditor's report when information that is not covered by the service auditor's report is not appropriately segregated and identified as such.

4.12 Paragraph 40 of SSAE No. 16 requires the service auditor to read other information, if any, included in a document containing management's

Performing an Engagement Under SSAE No. 16

description of the service organization's system and the service auditor's report to identify material inconsistencies. While reading the other information, the service auditor may become aware of an apparent misstatement of fact. In accordance with paragraph 41 of SSAE No. 16, the service auditor should discuss any such material inconsistencies or apparent misstatements of fact with management of the service organization, and if management refuses to correct the information, take appropriate action as identified in paragraphs .91–.94 of AT section 101, *Attest Engagements* (AICPA, *Professional Standards*).

Materiality Relating to the Fair Presentation of the Description of the Service Organization's System

4.13 Paragraph 17 of SSAE No. 16 requires the service auditor to evaluate materiality with respect to the fair presentation of the description of the service organization's system. The concept of materiality in the context of the fair presentation of the description relates to the information being reported on, not the financial statements of user entities. Materiality in this context primarily relates to qualitative factors, such as whether significant aspects of the processing have been included in the description or whether relevant information has been omitted or distorted. As outlined in paragraph A25 of SSAE No. 16, the concept of materiality takes into account that the service auditor's report provides information about the service organization's system to meet the common information needs of a broad range of user entities and their auditors who have an understanding of the manner in which the system is being used by a particular user entity for financial reporting. Similarly, this concept extends to a service auditor's report for a single user entity. Materiality also applies with respect to the subservice organization when the inclusive method is used. In other words, materiality is considered in the context of the fair presentation of the service organization's description of its system for both the service organization and subservice organization.

4.14 The following are some examples related to materiality with respect to the fair presentation of the description of the service organization's system:

> *Example 1.* Example Service Organization uses a subservice organization to perform all of its back-office functions and elects to use the carve-out method of presentation. Management's description of the service organization's system includes information about the nature of the services provided by the subservice organization and describes the monitoring the service organization performs and other controls the service organization implements with respect to the processing performed by the subservice organization. The description includes such information because it is likely to be relevant to user entities' internal control over financial reporting and, therefore, would be considered material to management's description of the service organization's system.
>
> *Example 2.* Example Service Organization is responsible for implementing general computer controls. The service organization's application controls cannot function without the underlying general computer controls; therefore, the general computer controls would be considered material to the description of the system and would be included in Example Service Organization's description of the system.

AAG-ASO 4.14

Example 3. Example Service Organization has multiple applications that enable management of the service organization to compare actual operating statistics with requirements in service level agreements with user entities. These applications do not process user entity transactions. Management may elect to exclude these applications from the description of Example Service Organization's system because they are not likely to be relevant to user entities' internal control over financial reporting and, therefore, are not material to the description.

Evaluating Whether Control Objectives Relate to Internal Control Over Financial Reporting

4.15 In determining whether management's description of the service organization's system is fairly presented, paragraph 19 of SSAE No. 16 requires the service auditor to determine whether the control objectives stated in management's description of the service organization's system are reasonable in the circumstances. Paragraph 2 of SSAE No. 16 states that the focus of SSAE No. 16 is on controls that are likely to be relevant to user entities' internal control over financial reporting. Accordingly, control objectives that are reasonable in the circumstances should relate to controls that are likely to be relevant to user entities' internal control over financial reporting and should include all such controls.

4.16 As discussed in paragraph 19(*a*) of SSAE No. 16, the service auditor should evaluate whether the control objectives stated in management's description of the service organization's system are reasonable in the circumstances. Paragraph A34 discusses several points that the service auditor may consider in making this determination, including whether the control objectives

- have been specified by the service organization or by outside parties, such as regulatory authorities, a user group, a professional body, or others.
- relate to the types of assertions commonly embodied in the broad range of user entities' financial statements to which controls at the service organization could reasonably be expected to relate (for example, assertions about existence and accuracy that are affected by controls that prevent or detect unauthorized access to the system). Although the service auditor ordinarily will not be able to determine how controls at a service organization specifically relate to the assertions embodied in individual user entities' financial statements, the service auditor's understanding of the nature of the service organization's system, including controls, and the services being provided is used to identify the types of assertions to which those controls are likely to relate.
- are complete. Although a complete set of control objectives can provide a broad range of user auditors with a framework to assess the effect of controls at the service organization on assertions commonly embodied in user entities' financial statements, the service auditor ordinarily will not be able to determine how controls at a service organization specifically relate to the assertions embodied in individual user entities' financial statements and cannot, therefore, determine whether control objectives are complete from

Performing an Engagement Under SSAE No. 16   **57**

the viewpoint of individual user entities or user auditors. If the control objectives are specified by an outside party, including control objectives specified by law or regulation, the outside party is responsible for their completeness and reasonableness.

4.17 The service auditor considers whether the control objectives included in the description represent control objectives that the service organization's controls are designed to achieve. For example, a fund accounting agent that is not responsible for valuing securities ordinarily would not have a control objective stating the following:

> Controls provide reasonable assurance that portfolio securities are accurately valued.

Instead, to more accurately reflect what the controls are designed to achieve the control objective may be revised to state as follows:

> Controls provide reasonable assurance that portfolio securities are valued using prices obtained from sources authorized by the customer.

Implementation of Service Organization Controls

4.18 Paragraph 20 of SSAE No. 16 requires the service auditor to determine whether the service organization's system has been implemented, that is, whether the system exists and relevant controls have been placed in operation.

4.19 Paragraph 20 of SSAE No. 16 states that the service auditor should determine whether controls have been implemented through inquiry in combination with other procedures. Such other procedures should include observation and inspection of records and other documentation of the manner in which the service organization's system operates and controls are applied. Paragraph A35 of SSAE No. 16 states that such procedures may also include reperformance.

4.20 Paragraph A35 of SSAE No. 16 also indicates that the service auditor's procedures to determine whether the system described by the service organization has been implemented may be similar to, and performed in conjunction with, procedures to obtain an understanding of the system. For example, when performing a walkthrough to verify the service auditor's understanding of the design of controls, the service auditor may also determine whether controls have been implemented. Performing a walkthrough entails asking relevant members of the service organization's management and staff to describe and demonstrate their actions in performing a procedure. A walkthrough generally includes tracing one or more transactions from initiation through how information is transferred to the reports and other information prepared for user entities, including the relevant information systems. Ordinarily, a service auditor also will obtain documentary evidence of the performance of controls or observe the controls being performed during the walkthrough. It also may be helpful to use flowcharts, questionnaires, or data flow diagrams to facilitate understanding the design of the controls.

4.21 An appropriately performed walkthrough provides an opportunity to verify the service auditor's understanding of the flow of transactions and the design of the controls. Probing questions, combined with other walkthrough procedures, enable the service auditor to gain a sufficient understanding of the processes and to determine whether procedures are actually performed as stated in the description of the service organization's system.

AAG-ASO 4.21

4.22 To be fairly presented, the description of the service organization's system should include only controls that have been implemented. If the service auditor determines that certain controls identified in management's description have not been implemented, the service auditor should ask management of the service organization to remove those controls from the description. In turn, the service auditor should consider only controls that have been implemented when assessing the suitability of the design and operating effectiveness of controls.

4.23 The fact that controls are implemented does not imply that they are suitably designed or operating with sufficient effectiveness to achieve the control objectives. The procedures the service auditor performs to assess the suitability of design and operating effectiveness of controls are discussed in paragraphs 4.42–.128 of this guide.

Changes to the Scope of the Engagement

4.24 Paragraph 12 of SSAE No. 16 states that if management requests a change in the scope of the engagement before the completion of the engagement, the service auditor should be satisfied that reasonable justification for the change exists before agreeing to the change. Paragraph A20 of SSAE No. 16 further states that a request to change the scope of the engagement to exclude certain control objectives because of the likelihood that the service auditor's opinion would be modified with respect to those control objectives may not be reasonable justification.

4.25 Consider the following two examples related to changes to control objectives:

> *Example 1.* After providing the description of its system to the service auditor, management of a transfer agent decides that it would like to remove a control objective related to new fund set up because only one fund was set up during the reporting period and management of the fund had performed its own testing. The service auditor concluded that the removal of the control objective related to new fund setup was reasonable in the circumstances because the objective was not relevant to a broad range of user entities during the examination period.
>
> *Example 2.* After the service auditor's testing identified deviations in controls related to the processing of contributions for pension plan participants that would have caused the service auditor to modify the service auditor's opinion, management of the service organization requested that the control objective related to the processing of contributions be removed from the description. In this situation, removal of the control objective from the description of the service organization's system would not be reasonable. If the service organization removes the control objective from the description, the service auditor may consider whether it is appropriate to continue with or withdraw from the engagement.

4.26 Paragraph A20 of SSAE No. 16 further states that a request to change the scope of an engagement from using the inclusive method of presentation to using the carve-out method of presentation, in effect, deleting the description of the subservice organization's system, its controls, and control objectives, may not have a reasonable justification if the request is made to prevent disclosure of deviations identified at the subservice organization. (See paragraph 5.49 for an illustrative explanatory paragraph that would be added to the service auditor's report when the service organization changes from the inclusive method to the carve-out method for a subservice organization without reasonable justification.)

4.27 Paragraph A21 of SSAE No. 16 states that there may be reasonable justification for a change from the inclusive method to the carve-out method if the service organization is unable to arrange for the service auditor to gain access to the subservice organization to perform tests of controls. A change from the inclusive method to the carve-out method may also have reasonable justification if the service organization is unable to obtain an appropriate assertion from management of the subservice organization.

Complementary User Entity Controls

4.28 The service organization may design its service with the assumption that certain controls will be implemented by the user entities. If such complementary user entity controls are necessary to achieve certain control objectives, paragraph 19(c) of SSAE No. 16 requires the service auditor to evaluate whether the service organization's description of its system adequately describes complementary user entity controls.

4.29 To evaluate whether complementary user entity controls included in the description are adequately described, the service auditor reads contracts with user entities to gain an understanding of the user entities' responsibilities and whether those responsibilities are appropriately described in management's description of the service organization's system.

4.30 For example, a service organization that provides payroll services to user entities and electronically receives payroll data from user entities would include the following control objective in its description:

> Controls provide reasonable assurance that input to the payroll application is authorized.

This control objective could not be achieved without the implementation of input controls at the user entities because transaction initiation and authorization rests with them. The service organization only can be responsible for determining that input transactions are received from authorized sources as established by the user entities. Accordingly, the description would include a complementary user entity control consideration, such as the following:

> Controls are implemented by user entities to provide reasonable assurance that input to the payroll application is authorized.

Alternatively, the control objective could be modified so that it could be achieved without a complementary user entity control, such as the following:

> Controls provide reasonable assurance that input is received from authorized sources.

4.31 Paragraph 5.50 of this guide describes how the service auditor modifies the service auditor's report when complementary user entity controls are necessary for one or more control objectives to be achieved and the service organization fails to include such complementary user entity control considerations in the description.

AAG-ASO 4.31

Subservice Organizations

4.32 During planning, management of the service organization determines whether the functions performed by subservice organizations are likely to be relevant to user entities' internal control over financial reporting and whether to use the inclusive or carve-out method of presentation.

4.33 The seventh bullet of paragraph A32 of SSAE No. 16 contains questions the service auditor may consider when evaluating whether the description is fairly presented with respect to subservice organizations when either the inclusive method or the carve-out method of presentation is used. Information in service level agreements and contracts between the service organization and the subservice organization may assist the service auditor in determining whether aspects of subservice organization controls are appropriately described.

4.34 Paragraph A7 of SSAE No. 16 indicates that if the service organization has used the inclusive method of presentation, the requirements of SSAE No. 16 also apply to the services provided by the subservice organization. The definition of inclusive method in paragraph 7 of SSAE No. 16 indicates that when the inclusive method is used, management's description of the service organization's system includes a description of the nature of the services provided by the subservice organization as well as the subservice organization's relevant control objectives and related controls. Accordingly, the service auditor should determine whether the description of the service organization's system includes that information.

4.35 If the description uses the inclusive method, the seventh bullet of paragraph A32 of SSAE No. 16 asks the service auditor to consider whether the description of the system separately identifies controls at the service organization and controls at the subservice organization. SSAE No. 16 does not prescribe how the description should be modified to differentiate between aspects of the description that address the service organization and aspects that address the subservice organization; however, example 2 of appendix B, "Illustrative Type 2 Reports," in this guide illustrates one method of doing so.

4.36 The definition of the carve-out method in paragraph 7 of SSAE No. 16 indicates that if the carve-out method is used, management's description of the service organization's system identifies the nature of the services performed by the subservice organization and excludes from the description and from the scope of the service auditor's engagement the subservice organization's relevant control objectives and related controls. Accordingly, if the service organization has used the carve-out method of presentation, the service auditor should determine whether the description identifies the nature of the services performed by the subservice organization.

4.37 The definition of carve-out method also states that if the carve-out method is used, the description of the service organization's system and the scope of the engagement would include controls at the service organization that monitor the effectiveness of controls at the subservice organization. Examples of monitoring controls include testing performed by members of the service organization's internal audit function at the subservice organization, reviewing output reports, holding periodic discussions with the subservice organization, making site visits, and reviewing reports on the subservice organization's system prepared pursuant to SSAE No. 16 or AT section 101.

4.38 When the carve-out method is used and the subservice organization has provided a type 1 or type 2 report to user entities, the service auditor should determine whether the service organization has included and addressed complementary user entity control considerations described in the subservice organization's type 1 or type 2 report or specified in the contract or service level agreement between the service organization and the subservice organization.

4.39 A service organization may use multiple subservice organizations and may prepare its description using the carve-out method of presentation for one or more subservice organizations and the inclusive method of presentation for others. The service auditor should determine whether the guidance concerning the inclusive method of presentation has been applied to all the subservice organizations for which the inclusive method is used and that the guidance concerning the carve-out method has been applied to all of the subservice organizations for which the carve-out method has been used.

4.40 Paragraph 5.51 of this guide addresses report modifications when the service organization has not disclosed that it uses subservice organizations to perform functions that are likely to be relevant to user entities' internal control over financial reporting.

Other Matters Relating to Fair Presentation

4.41 Although SSAE No. 16 does not address design deficiencies that could potentially affect processing in future periods, the service auditor may become aware of such design deficiencies. If management of the service organization does not intend to disclose the existence of these design deficiencies and their plans to correct the deficiencies, the service auditor may request that management of the service organization disclose this information in management's description of the service organization's system. This information may be disclosed in a section titled "Other Information Provided by the Service Organization." Paragraph 5.42 of this guide provides an illustrative paragraph that would be added to the service auditor's report when information that is not covered by the service auditor's report is presented and the service auditor disclaims an opinion on it.

Obtaining and Evaluating Evidence Regarding the Suitability of the Design of Controls

4.42 A control that is suitably designed is able to achieve the related control objective if it operates effectively. Paragraph 21 of SSAE No. 16 requires the service auditor to determine whether controls included in the service organization's description are suitably designed to achieve the related control objectives. This requirement is applicable to controls at the subservice organization if the inclusive method has been used. The service auditor determines which controls at the service organization are necessary to achieve the control objectives stated in management's description of the service organization's system and assesses whether those controls were suitably designed to achieve the control objectives by

    a. identifying the risks that threaten the achievement of the control objectives stated in management's description of the service organization's system as they relate to the user entities' financial statement assertions and *b.* evaluating the linkage of the controls identified in management's description of the service organization's system with those risks.

4.43 Management of a service organization is responsible for designing and implementing controls to achieve related control objectives, identifying the risks that threaten the achievement of those control objectives, and evaluating the linkage of the controls to the risks that threaten the achievement of the related control objectives. In many cases, the service auditor may be able to obtain management's documentation of its identification of risks and evaluation of the linkage of controls to those risks. In these instances, the service auditor may evaluate the completeness of management's identification of risks and the effectiveness of the controls in mitigating those risks.

4.44 Paragraph 17 of SSAE No. 16 requires the service auditor to evaluate materiality with respect to the design of controls to achieve the related control objectives. Paragraph A26 of SSAE No. 16 indicates that the service auditor considers materiality with respect to the suitability of the design of controls primarily by considering qualitative factors, such as whether

- management's description of the service organization's system includes the significant aspects of processing of significant transactions,
- management's description of the service organization's system omits or distorts relevant information, or
- the controls have the ability as designed to provide reasonable assurance that the control objectives stated in management's description of the service organization's system would be achieved.

4.45 Paragraph 9(*c*)(v) of SSAE No. 16 indicates that one of the conditions for engagement acceptance or continuance is that management of the service organization agree to the terms of the engagement by acknowledging and accepting its responsibility for identifying the risks that threaten the achievement of the control objectives stated in the description and designing, implementing, and documenting controls that are suitably designed and operating effectively to provide reasonable assurance that the control objectives stated in the description of the service organization's system will be achieved.

4.46 Paragraph A18 of SSAE No. 16 elaborates on the relationship between control objectives, risks, and controls.

> Control objectives relate to risks that controls seek to mitigate. For example, the risk that a transaction is recorded at the wrong amount or in the wrong period can be expressed as a control objective that transactions are recorded at the correct amount and in the correct period. Management is responsible for identifying the risks that threaten achievement of the control objectives stated in management's description of the service organization's system. Management may have a formal or informal process for identifying relevant risks. A formal process may include estimating the significance of identified risks, assessing the likelihood of their occurrence, and deciding about actions to address them. However, because control objectives relate to risks that controls seek to mitigate, thoughtful identification by management of control objectives when designing, implementing, and documenting the service organization's system may itself comprise an informal process for identifying relevant risks.

Performing an Engagement Under SSAE No. 16

4.47 In assessing the reasonableness of the control objectives, as discussed in paragraph A34 of SSAE No. 16, the service auditor considers whether the control objectives relate to the types of assertions commonly embodied in a broad range of user entity financial statements. Table 4-1, "Types of Assertions About Classes of Transactions and Events During a Period," and table 4-2, "Types of Assertions About Account Balances at the Period End," present the types of assertions that may exist in a user entity's financial statements, illustrative service organization control objectives that relate to those types of assertions, and the risks that threaten the achievement of those control objectives. Because the control objectives in the table are illustrative, they would need to be tailored to the specific circumstances.

4.48 Table 4-1 presents the categories of assertions that may exist in a user entity's financial statements and that may be affected when the service provided by the service organization involves processing transactions and recording events for user entities.[1]

Table 4-1

Types of Assertions[2] About Classes of Transactions and Events During a Period

User Entity Financial Statement Assertions	Illustrative Service Organization Control Objectives Controls provide reasonable assurance that...	Illustrative Risks That Threaten the Achievement of the Control Objective as They Relate to the User Entities' Financial Statements
Occurrence. Transactions and events that have been recorded have occurred and pertain to the entity.	transactions are authorized and received only from authorized sources.[3] transactions are validated[4] in a complete, accurate, and timely manner.[5]	Manual transactions are not reviewed and approved by authorized sources. Transaction access is not restricted to authorized individuals.

(continued)

---

[1] If the services provided by the service organization include preparation of user entity financial statements, the following user entity assertions about presentation and disclosure also may be relevant:

- *Occurrence and rights and obligations.* Disclosed events and transactions have occurred and pertain to the entity.
- *Completeness.* All disclosures that should have been included in the financial statements have been included.
- *Classification and understandability.* Financial information is appropriately presented and described and disclosures are clearly expressed.
- *Accuracy and valuation.* Financial and other information are disclosed fairly and at appropriate amounts.

[2] Paragraph .15 of AU section 326, *Audit Evidence* (AICPA, *Professional Standards*).

[3] Transaction data may be received in paper or electronic form, or by telephone, for example, by a call center. The service organization may have separate control objectives for each method of receipt.

[4] Validation includes determining that the recorded transaction has occurred and pertains to the user entity. It also includes correcting invalid data and properly reentering corrected data.

[5] A timely manner also includes recording the transaction in the correct period.

User Entity Financial Statement Assertions	Illustrative Service Organization Control Objectives Controls provide reasonable assurance that . . .	Illustrative Risks That Threaten the Achievement of the Control Objective as They Relate to the User Entities' Financial Statements
		Automated transactions are not validated against master files and transactions that do not correspond with data in the master files are not rejected.
Completeness. All transactions and events that should have been recorded have been recorded.	transactions are entered, processed, recorded, and reported in a complete manner.	After processing, transaction totals are not compared to the original batch total. Automated transactions are not compared to an authorized master file record and rejected if they do not match. Rejected transactions are not corrected and resubmitted. Duplicate transactions are not identified and rejected.
Accuracy. Amounts and other data relating to recorded transactions and events have been recorded appropriately.	transactions are entered, processed, recorded, and reported in an accurate manner.	Programmed calculations are mathematically incorrect. Transaction data does not match expected field values. Transaction data does not fall within predetermined limits. Expected transaction data is omitted.
Cutoff. Transactions and events have been recorded in the correct accounting period.	transactions are entered, processed, recorded, and reported in a timely manner.[6]	Rejected transactions are not corrected and posted in the appropriate period.

[6] See footnote 5.

User Entity Financial Statement Assertions	Illustrative Service Organization Control Objectives Controls provide reasonable assurance that...	Illustrative Risks That Threaten the Achievement of the Control Objective as They Relate to the User Entities' Financial Statements
Classification. Transactions and events have been recorded in the proper accounts.	*Note*: Entering, processing, recording, and reporting transactions in a complete, accurate, and timely manner includes appropriate classification to facilitate proper reporting by the user entity.	Transaction data is not systematically compared to a file of valid account numbers. Rejected transactions are not corrected and posted in the appropriate account.

4.49 Table 4-2 presents the categories of assertions that may exist in a user entity's financial statements and that may be affected when the service provided by the service organization involves maintaining balances for user entities, including detail trial balances or general ledgers.[7]

Table 4-2

Types of Assertions About Account Balances at the Period End

User Entity Financial Statement Assertions	Illustrative Service Organization Control Objectives Controls provide reasonable assurance that...	Illustrative Risks That Threaten the Achievement of the Control Objective as They Relate to the User Entities' Financial Statements
Existence. Assets, liabilities, and equity interests exist.	balances represent valid asset, liability, and equity interest balances and are classified properly.	Transactions are not systematically compared to a file of valid account numbers. Reconciliations of the subsidiary application to the general ledger are not performed.

(continued)

[7] See footnote 1.

User Entity Financial Statement Assertions	Illustrative Service Organization Control Objectives Controls provide reasonable assurance that . . .	Illustrative Risks That Threaten the Achievement of the Control Objective as They Relate to the User Entities' Financial Statements
Rights and obligations. The entity holds or controls the rights to assets, and liabilities are the obligations of the entity.	asset and liability balances relate to rights or obligations of the user entity.	Validity of each transaction is not reviewed and approved by an appropriate member of management.
Completeness. All assets, liabilities, and equity interests that should have been recorded have been recorded.	balances represent all asset, liability, and equity interest balances that should have been recorded.	Transactions are not batched and totaled. Rejected transactions are not corrected and resubmitted. Duplicate transactions are not identified and rejected.
Valuation and allocation. Assets, liabilities, and equity interests are included in the financial statements at appropriate amounts and any resulting valuation or allocation adjustments are appropriately recorded.	asset, liability, and equity interest balances are reported at accurate amounts.	Transaction access is not restricted to authorized individuals. Rejected transactions are not resubmitted and posted in the correct period. Reconciliations of the subsidiary application to the general ledger are not performed.

4.50 In addition, the control objectives would include general computer control objectives that are necessary to achieve the application control objectives (related to classes of transactions and events as well as account balances) and are therefore likely to be relevant to controls over financial reporting at user entities. General controls are assessed in relation to their effect on applications and data that are likely to be relevant to financial reporting at user entities. General control objectives and related controls are typically reported separately from application controls. Table 4-3, "General Computer Control Objectives," presents illustrative general computer control objectives and the risks that threaten their achievement.

Table 4-3

General Computer Control Objectives

	Illustrative Service Organization General Computer Control Objectives Controls provide reasonable assurance that...	Illustrative Risks That Threaten the Achievement of the General Computer Control Objective
Information Security	• logical access[8] to programs, data, and computer resources[9] is restricted to authorized and appropriate users.[10]	Unauthorized users gain access to the application and modify data or applications. Authorized users make unauthorized use of or modification to applications or application data. Segregation of duties is not effective or is not enforced by logical access security measures. Logical access security measures are bypassed through physical access to sensitive system resources, resulting in unauthorized access and changes to data or applications.

(continued)

---

[8] In assessing the logical access controls over programs, data, and computer resources, the service organization considers

- logical access controls that may affect the user entities' financial statements. Generally this would begin with the access controls directly over the application. If the effectiveness of application level security is dependent on the effectiveness of network and operating system controls, these are also considered. Controls over direct access to the databases or data files and tables are considered as well.
- the configuration and administration of security tools and techniques, and monitoring controls designed to identify and respond to security violations in a timely manner.

[9] Computer resources include, but are not limited to, computer equipment, network equipment, storage media, and other hardware supporting the services provided by the service organization.

[10] Many service organizations have features enabling customers to directly access programs and data. In assessing the logical access controls over programs and data, the service organization considers controls over security related to service organization personnel, the service organization's customers, and the customers' clients, as applicable, as well as the likely effect of these controls on user entities' financial statements.

AAG-ASO 4.50

	Illustrative Service Organization General Computer Control Objectives Controls provide reasonable assurance that . . .	Illustrative Risks That Threaten the Achievement of the General Computer Control Objective
	• physical access to computer and other resources[11] is restricted to authorized and appropriate personnel.	Physical media is taken or copied. Unauthorized use is made of system resources. Unauthorized physical access is not detected.
Change Management	• changes to application programs and related data management systems[12] are authorized, tested, documented, approved, and implemented to result in the complete, accurate, and timely[13] processing and reporting of transactions and balances.[14]	Application change process is not initiated when business rules, calculations, or processes change. Application specifications are inconsistent with needs, intent, or requirements. Application logic does not function as specified. Unauthorized changes are made to production applications. Application changes are not approved. Unauthorized changes to applications or application configurations are not detected.

---

[11] Computer resources include, but are not limited to, computer equipment, network equipment, storage media, and other hardware supporting the services provided by the service organization. Other resources include, but are not limited to, buildings, vaults, and negotiable instruments.

[12] Data management systems include database management systems, specialized data transport, or communications software (often called middleware), data warehouse software, and data extraction or reporting software. Controls over data management systems may enhance user authentication or authorization, the availability of system privileges, data access privileges, application processing hosted within the data management systems, and segregation of duties.

[13] Timeliness may be relevant in particular situations, for example, when emergency changes are needed or when changes that would likely affect the user entities' information systems are being implemented to meet contractual requirements. Controls for emergency changes typically will be different from those for planned changes.

[14] This control objective is quite broad and should be tailored to the service organization's environment. For example, if the service organization has different controls for developing new applications or for making changes to applications or databases, it might be clearer to have separate control objectives for each of these.

Performing an Engagement Under SSAE No. 16

Illustrative Service Organization General Computer Control Objectives Controls provide reasonable assurance that . . .	Illustrative Risks That Threaten the Achievement of the General Computer Control Objective
	Application configuration changes made to the system are not authorized or authorized changes are not made.
	Authorized application configuration changes are not entered accurately in the system.
	Application configuration changes are implemented before or after the appropriate time.
• network infrastructure[15] is configured as authorized to (1) support the effective functioning of application controls to result in valid, complete, accurate, and timely[16] processing and reporting of transactions and balances and (2) protect data from unauthorized changes.[17]	Unauthorized changes are made to application configurations.
	Unauthorized changes are made to Infrastructure and infrastructure configurations.
	Infrastructure and infrastructure configurations do not support the proper functioning of application processing, logical security, or availability of data and files, resulting in unauthorized access to applications or data.

(continued)

---

[15] Network infrastructure includes all of the hardware, software, operating systems, and communication components within which the applications and related data management systems operate.

[16] Timeliness may be relevant in particular situations, for example, when emergency changes are needed or when changes are being implemented to meet contractual requirements.

[17] Program change controls over network infrastructure include, as appropriate, the authorization, testing, documentation, approval, and implementation of changes to network infrastructure. In assessing change management, the service organization considers the configuration and administration of the security tools and techniques, and monitoring controls designed to identify exceptions to authorized network infrastructure, applications, and data management systems (for example, database structures) and act upon them in a timely manner. If the service organization has different controls for new implementations or making changes to the infrastructure, applications, or data management systems, it might be clearer to have separate control objectives that address the controls over each type of infrastructure. There also may be separate control objectives for controls over new implementations and controls over changes to existing resources.

AAG-ASO 4.50

	Illustrative Service Organization General Computer Control Objectives Controls provide reasonable assurance that...	Illustrative Risks That Threaten the Achievement of the General Computer Control Objective
		Network infrastructure is not updated on a timely basis to protect against known vulnerabilities.
		Emergency configuration changes are not authorized or appropriate.
		Unauthorized changes to infrastructure are not detected.
Computer Operations	• application and system processing[18] are authorized and executed in a complete, accurate, and timely manner, and deviations, problems, and errors are identified, tracked, recorded, and resolved in a complete, accurate, and timely manner.	Programs are not executed in the correct order.
		Programs are not executed within scheduled timeframes.
		Programs do not execute completely.
		Amended programs corrupt the data they were processing.
		Restarted programs result in incomplete processing or duplicate processing of data.
		Processing problems and errors are not detected or are not detected in a timely manner.
		Processing problems are not appropriately resolved in a timely manner.
		Controls are overridden.
		Emergency access privileges are misused.

---

[18] The processing in this control objective refers to the batch processing of data. It typically does not include the scheduling of file back-ups. Should the service organization have significant online, real-time processing, it may tailor this control objective or add a new control objective to address controls over the identification, tracking, recording, and resolution of problems and errors in a complete, accurate, and timely manner.

Illustrative Service Organization General Computer Control Objectives Controls provide reasonable assurance that...	Illustrative Risks That Threaten the Achievement of the General Computer Control Objective
• data transmissions between the service organization and its user entities and other outside entities are from authorized sources and are complete, accurate, secure, and timely.[19]	Data transmissions do not occur in a timely manner. Data transmissions are not received. Data transmissions are incomplete. Data transmissions are not accurate. Data is transmitted more than once.

4.51 Also, the service organization's control objectives may include other conditions that affect the effectiveness of application controls (related to classes of transactions, events, or account balances). For example, the effectiveness of application controls generally depends on the reliability of master data. Master data is the key information that is relatively constant and referenced or shared between multiple functions or applications (for example, a customer master record, which contains the customer number, shipping address, billing address, key contact information, and payment terms). Consequently, an additional control objective that generally may be necessary is: "Controls provide reasonable assurance that master data is valid, authorized, and established and maintained in a complete, accurate, and timely manner."

4.52 Paragraph A36 of SSAE No. 16 indicates that the risks that threaten the achievement of the control objectives stated in management's description of the service organization's system also encompass intentional and unintentional acts that threaten the achievement of the control objectives. The service auditor considers control objectives that may have a higher risk of being subjected to intentional and unintentional acts and evaluates whether management has addressed such risks in the description. Risks related to intentional acts may include management override of controls at the service organization, misappropriation of user entity assets by service organization personnel, and creation, by service organization personnel, of false or misleading documents or records of user entity transactions processed by the service organization.

4.53 Having identified the risks that threaten the achievement of the control objectives, the service auditor should evaluate whether the controls at the service organization are suitably designed to address the risks. Paragraph A37 of SSAE No. 16 indicates that from the perspective of the service auditor, a control is suitably designed if individually, or in combination with other controls, it would, when complied with satisfactorily, provide reasonable assurance that

---

[19] This control objective may also be presented as part of logical access security or as part of the business operations related to data input or reporting.

the control objective(s) stated in the description of the service organization's system are achieved.

4.54 In assessing the suitability of the design of the controls included in management's description, paragraph 21 of SSAE No. 16 also requires the service auditor to evaluate the linkage of those controls with the risks that threaten the achievement of the related control objectives. In doing so, the service auditor determines whether a control on its own or in combination with other controls, including aspects of the control environment, risk assessment, and monitoring, prevents, or detects and corrects, errors that could result in the nonachievement of the specified control objective.

4.55 If a control objective is composed of several elements (for example, the authorization, accuracy, completeness, and timeliness of transaction processing), the service auditor would need to link the applicable controls to each of the elements listed in the control objective. In addition, the service organization's processing may take different forms depending on how information is received from user entities. For example, transactions may be received by mail, phone, fax, voice response unit, or Internet. One or more controls may be designed to achieve the control objectives that support the way transactions are received.

4.56 To evaluate the suitability of the design of the service organization's controls, the service auditor considers the following information about the controls, which should be included in the description of the service organization's systems:

- The frequency or timing of the occurrence or performance of the control, by stating, for example: "Management reviews error reports monthly" or "The custodian specialist reviews reconciling items on a daily basis."

- The party responsible for conducting the activity, by stating, for example: "The Director of Trading reviews . . . " or "The accounting associate compares . . . "

- The specific activity being performed by the individual performing the control, by stating, for example: "Custodian cash positions are compared to the cash positions in the accounting system" or "The accounting manager reviews the outstanding receivables daily and signs off as evidence of review."

- The source of the information to which the control is applied, by stating, for example: "The custody clerk researches and resolves exceptions listed in the daily exception report."

4.57 Paragraph A39 of SSAE No. 16 states that controls may consist of a number of activities directed at the achievement of various control objectives. Consequently, if the service auditor concludes that certain controls are not suitably designed to achieve a particular control objective, but other controls are suitably designed to achieve that control objective, the service auditor need not mention the controls that are not suitably designed in the report. In contrast, if certain controls are not operating effectively to achieve a particular control objective, and other controls are operating effectively to achieve that control objective, the service auditor would need to identify those exceptions in the service auditor's description of tests of operating effectiveness as required by paragraph 52(*o*)(ii).

4.58 When the service organization uses a subservice organization and uses the carve-out method, the service auditor considers whether one or more controls at the subservice organization needs to be suitably designed in order for controls to be suitably designed to achieve one or more control objectives. Paragraph 5.55 of this guide describes how the service auditor modifies the service auditor's report when the service organization uses the carve-out method and controls at the subservice organization are necessary for the achievement of one or more control objectives.

4.59 The service auditor may determine that aspects of the service organization's control environment, risk assessment, information and communication, and monitoring are necessary for controls to be suitably designed to achieve the control objectives. The service auditor may conclude that controls are not suitably designed to achieve certain control objectives because of deficiencies in the control environment, risk assessment, information and communication, or monitoring.

4.60 The service auditor may conclude that there are no controls in place to support one or more elements of a control objective. For example, a service organization may include the following control objective in management's description of the service organization's system, "Controls provide reasonable assurance that user entity transactions are initially recorded completely, accurately, and in a timely manner." User entities may submit transaction processing requests by telephone or electronically. The service organization has identified in its description of the service organization's system controls that address the processing of electronic transaction requests received from user entities, but it has not identified controls that address transaction requests received via telephone. The service auditor would conclude that controls were not suitably designed to process transaction requests received via telephone.

4.61 A service auditor may have difficulty determining whether a control deficiency represents a deficiency in design or a deficiency in operation. If the deficiency is a deficiency in operation, the service organization might be able to correct the deficiency, for example, by designating a more qualified individual to perform the control. However, if the design of the control is deficient, it will not be effective no matter who performs the control. Accordingly, if upon identification of a deficiency, management of the service organization decides to implement a new control to remediate the deficiency, it is likely that the deficiency relates to the design of the control.

4.62 After performing the procedures and considering the matters described in paragraphs 4.42–.63, the service auditor considers whether the controls have the ability, as designed, to provide reasonable assurance that the control objectives stated in the description would be achieved. The service auditor considers whether design deficiencies resulting from a missing control or the ineffective design of a control are significant enough to conclude that the controls are not suitably designed to achieve one or more control objectives.

4.63 Paragraph 5.52 of this guide presents an illustrative explanatory paragraph that would be added to the service auditor's report when the service auditor determines that controls are not suitably designed to achieve one or more control objectives.

Obtaining and Evaluating Evidence Regarding the Operating Effectiveness of Controls in a Type 2 Engagement

4.64 Paragraph A40 of SSAE No. 16 states that from the viewpoint of the service auditor, a control is operating effectively if, individually or in combination with other controls, it provides reasonable assurance that the control objectives stated in management's description of the service organization's system are achieved. The objective of tests of controls is to evaluate how controls were applied, the consistency with which they were applied, and by whom or in what manner they were applied. When the service auditor employs the inclusive method, the service auditor considers the controls at both the service organization and the subservice organization.

4.65 Paragraph 17 of SSAE No. 16 instructs the service auditor to evaluate materiality with respect to the operating effectiveness of controls to achieve the related control objectives stated in the description. Paragraph A26 states that materiality with respect to the operating effectiveness of controls includes the consideration of quantitative factors, such as the tolerable rate of deviation (the maximum rate of deviations in the operation of the prescribed control that the service auditor is willing to accept without modifying the opinion relating to one or more elements of a control objective) and observed rate of deviation, as well as qualitative factors, such as the nature and cause of any observed deviations.

Determining Which Controls to Test

4.66 Paragraph 22 of SSAE No. 16 states that when performing a type 2 engagement, the service auditor should test those controls that the service auditor has determined are necessary to achieve the control objectives stated in management's description of the service organization's system and should assess their operating effectiveness throughout the period.

4.67 The service auditor may conclude that all or only a portion of the controls identified by management are necessary to achieve a control objective. If the service auditor determines that certain controls are not necessary to achieve a control objective, management may remove those controls from the description of the service organization's system or, if management of the service organization prefers to include the controls in the description of the system, the service auditor may indicate in the report that no testing was performed on them, so that user entities are clear about which controls were tested and which controls were not tested. In these cases, the service auditor is still responsible for determining that the controls that were not tested were fairly presented and implemented.

4.68 Paragraph 23 of SSAE No. 16 instructs the service auditor to inquire about changes in controls implemented during the period covered by the service auditor's report. If the service auditor believes the changes could be significant to user entities and their auditors, the service auditor should determine whether those changes have been included in management's description of the service organization's system and whether superseded controls could be relevant to the achievement of one or more control objectives. If so, the superseded controls would be included in the population of controls the service auditor would test. If the service organization has used the inclusive method, the service auditor would consider changes to controls at both the service organization and the subservice organization. Paragraph 5.39 of this guide describes reporting implications if such changes are not included in management's description of the service organization's system.

4.69 The service auditor considers the effect of design deficiencies on the tests of operating effectiveness. Although one control related to a given control objective may not be suitably designed, other controls may be suitably designed to address the given control objective. The service auditor tests the controls that are suitably designed, identifies in the report the controls that were tested, and determines the effect on the service auditor's report.

4.70 If design deficiencies in controls intended to achieve a given control objective are pervasive, the service auditor generally would not test the controls related to that objective for operating effectiveness.

4.71 Paragraph 5.56 contains an example of an explanatory paragraph that would be added to the service auditor's report when controls were not operating effectively.

Designing and Performing Tests of Controls

4.72 The service auditor is responsible for determining the nature (how the controls are tested), timing (when the controls are tested), and extent (the number of testing procedures performed or size of the sample) of testing necessary to provide sufficient appropriate evidence that the controls were operating effectively throughout the period covered by the report.

4.73 When determining the nature, timing, and extent of tests to be performed to obtain evidence of the operating effectiveness of controls, the service auditor considers the type of evidence that can be obtained from the service organization to demonstrate the operation of the control. The service auditor also considers whether a particular control achieves one or more elements of the control objective on its own or works in combination with other controls. If a combination of controls is necessary to achieve a given control objective, those controls are considered together and deviations are evaluated together. For example, in example 4 of appendix B of this guide, controls that achieve control objective 1 include controls over logical access, controls over program changes, and controls requiring signature verification or callback. The service auditor considers the effectiveness of all three of these controls together in assessing whether the control objective has been achieved.

4.74 The service organization's control environment, risk assessment, information and communication, and monitoring related to the service provided to user entities may enhance or mitigate the effectiveness of specific controls. If the service auditor determines that aspects of the control environment, risk assessment, information and communication, or monitoring are less effective, the service auditor generally would obtain more evidence of the operating effectiveness of the controls to determine whether a control objective has been achieved. In some situations, the service auditor may conclude that controls are not operating effectively to achieve certain control objectives because of deficiencies in the control environment, risk assessment, information and communication, or monitoring.

AAG-ASO 4.74

4.75 For example, management of Example Service Organization determines bonuses based on zero processing errors. In this environment, service organization personnel may be tempted to suppress errors in order to receive bonuses. The service auditor may substantially increase the extent of testing performed, perhaps even testing the entire population, to determine whether controls are operating effectively to achieve the control objective. If the service auditor is unable to obtain evidence of the operating effectiveness of controls, the service auditor may decide to modify the opinion.

4.76 Because of the pervasive effect that controls related to the control environment have, the service auditor ordinarily performs the testing in this area, rather than using the work of members of the service organization's internal audit function. However, the service auditor may consider certain work performed by members of the service organization's internal audit function in this area because it may indicate a need for increased testing of controls.

Nature of Tests of Controls

4.77 The nature and objectives of tests to evaluate the operating effectiveness of controls are different from those performed to evaluate the suitability of the design of controls. Paragraph 24 of SSAE No. 16 states that when designing and performing tests of controls, the service auditor should

    a. perform other procedures in combination with inquiry to obtain evidence about

        i. how the control was applied,

        ii. the consistency with which the control was applied, and

        iii. by whom or by what means the control was applied.

    b. determine whether the controls to be tested depend on other controls, and if so, whether it is necessary to obtain evidence supporting the operating effectiveness of those other controls.

    c. determine an effective method for selecting the items to be tested to meet the objectives of the procedure.

4.78 The other procedures the service auditor should perform in combination with inquiry to obtain evidence about the operating effectiveness of controls include

- observation of the application of the control,
- inspection of documents, reports, or electronic files that contain evidence of the performance of the control, and
- reperformance of the control.

4.79 Inquiry alone does not provide sufficient appropriate evidence of the operating effectiveness of controls. Some tests of controls provide more convincing evidence of the operating effectiveness of the controls than others. Performing inquiry combined with inspection or reperformance ordinarily provides more convincing evidence than performing inquiry and observation. For example, a service auditor may inquire about and observe a service organization's physical building security during the initial walkthroughs. Because an observation is pertinent only at the point in time at which it is made, the service auditor would supplement the observation with other procedures, which may include inspecting video tapes that monitor the entrance of the facility and comparing a sample of individuals who enter the building to the service organization's list of individuals authorized to access the building during that period to obtain sufficient appropriate evidence regarding the operating effectiveness of the controls.

4.80 The type of control being tested may affect the nature, timing, and extent of the testing performed by the service auditor. For example, for some controls, operating effectiveness is evidenced by documentation. In such circumstances, the service auditor may decide to inspect the documentation. Other controls may not leave evidence of their operation that can be tested at a later date and accordingly, the service auditor may need to test the operating effectiveness of such controls at various times throughout the period.

4.81 In determining the appropriate testing procedures, the service auditor determines whether evidence of the operating effectiveness of the control could exist regardless of whether or not evidence actually does exist. There may be instances in which evidence that would have demonstrated the operating effectiveness of the controls has been lost, misplaced, or inadvertently deleted by the service organization. In such instances, the service auditor evaluates the type of evidence available and whether the effectiveness of the control can be tested through other procedures, such as observation, that would provide sufficient evidence of the operating effectiveness of the control throughout the period. However, depending on the control activity and its significance to meeting the control objective, tests such as observation may not alone provide sufficient evidence.

4.82 When information produced by the service organization's information system is provided to the service auditor as a source for testing, the service auditor obtains evidence about the completeness and accuracy of that information. Such information may be provided in a report generated by manual or automated means using data prepared by management of the service organization as a result of providing services to user entities. These reports may be in several forms, including data listings, exception reports, or transaction reconciliations.

Timing of Tests of Controls

4.83 In determining the timing of tests of controls, the service auditor considers

- when the information will be available and when it will no longer be available, for example, that
  - electronic files may be overwritten after a period of time,
  - procedures may occur only at certain times during the period, and
  - certain test procedures may need to be performed after the end of the period, for example, reviewing the reconciliations of general ledger balances to external statements that are generated after the end of the period.
- the significance of the control being tested.

4.84 The service auditor may perform tests of controls at interim dates, at the end of the period, or after the end of the period if they relate to controls that were in operation during the period but do not leave evidence until after the end of the period. Performing procedures at an interim date may assist the service auditor in identifying, at an early stage of the examination, any potential deficiencies in design or operating effectiveness and, consequently, provides an opportunity for the service organization to resolve them prior to the end of the period, regardless of the service auditor's determination about whether they affect the service auditor's report. When the service auditor performs tests of the operating effectiveness at an interim period, the service auditor considers the extent of additional testing necessary for the remaining period.

Extent of Tests of Controls

4.85 The extent of the service auditor's testing relates to the size of the sample tested or the number of observations of a control activity. The service auditor determines the extent of testing using professional judgment after considering the tolerable rate of deviation, the expected rate of deviation, the frequency with which the control operates, the length of the testing period, the significance of the control to preventing, or detecting and correcting errors, and whether other controls support the achievement of the control objective.

4.86 The service auditor should test the operating effectiveness of the controls in effect throughout the period covered by the report and determine whether the control has occurred a sufficient number of times to be assessed as operating effectively. For example, if a report covers a period of six months and a control operates only annually, the service auditor may be unable to test the operating effectiveness of the control within the period. The shorter the test period, the more likely the service auditor will be unable to perform sufficient testing and obtain sufficient evidence to express an opinion on the operating effectiveness of controls.

4.87 Paragraph 22 of SSAE No. 16 states that evidence obtained in prior engagements about the satisfactory operation of controls in prior periods does not provide a basis for a reduction in testing in the current period, even if it is supplemented with evidence obtained during the current period. Sufficient, appropriate evidence about the operating effectiveness of controls throughout the current period is required for the service auditor to express an opinion on the operating effectiveness of controls.

4.88 Paragraph A43 of SSAE No. 16 states that knowledge of deviations observed in prior engagements may lead the service auditor to increase the extent of testing in the current period. For example, the service auditor's report on Example Service Organization's ABC System for the prior year was qualified relating to the operating effectiveness of controls over the accuracy of distribution transactions. In the current year, the service auditor learns that service organization management has made changes to controls to address the deficiencies. The service auditor may decide to increase the number of items to be tested in the current examination period knowing of the qualification in the prior year and the changes made to the controls, because observed prior year deviations increase the risk that the controls did not operate effectively in the current period.

4.89 If the service organization makes changes to controls during the period that are relevant to the achievement of the control objectives stated in the description and the service auditor believes the changes would be considered significant by user entities and their auditors, the service auditor should test the superseded controls before the change and the new controls after the change for the period each was in effect. For example, during the period June 1, 20X0, to May 31, 20X1, Example Service Organization decided to automate a control that was previously performed manually. The service organization automated the control on December 15, 20X0. The service auditor tests the manual control for the period from June 1, 20X0, to December 14, 20X0, considering the nature and frequency of the performance of the control, and then tests the automated control for the period from December 15, 20X0, to May 31, 20X1, again, giving consideration to the nature and frequency of the performance of the control. If the service auditor cannot test the superseded control, the service auditor should determine the effect on the service auditor's report.

4.90 If a control objective is composed of several elements (for example: "Controls provide reasonable assurance that transactions are authorized and entered into the order capture system completely, accurately, and on a timely basis."), the service auditor would need to link the applicable controls to each of the elements (authorization, completeness, accuracy, and timeliness) included in the control objective. The service auditor may determine that a deficiency exists in the design of the control that addresses the timeliness with which transactions are entered but that controls related to authorization, completeness, and accuracy are suitably designed. Because information about the design of controls related to authorization, completeness, and accuracy could be relevant to user entities, and those controls are suitably designed, the service auditor would test the operating effectiveness of those controls and would determine what effect the control that is not suitably designed will have on the service auditor's report.

4.91 If a control objective is composed of several elements and one of the elements is not achieved, the service auditor may

- conclude that the element of the control objective that is not achieved prevents the entire control objective from being achieved.
- suggest that the element of the control objective that was not achieved be disaggregated from the multiple-element control objective and be presented as a separate control objective. The service auditor would determine what effect the control that is not suitably designed will have on the service auditor's report for the disaggregated control objective.

Selecting Items to Be Tested

4.92 Paragraph 25 of SSAE No. 16 states that when determining the extent of tests of controls and whether sampling is appropriate, the service auditor should consider the characteristics of the population of the controls to be tested, including the nature of the controls, the frequency of their application, and the expected deviation rate. AU section 350, *Audit Sampling* (AICPA, *Professional Standards*), addresses planning, performing, and evaluating audit samples. In situations in which the service auditor determines that sampling is appropriate, the service auditor should apply the requirements in paragraphs .31–.43 of AU section 350 that address sampling in tests of controls. Paragraphs .01–.14 and .45–.46 of AU section 350 provide additional guidance regarding the principles underlying those paragraphs.

4.93 For tests of controls using sampling, the service auditor determines the tolerable rate of deviation and uses that rate to determine the number of items to be selected for a particular sample.

4.94 The service auditor's selection of sample items should result in a sample that is representative of the population. All items in the population should have an opportunity to be selected. Random-based selection of items represents one means of obtaining such samples.

4.95 Tests of automated application controls generally are tested only once or a few times if effective general computer controls are present.

Using the Work of the Internal Audit Function

4.96 In order for a service auditor to use specific work of the internal audit function, the service auditor should evaluate and perform procedures on that work to determine its adequacy for the service auditor's purposes. In doing so, the service auditor should evaluate whether

    a. the work was performed by members of the internal audit function having adequate technical training and proficiency;

    b. the work was properly supervised, reviewed, and documented;

    c. sufficient appropriate evidence has been obtained to enable the members of the internal audit function to draw reasonable conclusions;

    d. conclusions reached are appropriate in the circumstances and any reports prepared by members of the internal audit function are consistent with the results of the work performed; and

    e. any deviations or unusual matters disclosed by members of the internal audit function are properly resolved.

4.97 The nature, timing, and extent of the service auditor's procedures on specific work of the internal auditors will depend on the service auditor's assessment of the significance of that work to the service auditor's conclusions (for example, the significance of the risks that the controls tend to mitigate), the evaluation of the internal audit function, and the evaluation of the specific work of the internal auditors. Such procedures may include the following:

- Examination of items already examined by the internal auditors
- Examination of other similar items
- Observation of procedures performed by the internal auditors

4.98 The service auditor uses professional judgment in performing procedures to evaluate the work performed by the members of the service organization's internal audit function. The procedures performed generally include a combination of independent testing of the controls tested by members of the internal audit function and reperformance of their work. The service auditor is responsible for providing sufficient appropriate evidence for the opinion and determines the work to be performed. The service auditor has sole responsibility for the opinion expressed in the service auditor's report, and that responsibility is not reduced by the service auditor's use of the work of the internal audit function.

4.99 In considering whether to use the work of the internal audit function to obtain evidence regarding the operating effectiveness of controls, the service auditor considers the pervasiveness of the control and the potential for management override of the control (in addition to the degree of judgment and subjectivity required to evaluate the effectiveness of the control). As the significance of these factors increases, so does the need for the service auditor, rather than the internal audit function, to perform the tests, and conversely, as these factors decrease in significance, the need for the service auditor to perform the tests decreases.

4.100 If the quality and extent of the work performed by the members of the service organization's internal audit function is not performed to the same degree as the work the service auditor would have performed, the service auditor generally will perform additional tests and consider the extent to which to use the work of the internal audit function.

4.101 In reviewing internal audit reports, the service auditor evaluates test exceptions identified by the members of the service organization's internal audit function to determine whether to alter the nature, timing, and extent of the service auditor's procedures. The service auditor ordinarily corroborates exceptions identified by the members of the internal audit function and considers the extent of the exceptions, their nature and underlying cause, and whether additional procedures by the service auditor are necessary.

4.102 The service auditor ordinarily considers the adequacy of sampling procedures used by the members of the internal audit function and whether the sampling procedures used were appropriate and free from bias (that is, all items in the population should have an equal opportunity to be selected). AU section 350 provides additional information on sampling procedures.

4.103 If the size of the sample used by the members of the service organization's internal audit function is less than the sample size the service auditor would have used, the service auditor generally would select additional items to achieve the required sample size.

4.104 The service auditor may perform additional procedures to corroborate deviations identified by the members of the service organization's internal audit function by reperforming a sample of the work performed by the internal audit function. Typically, the service auditor does not solely use tests performed by members of the internal audit function to support the service auditor's opinion on the operating effectiveness of controls.

4.105 The responsibility to report on management's description of the service organization's system and the suitability of the design and operating effectiveness of controls rests solely with the service auditor and cannot be shared with the internal audit function. Therefore, the judgments about the significance of deviations in the design or operating effectiveness of controls, the sufficiency of tests performed, the evaluation of identified deficiencies, and other matters that affect the service auditor's report are those of the service auditor. In making judgments about the extent of the effect of the work of the internal audit function on the service auditor's procedures, the service auditor may determine, based on risk associated with the controls and the significance of the judgments relating to them, that the service auditor will perform the work relating to some or all of the controls rather than using the work performed by the internal audit function.

Direct Assistance

4.106 The service auditor may determine during planning that it will be effective and efficient to use the work of the internal audit function to provide direct assistance in performing tests of the operating effectiveness of controls under the direction of the engagement team. In such cases, the service auditor can take advantage of the internal audit function's familiarity with the service organization's procedures, records, and files to conduct tests efficiently. The service auditor should inform the members of the service organization's internal audit function of their responsibilities; the objectives of the procedures to be performed; the matters that may affect the nature, timing, or extent of the procedures; and how to communicate issues identified during testing.

4.107 When the service auditor uses members of the service organization's internal audit function to provide direct assistance, the service auditor should adapt and apply the requirements in paragraph .27 of AU section 322, *The Auditor's Consideration of the Internal Audit Function in an Audit of Financial Statements* (AICPA, *Professional Standards*), which states

> In performing the audit, the auditor may request direct assistance from the internal auditors. This direct assistance relates to work the auditor specifically requests the internal auditors to perform to complete some aspect of the auditor's work. For example, internal auditors may assist the auditor in obtaining an understanding of internal control or in performing tests of controls or substantive tests, consistent with the guidance about the auditor's responsibility in paragraphs .18 through .22. When direct assistance is provided, the auditor should assess the internal auditors' competence and objectivity (see paragraphs .09 through .11) and supervise, review, evaluate, and test the work performed by internal auditors to the extent appropriate in the circumstances. The auditor should inform the internal auditors of their responsibilities, the objectives of the procedures they are to perform, and matters that may affect the nature, timing, and extent of audit procedures, such as possible accounting and auditing issues. The auditor should also inform the internal auditors that all significant accounting and auditing issues identified during the audit should be brought to the auditor's attention.

Evaluating the Results of Tests of Controls

4.108 The service auditor evaluates the results of tests of controls and the significance of deviations noted. The service auditor may conclude that the controls are operating effectively to achieve the specified control objectives whether or not deviations have been identified or may conclude that the controls are not operating effectively if deviations are identified.

4.109 Paragraph 26 of SSAE No. 16 states that the service auditor should investigate the nature and cause of any deviations identified and determine whether

    a. identified deviations are within the expected rate of deviation and are acceptable. If so, the testing that has been performed provides an appropriate basis for concluding that the control operated effectively throughout the specified period.

    b. additional testing of the control or of other controls is necessary to reach a conclusion about whether the controls related to the control objectives stated in management's description of the service organization's system operated effectively throughout the specified period.

Performing an Engagement Under SSAE No. 16

c. the testing that has been performed provides an appropriate basis for concluding that the control did not operate effectively throughout the specified period.

4.110 Paragraph 27 of SSAE No. 16 states that if, as a result of performing the procedures identified in paragraph 26 of SSAE No. 16, the service auditor becomes aware that any identified deviations have resulted from intentional acts by service organization personnel, the service auditor should assess the risk that management's description of the service organization's system is not fairly presented, the controls are not suitably designed, and, in a type 2 engagement, the controls are not operating effectively.

4.111 Paragraph 5.56 of this guide contains an example of an explanatory paragraph that would be added to the service auditor's report when controls were not operating effectively to achieve one or more control objectives.

Documentation

4.112 Paragraphs 44–48 of SSAE No. 16 contain requirements for the service auditor to document the following:

- The nature, timing, and extent of the procedures performed, including the identifying characteristics of the specific items or matters being tested, who performed the work and the date such work was completed, and who reviewed the work performed and the date and extent of such review
- The results of the procedures performed and the evidence obtained
- Significant findings or issues arising during the engagement, the conclusions reached thereon, and significant professional judgments made in reaching those conclusions
- If the service auditor uses specific work of the internal audit function, conclusions reached regarding the evaluation of the adequacy of the work of the internal audit function and the procedures performed by the service auditor on that work
- Discussions of significant findings or issues with management and others, including the service auditor's final conclusion regarding a significant finding or issue, when the discussion took place, and with whom
- If the service auditor has identified information that is inconsistent with the service auditor's final conclusions, how the service auditor addressed the inconsistency

4.113 The service auditor should assemble the engagement file and complete this process no later than 60 days following the report release date. After completion of the engagement file, the service auditor should not delete or discard documentation before the end of the retention period. If the service auditor finds it necessary to modify existing documentation or add new documentation after the completion of the engagement file, the service auditor should document the reasons for making them and when and by whom they were made and reviewed. This guidance is an expansion of the "Attest Documentation" guidance included in paragraphs .100–.107 of AT section 101 and is similar to the documentation requirements related to audits of financial statements as provided in AU section 339, *Audit Documentation* (AICPA, *Professional Standards*, as amended). The service auditor also considers whether

AAG-ASO 4.113

certain industry segments (for example, government) may require additional documentation.

Extending or Modifying the Period

4.114 A service auditor may encounter situations in which management of a service organization requests that the period covered by an existing type 2 report be extended or modified; for example, the service auditor has previously reported on the period January 1, 20X1, to June 30, 20X1 (the original period), and management requests that the period be

- extended by three months to cover the period January 1, 20X1, to September 30, 20X1 (the extended period). In this case, six months of the extended period would have been tested, and three months of the extended period (new period) would not yet have been tested.
- modified to cover the period April 1, 20X1, to September 30, 20X1. In that case, three months of the modified period would have been tested, and three months of the modified period (new period) would not have been tested.

4.115 Prior to accepting an engagement in which the period covered by the service auditor's report is extended or modified, the service auditor would evaluate whether to accept the engagement.

4.116 Generally, the scope of the description of the system for the new period would be unchanged from the scope for the original period; therefore, portions, if not all, of the prior description of the system, including control objectives, controls, complementary user entity control considerations, and the service auditor's relevant tests and results, would be relevant to the engagement covering the extended or modified period.

4.117 Because the description of the service organization's system for the extended or modified period typically is consistent with that of the original period, the service auditor considers evidence obtained from tests of controls performed for the portion of the original period that is also included in the extended or modified period.

4.118 Thus, for example, if the service auditor performed tests of the operating effectiveness of controls during the original period for a sample of 13 items that relate to the period April 1, 20X1, through June 30, 20X1, the tests of operating effectiveness performed on the sample of 13 items could be used as evidence for the modified period.

4.119 The service auditor also inquires about any changes to the service organization's system that occurred during the new period, including changes to the services, control environment, controls, user entities, and personnel, and performs such additional procedures as he or she considers necessary. Information obtained from inquiry and other procedures is taken into consideration in developing the examination plan and assessing engagement risk.

4.120 The service auditor obtains evidence about the nature and extent of any changes to controls that occurred during the new period. If controls changed during that period, the service auditor would ordinarily test the controls in existence before the change and the controls in existence after the change.

4.121 The service auditor is not precluded from performing additional tests for the portion of the modified or extended period included in the original period and considers the results of those tests along with any additional information of which he or she becomes aware that may affect his or her conclusion about the fairness of the presentation of the description of the system, the suitability of the design of the controls, or the operating effectiveness of the controls for the modified or extended period.

4.122 Conclusions reached during the original period are taken into consideration, in addition to the results of tests performed and other evidence obtained related to the new period, when forming the service auditor's opinion. In making a determination about the nature and extent of the additional evidence needed for the extended or modified period, the service auditor may consider

- the control environment.
- the significance of the assessed risks.
- the specific controls that were tested during the portion of the original report period included in the new period and the nature and extent of the evidence obtained for that period.
- the nature, timing, and extent of procedures performed for the portion of the original period included in the new period.
- the length of the extended or modified period.

4.123 If there have been major changes in the service organization's system, it may not be appropriate to perform an engagement for an extended or modified period. For example, if a service organization converted from one application processing system to another during the new period, and it made significant modifications to the controls, the service auditor may decide that communicating information about changes in controls may present challenges for user entities and, therefore, may decide that an engagement covering an extended or modified period is not appropriate.

Management's Written Representations for the Extended or Modified Period

4.124 Paragraphs 5.69–.80 contain information about the requirement to obtain management's written representations. When the engagement covers a modified or extended period, the service auditor should obtain management's written representations in the form of a representation letter addressed to the service auditor and dated as of the same date as the service auditor's report that covers the entire extended or modified period (that is, the portion of the original period included in the modified or extended period plus the new period).

Reports of Deficiencies

4.125 The service auditor assesses any deficiencies identified in the original period and corrected during the new period to determine their overall effect on, and whether disclosures are required in, the service auditor's report. Similarly, deficiencies noted in the extended or modified period are also evaluated to determine their effect on the service auditor's report.

4.126 Any deficiencies identified in the portion of the original period that is included in the extended or modified period would be included in the report on the extended or modified period, even if they were corrected during the extended or modified period. The service auditor considers the status of any exceptions, deficiencies, or other matters noted in the portion of the original period that is also included in the extended or modified period, plus any exceptions, deficiencies, or other matters noted during the new period. For example, assume that the original report covered the period January 1, 20X1, to June 30, 20X1, and included a deficiency in operating effectiveness. Also assume that the deficiency was corrected on August 15, 20X1. For a report covering an examination period January 1 through September 30, the deficiency in operating effectiveness would be reported for the period from January 1 through September 30, 20X1. No reference to the original report is made in the extended or modified report.

4.127 For deficiencies reported in the original report that have not been corrected, the service auditor may evaluate the reasons that the deficiency has not been corrected and consider the effect on the engagement.

4.128 The service auditor may use evidence obtained for the original period that is included in the extended or modified period. Assume that the original period covered by the report is January 1, 20X1, to August 31, 20X1, and the modified period is April 1, 20X1, to December 31, 20X1. Of the modified period, 5 months were tested, and 4 months were untested. In the original period, 25 items were tested, 12 of which relate to the 5 months that were included in the modified period. There was 1 test exception noted for those 12 items. Thirteen items were tested for the modified period, and 1 exception was identified. The results of tests reported would identify the total number of exceptions identified based on the total number of tests performed (for example, "Two exceptions were identified in a sample of 25 items selected for testing. The service auditor's conclusion on the achievement of the control objective would be based on an exception rate of 2 of 25.").

Examination Quality Control

4.129 The service auditor should implement procedures to determine that the examination is effective in complying with relevant professional standards and the service auditor's report is accurate and complete. Such procedures should consider applicable standards provided under AT section 101. As discussed in paragraphs .16–.18 of that standard, the service auditor's firm has a responsibility to adopt a system of quality control in the conduct of its attest practice. The service auditor should follow its firm's established quality control policies and procedures to provide reasonable assurance that the service auditor complies with the attestation standards in its SSAE No. 16 attest engagements.

4.130 Of the six elements of a system of quality control identified in Statement on Quality Control Standards (SQCS) No. 7, *A Firm's System of Quality Control* (AICPA, *Professional Standards*, QC sec. 10A), the "Engagement Performance" element is the most relevant to the service auditor during the performance phase of a SSAE No. 16 examination. Policies and procedures related to this element should address

    a. engagement performance (for example, processes for complying with applicable engagement standards, appropriate documentation of the work performed, and appropriate communication of the results of the engagement),

Performing an Engagement Under SSAE No. 16

    b. supervision responsibilities (for example, considering whether sufficient time exists to complete the engagement, considering whether the work is being carried out in accordance with the planned approach, and addressing significant issues arising during the engagement), and

    c. review responsibilities (for example, considering whether the work performed supports the conclusions reached and is appropriately documented, whether evidence obtained is sufficient and appropriate to support the report, and whether the objectives of the engagement procedures have been achieved).

4.131 SQCS No. 7 additionally states that the firm should establish criteria against which all engagements are to be evaluated to determine whether an engagement quality control review should be performed. If the engagement meets the established criteria, the nature, timing, and extent of the engagement quality control review should follow the guidance discussed in paragraphs .85–.91 of SQCS No. 7.

4.132 If the use of the internal audit function has been contemplated in the performance of the examination procedures, the service auditor should apply the quality control provisions of AU section 322. See discussion related to the use of the internal audit function in paragraphs 3.95–.104, 4.96–.107, and 5.08–.12 of this guide.

Chapter 5
Reporting and Completing the Engagement

In reporting on and completing a type 1 or type 2 engagement, both the service organization and the service auditor have specific responsibilities. This chapter describes those responsibilities and identifies matters the service auditor considers and procedures the service auditor performs to prepare the service auditor's report and complete the engagement. This chapter principally focuses on type 2 reports.

Responsibilities of the Service Auditor

5.01 The service auditor's responsibilities for reporting on the engagement include preparing

- a written description of the tests of controls performed by the service auditor and the results of those tests and
- the service auditor's report, including all of the report elements for a type 2 report identified in paragraph 52 of Statement on Standards for Attestation Engagements (SSAE) No. 16, *Reporting on Controls at a Service Organization* (AICPA, *Professional Standards*, AT sec. 801) (and paragraph 53 for a type 1 report), and modifying the report if the service auditor determines it is appropriate to do so.

Describing Tests of Controls and the Results of Tests

5.02 Paragraph 52(*o*) of SSAE No. 16 states that a service auditor's type 2 report should contain a reference to a description of the service auditor's tests of controls and results thereof. The description should identify the controls that were tested, whether the items tested represent all or a selection of the items in the population, and the nature of the tests performed in sufficient detail to enable user auditors to determine the effect of such tests on their risk assessments. See table 5-1, "Information to Be Included in the Description of Tests of Controls."

5.03 Materiality with respect to the operating effectiveness of controls includes the consideration of both quantitative and qualitative factors, for example, the tolerable rate and observed rate of deviation (a quantitative matter) and the nature and cause of any observed deviations (a qualitative matter).

5.04 The concept of materiality is not applied when reporting the results of tests of controls for which deviations have been identified because the service auditor does not have the ability to determine whether a deviation will be relevant to a particular user entity. Consequently, the service auditor reports all deviations. If the service auditor has not identified any deviations, the service auditor may document those results with a phrase such as "No exceptions noted" or "No deviations noted." Appendix B, "Illustrative Type 2 Reports," in this guide provides a number of examples of descriptions of tests of controls in which no deviations have been identified.

5.05 The description of tests of controls need not be a duplication of the service auditor's detailed audit program which might make the report too voluminous for user auditors and provide more than the required level of detail.

The service auditor is not required to indicate the size of the sample unless deviations were identified during testing.

5.06 If deviations have been identified, paragraph 52(*o*)(ii) of SSAE No. 16 requires the service auditor's description of tests of controls and results to identify the extent of testing performed by the service auditor that led to the identification of the deviations, including the number of items tested and the number and nature of the deviations noted, even if, on the basis of tests performed, the service auditor concludes that the related control objective was achieved.

Table 5-1

Information to Be Included in the Description of Tests of Controls

Information to Be Disclosed	If No Deviations Were Identified	If Deviations Were Identified
The controls that were tested	Required	Required
Whether the items tested represent all or a selection of the items in the population,	Required	Required
The nature of the tests performed	Required	Required
The number of items tested		Required
The number and nature of the deviations		Required
Causative factors (for identified deviations)		Optional[1]

5.07 The following example illustrates the documentation of tests of controls for which deviations have been identified. It is assumed that in each situation other relevant controls and tests of controls would also be described.

> *Control Objective*: Controls provide reasonable assurance that trades are authorized, processed, and recorded in a complete, accurate, and timely manner.
>
> *Example Service Organizations Controls*: Trades are initiated only upon receipt of a trade authorization form signed by an employee of the user entity who has been specifically designated by the user entity to authorize trades.
>
> *Service Auditor's Tests of Controls*: Inquired of the trading desk clerks about the procedures performed upon receipt of trade authorizations. Inspected a sample of trade authorizations for the signatures of authorized user entity employees, comparing the signature on the trade authorization to a list of designated employees authorized to initiate trades for the user entity.

---

[1] Paragraph A65 of Statement on Standards for Attestation Engagements (SSAE) No. 16, *Reporting on Controls at a Service Organization* (AICPA, *Professional Standards*, AT sec. 801), indicates that it assists users of the report in understanding identified deviations if the service auditor's report includes information about causative factors, to the extent the service auditor has identified such factors.

Reporting and Completing the Engagement 91

Results of Tests of Controls: One of the n^2 trade authorizations sampled was missing the signature of an authorized user entity employee. The trading desk clerk stated that an authorized user entity employee had called to say that the trade had been approved, but the employee forgot to sign the trade authorization. Furthermore, another of the n trade authorizations sampled was signed, but the name of the individual who signed it was not on the list of authorized employees at the time. Observed that the name of that individual was added to the list of authorized user entity employees two weeks after the trade request had been approved. No other exceptions were noted.

Describing Tests of Controls and Results of Tests When Using the Internal Audit Function

5.08 If the work of the internal audit function has been used, the service auditor should not make reference to that work in the service auditor's opinion. Notwithstanding its degree of autonomy and objectivity, the internal audit function is not independent of the service organization. The service auditor has sole responsibility for the opinion expressed in the service auditor's report, and, accordingly, that responsibility is not reduced by the service auditor's use of the work of the internal audit function.

5.09 Paragraph 34 of SSAE No. 16 states that if the work of the internal function has been used to perform tests of controls (in other than a direct assistance capacity), the part of the service auditor's report that describes the service auditor's tests of controls and results should include a description of the work performed by the internal audit function and the service auditor's procedures with respect to that work. If the service auditor uses members of the service organization's internal audit function to provide direct assistance, including assistance in performing tests of controls that are designed by the service auditor and performed under the direction, supervision, and review of the service auditor, the description of tests of controls and results need not distinguish between the tests performed by members of the internal audit function and the tests performed by the service auditor because when the internal audit function provides direct assistance, the work performed by the internal audit function undergoes the same scrutiny as if it were performed by the service auditor's staff.

5.10 Paragraph A50 of SSAE No. 16 additionally states that the service auditor's description of tests of controls performed by the internal audit function and the service auditor's procedures performed with respect to that work may be presented in a number of ways, for example, by including introductory material in the description of tests of controls indicating that certain work of the internal audit function was used in performing tests of controls or by specifically identifying the tests performed by the internal audit function and attributing those tests to the internal audit function.

5.11 The following are examples of introductory material that may be included in the description of tests of controls and results to inform readers that the service auditor has used the work of the internal audit function to perform tests of controls.

---

[2] The letter "n" is used to represent the size of the sample.

AAG-ASO 5.11

Example 1. Throughout the examination period, members of XYZ Service Organization's internal audit function performed tests of controls related to the control objectives that address withdrawals, corporate actions, and dividends. Members of the internal audit function observed the control being performed, inspected documentation of and reperformed the control activities, and did not identify any deviations in testing. We reperformed selected tests that had been performed by members of the internal audit function and found no exceptions.

Example 2. Members of XYZ Service Organization's internal audit function performed tests of controls for the following control objectives:

- Controls provide reasonable assurance that withdrawals are authorized and processed in a complete, accurate, and timely manner.
- Controls provide reasonable assurance that corporate actions are processed and recorded in a complete, accurate, and timely manner.
- Controls provide reasonable assurance that dividends are processed and recorded in a complete, accurate, and timely manner.

The tests performed by members of the internal audit function included inquiry of relevant parties who performed the control activities observation of the control being performed at different times during the examination period and inspection of the documentation for a sample of transactions. No deviations were noted by members of the internal audit function. We tested the work of members of the internal audit function through a combination of independent testing and reperformance and noted no exceptions.

5.12 The following are examples of descriptions of tests of controls and results that identify the tests performed by the internal audit function and attribute that work to them.

Example 1. When withdrawal requests are received, the name of the individual requesting the withdrawal is compared to a client-provided list of individuals authorized to make such requests. The employee who performs this control initials the request form to indicate that the comparison has been performed. Requests from individuals whose names are not on the client-provided list are rejected and sent back to the client.

Tests performed by the internal audit function

- Inquired of the employee responsible for performing the control regarding the procedures followed when a withdrawal request is received.
- Observed on multiple occasions throughout the examination period of the employee performing the control.
- For a sample of withdrawals made during the examination period, compared the name on the withdrawal request to the client-provided list of individuals authorized to make such requests.

Tests performed by the service auditor

- Inquired of the employee who performs the control regarding the procedures followed when a withdrawal request is received.
- For a sample of items tested by members of the internal audit function, reperformed the control.
- For an additional sample of withdrawals made during the examination period, compared the name on the withdrawal request form to the client-provided list of employees authorized to make such requests.

Results of tests

- No exceptions noted.

Example 2. When withdrawal requests are received, the name of the individual requesting the withdrawal is compared to a client-provided list of employees authorized to make such requests. The employee performing this control initials the request form or electronic request to indicate that the comparison has been performed. Requests from individuals who are not on the client-provided list are rejected and sent back to the client.

Tests performed

- Members of the internal audit function inquired of the employee responsible for performing the control regarding the procedures followed when withdrawal requests are received.
- Members of the internal audit function made multiple observations throughout the examination period of the employee performing the control.
- For a sample of withdrawals during the examination period, both members of the internal audit group and the service auditor compared the name on the withdrawal request form or electronic request to the client-provided list of individuals authorized to make such requests and noted no exceptions.
- The service auditor reperformed the testing for a sample of items tested by members of the internal audit group.

Results of tests

- No exceptions noted.

Elements of the Service Auditor's Report

5.13 Paragraph 52 of SSAE No. 16 identifies the elements that should be included in a type 2 service auditor's report, and paragraph 53 of SSAE No. 16 identifies the elements that should be included in a type 1 report.

5.14 The following chart identifies where each required element of a type 2 service auditor's report is illustrated in this guide, primarily referencing appendix B, which contains illustrative type 2 reports. A service auditor's type 2

AAG-ASO 5.14

report should contain all of the elements identified in paragraph 52 of SSAE No. 16. Illustrative reports are shown in paragraph A68 of SSAE No. 16.

Paragraph Containing the Requirement in SSAE No. 16	Illustration of the Required Element in This Guide	Required Element and Additional Comments
52(*a*)	Appendix B, Example 1	A title that includes the word independent.
52(*b*)	Appendix B, Example 1	An addressee. (In most cases, the service auditor is engaged by the service organization and would address the service auditor's report to management of the service organization. However, the service auditor may be engaged by one or more user entities or the board of directors of the service organization and, in such cases, would address and provide the report to the party that engaged the service auditor.)
52(*c*)(i)	Appendix B, Example 1	Identification of management's description of the service organization's system and the function performed by the system.
52(*c*)(ii)	Paragraph 5.17	Any parts of management's description of the service organization's system that are not covered by the service auditor's report.
52(*c*)(iii)	Paragraph 5.20	Any information included in a document containing the service auditor's report that is not covered by the service auditor's report.
52(*c*)(iv)	Appendix B, Example 1	The criteria. (The criteria are identified in management's assertion and incorporated by reference in the service auditor's report.)
52(*c*)(v)(1)	Appendix B, Example 3	Services performed by a subservice organization and whether the carve-out or inclusive method was used. If the carve-out method was used, a statement that the description of the service organization's system excludes control objectives and controls at the subservice organization and that the service auditor's procedures do not extend to the subservice organization.

AAG-ASO 5.14

Paragraph Containing the Requirement in SSAE No. 16	Illustration of the Required Element in This Guide	Required Element and Additional Comments
52 (c)(v)(2)	Appendix B, Example 2	Services performed by a subservice organization and whether the carve-out or inclusive method was used. If the inclusive method was used, a statement that the description of the service organization's system includes the subservice organization's control objectives and controls and that the service auditor's procedures included procedures related to the subservice organization.
52(d)	Appendix B, Example 1	If the description refers to the need for complementary user entity controls, a statement that the service auditor has not evaluated the suitability of design or operating effectiveness of complementary user entity controls, and that the control objectives can be achieved only if complementary user entity controls are suitably designed and operating effectively along with controls at the service organization.
52(e)	Appendix B, Example 1	A reference to management's assertion and a statement that management is responsible for
52(e)(i)	Appendix B, Example 1	• preparing the description of the service organization's system and the assertion, including the completeness, accuracy, and method of presentation of the assertion and description. Paragraph A60 states that management's assertion may be presented in or attached to the description.
52(e)(ii)	Appendix B, Example 1	• providing the services covered by the description of the service organization's system.

(continued)

AAG-ASO 5.14

Paragraph Containing the Requirement in SSAE No. 16	Illustration of the Required Element in This Guide	Required Element and Additional Comments
52(e)(iii)	Appendix B, Example 1	• specifying the control objectives, unless the control objectives are specified by law, regulation, or another party, and stating them in the description of the service organization's system.
52(e)(iv)	Appendix B, Example 1	• identifying the risks that threaten the achievement of the control objectives.
52(e)(v)	Appendix B, Example 1	• selecting the criteria.
52(e)(vi)	Appendix B, Example 1	• designing, implementing, and documenting controls that are suitably designed and operating effectively to achieve the related control objectives stated in the description.
52(f)	Appendix B, Example 1	An enumeration of the service auditor's responsibilities.
52(g)	Appendix B, Example 1	A statement that the examination was conducted in accordance with AICPA Attestation Standards.
52(h)	Appendix B, Example 1	A statement that the examination entails performing procedures to obtain evidence about the fairness of the presentation of the description, and the suitability of the design and operating effectiveness of the controls, including
52(i)	Appendix B, Example 1	• assessing the risks that the description is not fairly presented and that controls were not suitably designed or operating effectively.
52(j)	Appendix B, Example 1	• testing the operating effectiveness of controls.
52(k)	Appendix B, Example 1	• evaluating the overall presentation of management's description and the suitability of the control objectives.

AAG-ASO 5.14

Reporting and Completing the Engagement

Paragraph Containing the Requirement in SSAE No. 16	Illustration of the Required Element in This Guide	Required Element and Additional Comments
52(*l*)	Appendix B, Example 1	A statement that the service auditor believes the examination provides a reasonable basis for the opinion.
52(*m*)	Appendix B, Example 1	A statement about the inherent limitations of controls and the risk of projecting to the future any evaluation of the description of the service organization's system or the suitability of the design or operating effectiveness of the controls.
52(*n*)	Appendix B, Example 1	The service auditor's opinion on whether, in all material respects, based on the criteria described in management's assertion
52(*n*)(i)	Appendix B, Example 1	• management's description of the service organization's system fairly presents the service organization's system that was designed and implemented throughout the specified period.
52(*n*)(ii)	Appendix B, Example 1	• the controls related to the control objectives stated in management's description of the service organization's system were suitably designed to provide reasonable assurance that those controls would be achieved if the controls operated effectively throughout the specified period.
52(*n*)(iii)	Appendix B, Example 1	• the controls the service auditor tested, which were those necessary to provide reasonable assurance that the control objectives stated in management's description of the service organization's system were achieved, operated effectively throughout the specified period.

(continued)

AAG-ASO 5.14

Paragraph Containing the Requirement in SSAE No. 16	Illustration of the Required Element in This Guide	Required Element and Additional Comments
52(n)(iv)	Appendix B, Example 1	If the application of complementary user entity controls is necessary to achieve the related control objectives stated in management's description of the service organization's system, a reference to this condition.
52(o)	Appendix B, Example 1	A reference to the service auditor's tests of controls and results thereof.
52(o)(i)	Appendix B, Example 1	Identification of the controls that were tested, whether the items tested represent all or a selection of the items in the population, and the nature of tests in sufficient detail to enable user auditors to determine the effect of such tests on their risk assessments.
52(o)(ii)	Paragraph 5.07	If deviations have been identified in the operation of controls included in the description, the extent of testing performed by the service auditor that led to the identification of deviations (including the number of items tested) and the number and nature of the deviations noted (even if, on the basis of tests performed, the service auditor concludes that the related control objectives were achieved).
52(p)	Appendix B, Example 1	A statement restricting the use of the service auditor's report to management of the service organization, user entities of the service organization's system during some or all of the period covered by the service auditor's report, and the independent auditors of such user entities. (Paragraph A64 of SSAE No. 16 states that a user entity of the service organization is also considered a user entity of the subservice organization if controls at the subservice organization are relevant to the user entity's internal control over financial reporting and may be included in the group to whom use of the service auditor's report is restricted.)

Paragraph Containing the Requirement in SSAE No. 16	Illustration of the Required Element in This Guide	Required Element and Additional Comments
52(q)	Appendix B, Example 1	The date of the service auditor's report. (Paragraph 54 of SSAE No. 16 states that the service auditor should date the report no earlier than the date on which the service auditor has obtained sufficient appropriate evidence to support the service auditor's opinion.)
52(r)	Appendix B, Example 1	The name of the service auditor and the city and state where the service auditor maintains the office that has responsibility for the engagement.

Information Not Covered by the Service Auditor's Report

5.15 Paragraph 52(c)(ii) of SSAE No. 16 requires the service auditor's type 2 report to identify any parts of management's description of the service organization's system that are not covered by the service auditor's report. Typically, this would be information that is beyond the scope of the engagement that the service organization wishes to communicate to user entities. Examples of such information include the following:

- Future plans for new systems
- Other services provided by the service organization that are not included in the scope of the engagement
- Qualitative information, such as marketing claims, that may not be objectively measurable
- Information related to the privacy of personally identifiable or medical information
- Information that would not be considered relevant to user entities' internal control over financial reporting, such as information about the service organization's business continuity plans
- Responses from management to address control improvement recommendations

5.16 One way of presenting information that is not covered by the service auditor's report is to include the information in a separate section of the description, for example, in a section titled "Other Information Provided by the Service Organization."

5.17 The following is an example of an explanatory paragraph that could be added to the report to identify such information:

> The information in section 5 of management's description of the service organization's system, "Other Information Provided by XYZ Service Organization," that describes XYZ Service Organization's inventory application, is presented by management of XYZ Service Organization

AAG-ASO 5.17

to provide additional information and is not a part of XYZ Service Organization's description of its payroll system made available to user entities during the period June 1, 20X0, to May 31, 20X1. Information about XYZ Service Organization's inventory application has not been subjected to the procedures applied in the examination of the description of the payroll system and of the suitability of the design and operating effectiveness of controls to achieve the related control objectives stated in the description of the payroll system.

5.18 The service auditor also has the option of disclaiming an opinion on information that is not covered by the service auditor's report by adding the words "and, accordingly, we express no opinion on it" at the end of the explanatory paragraphs illustrated in paragraph 5.17.

5.19 Paragraph 52(*c*)(iii) of SSAE No. 16 requires the service auditor's report to identify any information included in a document containing the service auditor's report that is not covered by the service auditor's report. Paragraph A56 indicates that such information may be provided by the service organization or by another party. Examples of such information include a

- report comparing the service organization's performance to its commitments to user entities per service level agreements or a newsletter containing information about events at the service organization,
- description of a subsequent event that does not affect the functions and processing performed by the service organization during the period covered by the service auditor's report but may be of interest to user entities, or
- description of future planned system conversions.

5.20 The following is an example of an explanatory paragraph that would be added to the service auditor's report to identify such information:

The type 2 report that addresses Computer Subservice Organization's IT Controls, on pages 8–10, has been provided by XYZ Service Organization to provide additional information and is not a part of XYZ Service Organization's description of its payroll system made available to user entities during the period June 1, 20X0, to May 31, 20X1. The type 2 report for Computer Subservice Organization has not been subjected to the procedures applied in the examination of the description of the payroll system and of the suitability of the design and operating effectiveness of controls to achieve the related control objectives stated in the description of the payroll system.

5.21 The service auditor has the option of disclaiming an opinion on information included in a document containing the service auditor's report that is not covered by the service auditor's opinion by adding the phrase "and, accordingly, we express no opinion on it" at the end of the explanatory paragraph illustrated in paragraph 5.20.

Modifications to the Service Auditor's Report

5.22 Paragraph 55 of SSAE No. 16 states that the service auditor's opinion should be modified and the service auditor's report should contain a clear description of all the reasons for the modification, if the service auditor concludes that

Reporting and Completing the Engagement

  a. management's description of the service organization's system is not fairly presented, in all material respects;
  b. the controls are not suitably designed to provide reasonable assurance that the control objectives stated in management's description of the service organization's system would be achieved if the controls operated as described;
  c. in the case of a type 2 report, the controls did not operate effectively throughout the specified period to achieve the related control objectives stated in management's description of the service organization's system; or
  d. the service auditor is unable to obtain sufficient, appropriate evidence.

The objective of including a clear description of each of the reasons for the modification is to enable report users to develop their own assessments of the effect of deficiencies on user entities' internal control over financial reporting. If the explanatory paragraph describing the deficiency is not otherwise clear regarding the effect of the deficiency on each of the components of the service auditor's opinion, the service auditor may wish to add language such as the following to the explanatory paragraph, "We did not perform procedures to determine whether controls were suitably designed and operating effectively . . ." Appendix B, "Illustrative Service Auditor's Reports," of SSAE No. 16 provides examples of elements of modified service auditor's reports. Examples of explanatory paragraphs that describe such modifications are provided in paragraphs 5.15–.63 of this guide.

5.23 When determining whether to modify the service auditor's opinion, the service auditor considers the individual and aggregate effect of identified deficiencies and deviations in management's description of the service organization's system and the suitability of the design and operating effectiveness of the controls throughout the specified period. The service auditor considers quantitative and qualitative factors such as the following:

- The likelihood that the deficiencies or deviations will result in errors or misstatements in the user entity's data
- The magnitude of the errors or misstatements that could occur in the user entity's financial statements as a result of the deficiencies or deviations
- The tolerable rate of deviations that the service auditor has established
- The pervasiveness of the deficiencies or deviations
- Whether user entities and user auditors could be misled if the service auditor's opinion or individual components of the opinion were not modified

5.24 If a modified opinion is appropriate, the service auditor determines whether to issue a qualified opinion, an adverse opinion, or a disclaimer of opinion.

5.25 The service auditor considers the need to express a qualified opinion if the deficiencies or deviations in management's description of the service organization's system, the suitability of the design of the controls, or the operating effectiveness of the controls are limited to one or more, but not all, aspects of the description of the service organization's system or control objectives and

AAG-ASO 5.25

do not affect the service auditor's opinion on other aspects of the description of the service organization's system or other control objectives.

5.26 When the service auditor has determined that a qualified opinion is appropriate, in addition to adding an explanatory paragraph to the service auditor's report, the service auditor should modify the opinion paragraph of the service auditor's report as follows (New language is shown in boldface italics.):

> In our opinion, *except for the matter referred to in the preceding paragraph,* in all material respects, and based on the criteria described in [*service organization's*] assertion on page [*aa*], . . .

5.27 The service auditor considers the need to issue an adverse opinion if the deficiencies or deviations in management's description of the service organization's system, the suitability of the design of the controls, or the operating effectiveness of the controls are pervasive throughout the description or across all or most of the control objectives.

Adverse Opinion

5.28 When the service auditor has determined that an adverse opinion is appropriate, in addition to adding an explanatory paragraph to the service auditor's report, the service auditor should modify the opinion paragraph of the service auditor's report, assuming an adverse opinion on all three components of the opinion. The following is an example of such a paragraph (New language is shown in boldface italics; deleted language is shown by strikethrough):

> In our opinion, *because of the matter referred to in the preceding paragraph,* in all material respects and based on criteria described in [*name of service organization's*] assertion on page [*xx*]
>
> - the description *does not* fairly presents the [*type or name of system*] that was designed and implemented throughout the period.
> - the controls related to the control objectives stated in the description were *not* suitably designed to provide reasonable assurance that the control objectives would be achieved if the controls operated effectively throughout the period [*date*] to [*date*].
> - the controls tested, which were those necessary to provide reasonable assurance that the control objectives stated in the description were achieved, *did not* operated effectively throughout the period from [*date*] to [*date*].

Disclaimer of Opinion

5.29 In some circumstances the service auditor may decide to disclaim an opinion because he or she is unable to obtain sufficient appropriate evidence. In those circumstances, the service auditor's opinion should be modified and the service auditor's report should contain a clear description of all the reasons for the modification. If the service auditor plans to disclaim an opinion and the limited procedures performed by the service auditor caused the service auditor to conclude that certain aspects of management's description of the service organization's system are not fairly presented, certain controls are not suitably designed, or that certain controls did not operate effectively, the service auditor should identify these findings in the service auditor's report.

Reporting and Completing the Engagement

The following are other situations in which the service auditor should disclaim an opinion:

- Management refuses to provide a written assertion (after initially agreeing to do so), and law or regulation does not allow the service auditor to withdraw from the engagement. This is cited in paragraph 11 of SSAE No. 16.

- Management refuses to provide a representation reaffirming its written assertion included in or attached to its description, or a representation stating that it has provided the service auditor with all relevant information and access agreed to. Paragraph 39 of SSAE No. 16 indicates that another option in these circumstances is for the service auditor to withdraw from the engagement.

5.30 Paragraph 57 of SSAE No. 16 states that if the service auditor disclaims an opinion, the service auditor's report should not identify the procedures that were performed nor include statements describing the characteristics of a service auditor's engagement, because to do so might overshadow the disclaimer. When disclaiming an opinion, in addition to adding an explanatory paragraph to the service auditor's report, the service auditor should also modify the opinion paragraph of the service auditor's report by adding a sentence such as the following at the end of the opinion paragraph:

> Because of the matter described in the preceding paragraph, the scope of our work was not sufficient to enable us to express, and we do not express, an opinion.

5.31 A modified opinion on an individual component of the service auditor's opinion (for example, management's description of the service organization's system is not fairly presented in all material respects) may affect the other components of the opinion (the opinion on the suitability of the design or operating effectiveness of controls). For example, a service auditor may determine that an adverse opinion on the fair presentation of the description of the service organization's system is appropriate because the description includes a number of controls for each control objective that have not been implemented, and management will not amend the description to reflect this problem. Because many of the controls that are needed to achieve the related control objectives have not been implemented, an adverse opinion on the suitability of the design of the controls and operating effectiveness of the controls is also appropriate. Another example is a situation in which the service auditor has concluded that the description is fairly presented but the service auditor has determined that a qualified opinion on the suitability of the design of the controls is appropriate because, as designed, certain controls do not achieve the related control objective. The service auditor would also conclude that the qualification applies to the operating effectiveness of the controls, because even if the controls are operating as designed, the controls would not be operating effectively to achieve the control objectives due to their inappropriate design. In all of these situations, the service auditor should include an explanatory paragraph in the report that describes all of the reasons for the modification.

5.32 Although the service auditor may qualify the opinion on the fairness of the presentation of management's description of the service organization's system because of an omission of a control objective, the omission would not

AAG-ASO 5.32

necessarily affect the service auditor's opinion on the suitability of the design or operating effectiveness of the controls because those opinions relate only to control objectives included in management's description. The service auditor cannot report or comment on the suitability of the design or operating effectiveness of controls intended to achieve control objectives that are not included in management's description of the service organization's system. The service auditor is not responsible for identifying or testing controls that might achieve the omitted control objective(s).

Illustrative Explanatory Paragraphs: Description Is Not Fairly Presented

5.33 A number of situations are presented in chapter 4, "Performing an Engagement Under Statement on Standards for Attestation Engagement No. 16," of this guide in which the service auditor determines that the description is not fairly presented. In practice, if the service auditor makes such a determination, the service auditor works with the service organization by informing management of the service organization of the changes that need to be made for the description to be fairly presented. The following paragraphs contain examples of explanatory paragraphs that would be inserted before the modified opinion paragraph of the service auditor's report if management is unwilling to amend a description that is not fairly presented.

Description Includes Controls That Have Not Been Implemented

5.34 The following is an example of an explanatory paragraph that would be added to the service auditor's report when the description includes controls that have not been implemented:

> The accompanying description of the XYZ System states that Example Service Organization uses operator identification numbers and passwords to prevent unauthorized access to its system. Our testing determined that operator identification numbers and passwords are used in applications A and B, but are not used in applications C and D.

Description Includes Subjective Information

5.35 The following is an example of an explanatory paragraph that would be added to the service auditor's report when the description of the service organization's system includes subjective information:

> On page XX of the attached description, Example Trust Organization states that its savings system is the industry's best system and is staffed by the most talented IT personnel. Because no criteria have been established for these attributes of the system or personnel, these statements are not relevant to user entities' internal control over financial reporting and cannot be objectively evaluated within the scope of this examination.

Description Omits Control Objectives and Related Controls Required for Other Controls to Be Suitably Designed and Operating Effectively

5.36 The following is an example of an explanatory paragraph that would be added to the service auditor's report when the description of the service organization's system omits control objectives and related controls needed for other controls included in the description to be suitably designed and operating effectively:

> The description of Example Trust Organization's savings system includes application controls related to the savings system. These controls depend on the effective operation of general computer controls, which have not been included in the description.

Description Omits Information Relevant to User Entities' Internal Control

5.37 The following is an example of an explanatory paragraph that would be added to the service auditor's report when the description of the service organization's system omits information that may be relevant to user entities' internal control over financial reporting:

> The accompanying description of Example Service Organization's XYZ1 and XYZ2 systems does not include information about the automated interfaces between the XYZ1 and XYZ2 systems. We believe that such information about the automated interfaces should be included in management's description of its system because it is relevant to user entities' internal control over financial reporting.

Description Omits Information About Relevant Subsequent Events

5.38 The following is an example of an explanatory paragraph that would be added to the service auditor's report when the description of the service organization's system omits information about a subsequent event that affects the functions and processing performed by the service organization during the period covered by the service auditor's report:

> Subsequent to the examination, XYZ Service Organization's management discovered that a supervisor had provided all of the programmers with access to the production data files for the month of July. This information should be included in XYZ's description of its system because providing programmers with access to production data files could enable programmers to modify data, which would be relevant to user entities internal control over financial reporting.

Description Omits Relevant Changes to Controls

5.39 The following is an example of an explanatory paragraph that would be added to the service auditor's report when the description does not address relevant changes to the service organization's controls:

> The accompanying description states that the quality assurance group reviews a random sample of work performed by input clerks to determine the degree of compliance with the service organization's input requirements. Inquiries of staff personnel indicate that this control was first implemented on July 1, 20X0, which would be relevant to user entities' internal control over financial reporting during the first six months of the year.

Description Includes Information Not Relevant to User Entities' Internal Control That Is Not Appropriately Segregated

5.40 The following is an example of an explanatory paragraph that would be added to the service auditor's report when the description includes information that is not relevant to user entities' internal control over financial reporting and the service organization refuses to place the information in a separate section of the description identified as, for example, "Other Information Provided by XYZ Service Organization," or otherwise exclude it from the description altogether:

> The accompanying description includes the procedures the organization performs to comply with Health Insurance Portability and Accountability Act (HIPAA) regulations. Such information is not relevant to user entities' internal control over financial reporting and should not be included in the description.

In these circumstances, because management refuses to move the other information to a separate section of the type 1 or type 2 report, the service auditor may wish to disclaim an opinion on that information by adding the words "and, accordingly, we express no opinion on it" at the end of the explanatory paragraph.

Description Includes Control Objective Not Relevant to User Entities' Internal Control

5.41 The following is an example of an explanatory paragraph that would be added to the service auditor's report when the description includes a control objective that is not relevant to user entities' internal control over financial reporting:

> The accompanying description includes Control Objective 5, "Controls provide reasonable assurance that data will be recovered in the event of a power system failure." This control objective should not be included in the description because it is not relevant to user entities' internal control over financial reporting during the period April 1, 20X1, to May 31, 20X2.

Disclaimer on Information Included in Description That Is Not Covered by the Service Auditor's Report

5.42 The following is an example of an explanatory paragraph that would be added to the service auditor's report when the description includes information that is not covered by the service auditor's report and the service auditor is disclaiming an opinion on that information.

> Example Service Organization has included information about its inventory application on page XX of its description. This information has not been subjected to the procedures applied in the examination of the payroll system, and accordingly, we express no opinion on it.

Description Includes Control Objective That Is Not Objectively Stated

5.43 The following is an example of an explanatory paragraph that would be added to the service auditor's report when the description includes a control objective that is not objectively stated:

> Page XX of the description includes Control objective 10, "Controls are adequate to restrict access to computer resources." The wording of this control objective is not sufficiently objective for use in evaluating the design or operating effectiveness of controls related to the control objective.

Description Omits Certain Control Objectives Established by an Outside Party

5.44 The following is an example of an explanatory paragraph that would be added to the service auditor's report when the control objectives have been established by an outside party and the description omits one or more of the control objectives specified by the outside party:

> The set of control objectives specified by Outside User Group includes the control objective, "Controls provide reasonable assurance that investment purchases and sales are authorized." Example Trust Organization has not included or addressed this control objective in its description of Example Trust Organization's savings system.

Set of Control Objectives Established by Outside Party Omits a Control Objective Necessary to Achieve Other Control Objectives

5.45 The following is an example of an explanatory paragraph that would be added to the service auditor's report when the set of control objectives established by an outside party omits control objectives that the service auditor believes are needed to achieve other control objectives:

> The set of control objectives specified by Outside User Group does not include a control objective that addresses the authorization, testing, documentation, and implementation of changes to existing applications. Such a control objective and the related controls are necessary for other control objectives related to the application to be achieved. Example Trust Organization has included this control objective and described the controls to address this control objective in its description of Example Trust Organization's system.

Description Includes an Incomplete Control Objective

5.46 The following is an example of an explanatory paragraph that would be added to the service auditor's report when the description of the service organization's system includes an incomplete control objective:

> Control Objective 5 in Example Service Organization's description of its system is: "Controls provide reasonable assurance that loan payments received from user entities are completely and accurately recorded." This control objective should be amended to address the timeliness of the recording of loan payments because of its relevance to user entities' internal control over financial reporting.

Description Omits a Relevant Control Objective

5.47 The following is an example of an explanatory paragraph that would be added to the service auditor's report when the service organization's description omits a relevant control objective:

> Example Trust Organization's description of its system does not include a control objective and related controls that address the restriction of logical access to system resources (for example, programs, data, tables, and parameters) to authorized individuals. This control objective should be included because of its relevance to user entities' internal control over financial reporting.

Service Organization Revises a Control Objective During the Engagement Without Reasonable Justification

5.48 The following is an example of an explanatory paragraph that would be added to the service auditor's report when the service organization revises a control objective during the engagement without reasonable justification for doing so:

> Example Trust Organization's description of its system, dated April 1, 20X1, includes the following control objective: "Controls provide reasonable assurance that changes to existing applications are authorized, tested, documented, and implemented in a complete, accurate and timely manner." After informing management that the results of our testing indicated that controls over the authorization of changes to existing applications were not suitably designed, management deleted the word "authorized" from the aforementioned control objective. As modified, the control objective is not sufficiently complete.

Service Organization Changes from Inclusive Method to Carve-Out Method Without Reasonable Justification

5.49 The following is an example of an explanatory paragraph that would be added to the service auditor's report when the service organization changes from the inclusive method of presentation to the carve-out method of presentation for a subservice organization, without reasonable justification:

> As indicated in the description, Example Trust Organization uses a subservice organization for computer processing. Example Trust Organization elected to change from the inclusive method of presentation to the carve-out method of presentation after our testing indicated that controls at the subservice organization, intended to restrict access to the subservice organization's system to authorized and approved individuals, had not been implemented. As a result, this information would be relevant to user entities' internal control over financial reporting.

Description Omits Complementary User Entity Controls

5.50 The following is an example of an explanatory paragraph that would be added to the service auditor's report when the description omits complementary user entity controls that are required to achieve the control objectives:

> Example Service Organization has omitted from its description a statement indicating that user entities should have controls in place that limit access to user defined indexes to authorized individuals. Such complementary user entity controls are necessary for controls to be considered suitably designed and operating effectively to achieve control objective 11. This information about the need for such complementary user entity controls would be relevant to user entities' internal control over financial reporting.

Description Does Not Disclose That Service Organization Uses a Subservice Organization

5.51 The following is an example of an explanatory paragraph that would be added to the service auditor's report when the functions and processing performed by a subservice organization are significant to the processing of

Reporting and Completing the Engagement

user entities' transactions, and the service organization has not disclosed the existence of a subservice organization and the functions it performs:

> Example Trust Organization's description does not indicate that it uses a subservice organization for computer processing, which could be significant to user entities' internal control over financial reporting because controls at the subservice organization are relevant to changes to programs as well as physical and logical access to system resources.

Illustrative Explanatory Paragraphs: Controls Are Not Suitably Designed

Controls Are Not Suitably Designed to Achieve the Control Objectives

5.52 The following is an example of an explanatory paragraph that would be added to the service auditor's report when the service auditor concludes that controls are not suitably designed to achieve one or more of the specified control objectives:

> The accompanying description of the XYZ System states on page [mn] that Example Service Organization reconciles the list of loan payments received with the Loan Payment Summary Report. The Organization's reconciliation procedures, however, do not include a control for follow-up on reconciling items and independent review and approval of the reconciliations. As a result, the controls are not suitably designed and not operating effectively to achieve the control objective, "Controls provide reasonable assurance that output is complete, accurate, reconciled, and independently reviewed and approved."

Part of the Control Objective Is Not Achieved Because Certain Controls Are Missing

5.53 The following is an example of an explanatory paragraph that would be added to the service auditor's report when certain controls that are needed to achieve a portion of a control objective are missing:

> Example Service Organization has controls in place to ascertain that total contributions received are recorded in the correct amount. However, there are no controls in place to ascertain that contributions received are recorded in the correct user account. As a result, the design of Example Service Organization's controls does not provide reasonable assurance that the following control objective was achieved solely as it relates to the accuracy of processing contributions during the period, "Controls provide reasonable assurance that contributions received are processed and recorded in a complete, accurate, and timely manner."

Scope Limitation Related to Suitably of Design of Controls

5.54 The following is an example of an explanatory paragraph that would be added to the service auditor's report when the service auditor is unable to obtain sufficient evidence that controls were suitably designed to achieve a specified control objective:

> Page [mn] of the accompanying description of the XYZ System states that Example Service Organization reconciles the list of loan payments received with the Loan Payment Summary Report. The Organization's

AAG-ASO 5.54

reconciliation procedures changed on July 15, 20X0, and sufficient evidence that independent review and approval of the reconciliations occurred prior to July 15, 20X0, could not be obtained. As a result, we were unable to determine whether controls were suitably designed and operating effectively during the period January 1 to July 14, 20X0, to achieve the control objective, "Controls provide reasonable assurance that output is complete, accurate, reconciled, and independently reviewed and approved."

Service Organization Uses Carve-Out Method; Achievement of Service Organization Control Objective Requires Controls at Subservice Organization

5.55 When a service organization uses a subservice organization and uses the carve-out method of presentation, certain control objectives included in the description may only be able to be achieved if controls at the subservice organization are suitably designed and operating effectively. Following is a modification of the scope paragraph of a type 2 report if the description refers to the need for controls at the subservice organization (new language is shown in boldface italics):

> We have examined XYZ Service Organization's description of its [*type or name of*] system for processing user entities' transactions [*or identification of the function performed by the system*] throughout the period [*date*] to [*date*] (description) and the suitability of the design and operating effectiveness of controls to achieve the related control objectives stated in the description. ***The description indicates that certain control objectives specified in the description can be achieved only if controls at the subservice organization contemplated in the design of XYZ Service Organization's controls are suitably designed and operating effectively, along with related controls at the service organization. We have not evaluated the suitability of the design or operating effectiveness of such subservice organization controls.***

Following is a modification of the applicable subparagraphs of the opinion paragraph of a type 2 service auditor's report if the application of controls at the subservice organization is necessary to achieve the related control objectives stated in the description of the service organization's system.

> b. the controls related to the control objectives stated in the description were suitably designed to provide reasonable assurance that the control objectives would be achieved if the controls operated effectively throughout the period [*date*] to [*date*] ***and subservice organizations applied the controls contemplated in the design of XYZ Service Organization's system throughout the period [date] to [date].***
>
> c. the controls tested, which ***together with the subservice organization's controls referred to in the scope paragraph of this report, if operating effectively,*** were those necessary to provide reasonable assurance that the control objectives stated in the description were achieved, operated effectively throughout the period [*date*] to [*date*].

Illustrative Explanatory Paragraphs: Controls Were Not Operating Effectively

5.56 The service auditor may conclude that controls were not operating with sufficient effectiveness to achieve one or more of the specified control objectives. The following is an example of an explanatory paragraph that would be added to the service auditor's report when controls were not operating effectively throughout the specified period to achieve one or more control objectives:

> The service organization states in its description that it has controls in place to reconcile securities account master files to subsidiary ledgers, to follow up on reconciling items, to perform surprise annual physical counts, and to independently review its reconciliation procedures. However, as noted at page [mn] of the description of test of controls and results, controls related to the reconciliations and annual physical counts were not performed during the period April 1, 20X1, to December 31, 20X1. As a result, controls were not operating effectively to achieve the control objective, "Controls provide reasonable assurance that securities account master files are properly reconciled to subsidiary ledgers and surprise annual physical counts are performed."

Scope Limitation Related to Operating Effectiveness of Controls

5.57 The following is an example of an explanatory paragraph that would be added to the service auditor's report if the service auditor is unable to obtain sufficient appropriate evidence regarding the operating effectiveness of controls to achieve a specified control objective:

> Example Trust Organization states in its description of its savings system that it has automated controls in place to reconcile loan payments received with the Loan Payment Summary Report. However, electronic records of the performance of this reconciliation for the period January 1, 20X1, to July 31, 20X1 were deleted as a result of a computer processing error and, therefore, tests of operating effectiveness could not be performed for that period. Consequently, we were unable to determine whether the control objective, "Controls provide reasonable assurance that loan payments received are properly recorded," was achieved throughout the period January 1, 20X1, to July 31, 20X1.

Various Control Objectives in Place for Different Periods

5.58 If various control objectives were in place for different periods, the service auditor's report discloses the applicable periods. The following is an example of (*a*) an explanatory paragraph that would be added to the service auditor's report and (*b*) the revisions that would be made to the service auditor's opinion when the periods covered by various control objectives differ and the tests of controls cover those differing periods.

> As indicated in XYZ Service Organization's description of its system, control objectives 1–10 were implemented and the related controls were in operation during the period January 1, 20X1, to October 31, 20X1; whereas control objectives 11–13 were implemented and the related controls were in operation during the period November 1, 20X1, to December 31, 20X1. Our tests of operating effectiveness covered the period during which the applicable control objectives were implemented and the related controls were in operation.

Opinion

In our opinion, in all material respects, based on the criteria described in XYZ Service Organization's assertion on page [*aa*],

    a. the description fairly presents the [*type or name of*] system that was designed and implemented throughout the period January 1, 20X1, to October 31, 20X1, as it relates to control objectives 1 through 10, and throughout the period November 1, 20X1, to December 31, 20X1, as it relates to control objectives 11 through 13

    b. the controls related to the control objectives stated in the description were suitably designed to provide reasonable assurance that the control objectives would be achieved if the controls operated effectively throughout the period January 1, 20X1, to October 31, 20X1, for control objectives 1 through 10 and throughout the period November 1, 20X1, to December 31, 20X1, for control objectives 11 through 13

    c. the controls tested, which were those necessary to provide reasonable assurance that the control objectives stated in the description were achieved, operated effectively throughout the period January 1, 20X1, to October 31, 20X1, for control objectives 1 through 10 and operated effectively throughout the period November 1, 20X1, to December 31, 20X1, for control objectives 11 through 13.

Illustrative Explanatory Paragraphs: Disclaimer of Opinion

5.59 A disclaimer of opinion states that the service auditor does not express an opinion on the fair presentation of the description or on the suitably of the design and operating effectiveness of the controls. If the service auditor disclaims an opinion, the service auditor's report provides all of the substantive reasons for the disclaimer. A disclaimer is appropriate when the auditor has not performed an examination sufficient in scope to enable him or her to form an opinion on whether the description is fairly presented and the controls are suitably designed and operating effectively.

5.60 When disclaiming an opinion, the service auditor does not identify the procedures that were performed nor include the paragraph describing the characteristics of a service auditor's examination (that is, the scope paragraph of the service auditor's standard report); to do so may tend to overshadow the disclaimer. In addition, the service auditor also discloses any other reservations he or she has regarding the fair presentation of the description and suitability of the design and operating effectiveness of the controls.

Management Will Not Provide Written Representations

5.61 The following is an example of the modifications that would be made to the service auditor's report when disclaiming an opinion because management will not provide one or more of the written representations requested by the service auditor (New language is shown in boldface italics; deleted language is shown by strikethrough):

Reporting and Completing the Engagement

Scope

We ~~have~~ **were engaged to** examined XYZ Service Organization's description of its [*type or name of*] system for processing user entities' transactions [*or identification of the function performed by the system*] throughout the period [*date*] to [*date*] (description) and the suitability of the design and operating effectiveness of controls to achieve the related control objectives stated in the description.

Service organization's responsibilities

~~On page XX of the description, XYZ Service Organization has provided an assertion about the fairness of the presentation of the description and suitability of the design and operating effectiveness of the controls to achieve the related control objectives stated in the description.~~ XYZ Service Organization is responsible for preparing the description and for **providing** ~~the~~ **an** assertion **about the fairness of the presentation of the description and the suitability of the design and operating effectiveness of the controls to achieve the related control objectives stated in the description,** including the completeness, accuracy, and method of presentation of the description and the assertion~~,~~. **XYZ Service Organization is also responsible for** providing the services covered by the description, specifying the control objectives and stating them in the description, identifying the risks that threaten the achievement of the control objectives, selecting the criteria, and designing, implementing, and documenting controls to achieve the related control objectives stated in the description.

Service auditor's responsibilities

Our responsibility is to express an opinion on the fairness of the presentation of the description and on the suitability of the design and operating effectiveness of the controls to achieve the related control objectives stated in the description, based on our examination. ~~We conducted our examination in accordance with attestation standards established by the American Institute of Certified Public Accountants. Those standards require that we plan and perform our examination to obtain reasonable assurance about whether, in all material respects, the description is fairly presented and the controls were suitably designed and operating effectively to achieve the related control objectives stated in the description throughout the period [date] to [date].~~

[*The second paragraph identifying the service auditor's responsibilities is omitted*]

Management of Example Service Organization did not provide us with certain written representations that we requested to reaffirm its assertion and to represent that it has provided us with all relevant information, among other matters, upon which we would base our opinion. Since the service organization did not provide us with the requested representations, the scope of our work was not sufficient to enable us to express, and we do not express, an opinion on the fairness of the presentation of the description and on the suitability of the design and operating effectiveness of the controls.

Management Will Not Provide a Written Assertion, Law or Regulation Does Not Permit Service Auditor to Withdraw From Engagement

5.62 The following is an example of an explanatory paragraph that would be added to the service auditor's report when management does not provide a written assertion and law or regulation does not permit the service auditor to withdraw from the engagement:

> The accompanying description of Example Service Organization's XYZ system does not include management's assertion. A written assertion by management is required to perform an engagement in accordance with attestation standards established by the American Institute of Certified Public Accountants.

Illustrative Explanatory Paragraph: Management's Assertion Does Not Reflect Deviations Identified in Service Auditor's Report

5.63 Paragraph 3.75 states that management's assertion would be expected to disclose any deviations in the subject matter (that is, the fairness of the presentation of the description, the suitability of the design of the controls, and the operating effectiveness of the controls) identified in a modified service auditor's report. If the service auditor has determined that a modified report is appropriate for reasons such as those addressed in paragraphs 5.22–.61, and management of the service organization will not modify its written assertion to reflect the deviations in the subject matter identified in the service auditor's report, the service auditor should add an additional explanatory paragraph to the report indicating that the deficiencies identified in the service auditor's report have not been identified in management's assertion. The following is an illustrative explanatory paragraph that a service auditor would add to the report if controls were not operating effectively, followed by an additional illustrative explanatory paragraph indicating that management's assertion has not been modified to reflect the matter described in the first explanatory paragraph.

> The service organization states in its description that it has controls in place to reconcile securities account master files to subsidiary ledgers, to follow up on reconciling items, to perform surprise annual physical counts, and to independently review its reconciliation procedures. However, as noted on page [*mn*] of the description of test of controls and results, controls related to the reconciliations and annual physical counts were not performed during the period April 1, 20X1, to December 31, 20X1. As a result, controls were not operating effectively to achieve the control objective, "Controls provide reasonable assurance that securities account master files are properly reconciled to subsidiary ledgers and surprise annual physical counts are performed."

> Management of Example Service Organization has not identified the deficiencies noted in the preceding paragraph in its assertion regarding the operating effectiveness of its controls.

Paragraphs 5.89–.93 discuss modifications to management's assertion.

Intended Users of the Report

5.64 Paragraphs 52(*p*) and 53(*o*) of SSAE No. 16 indicate that a service auditor's report should contain a statement restricting the use of the report to specified parties, including management of the service organization, user entities of the service organization's system and the independent auditors of such user entities. The user entities to whom use of the report is restricted include user entities of the service organization ("during some or all of the period covered by the report" for a type 2 report and "as of the ending date of the period covered by the report" for a type 1 report) It does not include *potential* users of the service organization.

5.65 Paragraph A64 of SSAE No. 16 states that a user entity of a service organization is also considered a user entity of the service organization's subservice organization if controls at the subservice organization are relevant to the user entity's internal control over financial reporting. In such case, the user entity is referred to as an indirect or downstream user entity of the subservice organization. Consequently, an indirect or downstream user entity may be included in the group to whom use of the service auditor's report is restricted if controls at the service organization are relevant to the indirect or downstream user entity's internal control over financial reporting. For example, a company (user entity) that has a self-insured health plan outsources the processing of its medical claims to a health insurance company that processes medical claims. In turn, the claims processor outsources the processing of pharmacy claims to a pharmacy benefits manager. Management of the pharmacy benefits manager engages a service auditor to report on the pharmacy benefits manager controls over the processing of pharmacy claims. Because the processing of pharmacy claims may be relevant to the user entity's internal control over financial reporting, the user entity is considered an indirect or downstream user entity of the pharmacy benefits manager and, therefore, a member of the group to whom use of the pharmacy benefits manger's report is restricted.

5.66 The requirement to restrict the use of the report is based on paragraph .79 of AT section 101, *Attest Engagements* (AICPA, *Professional Standards*), which requires that use of a practitioner's report be restricted to specified parties when the criteria used to evaluate or measure the subject matter are available only to specified parties or appropriate only for a limited number of parties who either participated in their establishment or can be presumed to have an adequate understanding of the criteria. Paragraph A61 of SSAE No 16 indicates that the criteria used for engagements to report on controls at a service organization are relevant only for the purpose of providing information about the service organization's system, including controls, to those who have an understanding of how the system is used for financial reporting by user entities.

Report Date

5.67 As stated in paragraph 52 of SSAE No. 16, the service auditor should date the service auditor's report no earlier than the date on which the service auditor has obtained sufficient appropriate evidence to support the service auditor's opinion.

Completing the Engagement

5.68 Procedures that usually are performed toward the end of a service auditor's engagement include

- obtaining representations from management of the service organization and
- inquiring about subsequent events and evaluating the need for disclosure of such events.

If the service auditor wishes to do so, providing recommendations to management of the service organization, generally related to controls that affect user entities' internal control over financial reporting.

Obtaining Written Representations

5.69 As indicated in paragraph 9(*c*)(vi)(4) of SSAE No. 16, one of the conditions for accepting or continuing an engagement to report on controls at a service organization is that management of the service organization agrees to the terms of the engagement by acknowledging and accepting its responsibility for providing the service auditor with written representations at the conclusion of the engagement.

5.70 Paragraph 36 of SSAE No. 16 requires the service auditor to request from management written representations that address the matters listed in the paragraph. Although paragraph 36 indicates that the request should be made to management, paragraph 8 of SSAE No 16 indicates that the service auditor should determine the appropriate person(s) within the service organization's management or governance structure with whom to interact and when doing so, should consider which person(s) have the appropriate responsibilities for and knowledge of the matters concerned. In addition, paragraph A52 of SSAE No. 16 states that in certain circumstances, the service auditor may obtain written representations from parties in addition to management of the service organization, such as those charged with governance.

5.71 In some cases the party making the assertion may be indirectly responsible for and knowledgeable about specified matters covered in the representations. For example, the CEO of the service organization may be knowledgeable about certain matters through personal experience and about other matters through employees who report to the CEO. The service auditor may request that individuals who are directly or indirectly responsible for and knowledgeable about matters covered in the written representations provide their own representations.

5.72 Paragraph 37 of SSAE No. 16 indicates that if a service organization uses a subservice organization, and management's description of the service organization's system uses the inclusive method, the service auditor also should obtain written representations from management of the subservice organization. The subservice organization's written representations should address the matters identified in paragraph 36 of SSAE No. 16.

5.73 Paragraph A54 of SSAE No. 16 states that if the service auditor is unable to obtain written representations regarding relevant control objectives and related controls at the subservice organization, management of the service organization would be unable to use the inclusive method but may be able to use the carve-out method.

5.74 Paragraph A55 states that the service auditor may consider it necessary to request written representations about matters in addition to those listed in paragraph 36 of SSAE No. 16. This would be determined based on the facts and circumstances of the particular engagement, for example, if changes to the service organization's controls have occurred during the period covered by the service auditor's report, there might be a need to obtain representations that address the period before the change and the period after the change.

5.75 Paragraph 36 of SSAE No. 16 requires the service auditor to request written representations from management that

Reporting and Completing the Engagement

a. reaffirm its assertion included in or attached to the description of the service organization's system,

b. it has provided the service auditor with all relevant information and access agreed to, and[3]

c. it has disclosed to the service auditor any of the following of which it is aware:

  i. Instances of noncompliance with laws and regulations or uncorrected errors attributable to the service organization that may affect one or more user entities

  ii. Knowledge of any actual, suspected, or alleged intentional acts by management or the service organization's employees that could adversely affect the fairness of the presentation of management's description of the service organization's system or the completeness or achievement of the control objectives stated in the description

  iii. Design deficiencies in controls

  iv. Instances when controls have not operated as described

  v. Any events subsequent to the period covered by management's description of the service organization's system up to the date of the service auditor's report that could have a significant effect on management's assertion

5.76 Paragraph A53 of SSAE No. 16 clarifies that the written representations required by paragraph 36 of SSAE No. 16 are separate from and in addition to management's written assertion.

5.77 Paragraph 38 of SSAE No. 16 states that the written representations should be in the form of a representation letter addressed to the service auditor and dated as of the same date as the service auditor's report.

5.78 Paragraph 39 of SSAE No. 16 states that if management does not provide one or more of the requested representations, the service auditor should do the following:

a. Discuss the matter with management

b. Evaluate the effect of such refusal on the service auditor's assessment of the integrity of management and evaluate the effect that this may have on the reliability of management's representations and evidence in general

c. Take appropriate actions, which may include disclaiming an opinion or withdrawing from the engagement

5.79 Paragraph 39 further indicates that if management refuses to provide the service auditor with (a) representations that reaffirm its assertion or (b) a representation that it has provided the service auditor with all relevant information and access agreed to, the service auditor should disclaim an opinion or withdraw from the engagement. (See paragraphs 36[a]–[b] of SSAE No. 16.) This is the case because these representations are fundamental to the engagement and affect all of the other representations.

5.80 Because management's written representations are an important consideration when forming the service auditor's opinion, the service auditor

---

[3] See paragraph 9(c)(vi)(1) of SSAE No. 16.

would not ordinarily be able to issue the report until he or she had received the representation letter. Illustrative representation letters for a service auditor's engagement are presented in appendix C, "Representation Letters," of this guide.

Subsequent Events

5.81 Paragraph 42 of SSAE No. 16 requires the service auditor to make inquiries about whether management is aware of any events subsequent to the period covered by management's description of the service organization's system up to the date of the service auditor's report that could have a significant effect on management's assertion. If the service auditor becomes aware, through inquiry or otherwise, of such an event, or any other event that is of such a nature and significance that its disclosure is necessary to prevent users of the report from being misled, and information about that event is not disclosed by management in its description, the service auditor should disclose such event in the service auditor's report. The service auditor is responsible for determining the effect of the event on the service auditors' report, whether or not management appropriately discloses the event.

5.82 The following are examples of subsequent events that could affect management's assertion or management's description of the service organization's system:

- A defalcation occurred at the service organization.
- After the period covered by the service auditor's report, it was discovered that the signatures on a number of nonautomated trade execution instructions submitted during the examination period that appeared to be authenticated by signature verification had been forged.
- After the period covered by the service auditor's report, management discovered that during the last quarter of the period covered by the service auditor's report the IT security director had provided all of the programmers with access to the production data files enabling them to modify data.

5.83 If the subsequent event affects the functions and processing performed by the service organization as described in management's description of the service organization's system for the period covered by the service auditor's report and is significant to the processing of user entities' transactions, and the service organization does not disclose the subsequent event in its description, the service auditor requests that management amend the description of the service organization's system to disclose the required information. If management does not amend the description, the service auditor may modify the opinion on the fairness of the presentation of the description and should disclose the subsequent event in the service auditor's report. Paragraph 5.38 of this guide presents an illustrative explanatory paragraph that would be added to the service auditor's report when the description omits information about a subsequent event that affects the functions and processing performed by the service organization during the period covered by the service auditor's report.

5.84 Situations may exist in which the event discovered subsequent to the period covered by management's description of the service organization's system up to the date of the service auditor's report would likely have no effect on management's assertion because the underlying situation did not occur or exist until after the period covered by management's description of the service organization's system; however, the matter may be sufficiently important for disclosure by management in its description and potentially by the service auditor in an emphasis paragraph of the service auditor's report. The following are examples of such subsequent events:

- The service organization was acquired by another entity.
- The service organization experienced a significant operating disruption.
- A data center hosting service organization that provides applications and technology that enable user entities to process financial transactions made significant changes to its information systems including a system conversion or significant outsourcing of operations.

5.85 The service organization may wish to disclose such events in a separate section of the description of the service organization's system titled, for example, "Other Information Provided by the Service Organization," as described in paragraph 5.16 of this guide.

5.86 Paragraph 43 of SSAE No. 16 states that the service auditor has no responsibility to keep informed of events subsequent to the date of the service auditor's report; however, after the release of the service auditor's report, the service auditor may become aware of conditions that existed at the report date that might have affected management's assertion and the service auditor's report had the service auditor been aware of them. The evaluation of such subsequent information is similar to the evaluation of information discovered subsequent to the date of the report on an audit of financial statements, as described in AU section 561, *Subsequent Discovery of Facts Existing at the Date of the Auditor's Report* (AICPA, *Professional Standards*). The service auditor should adapt and apply the guidance in AU section 561.

Service Auditor's Recommendations for Improving Controls

5.87 Although it is not the objective of a service auditor's engagement, a service auditor may develop recommendations to improve a service organization's controls. The service auditor and management of the service organization agree on whether and how such recommendations will be communicated. Typically, the service auditor includes this information in a separate written communication provided only to the service organization's management. Management's responses to such recommendations also may be included. If included in the service auditor's report, it typically is placed in a separate section titled, "Other Information Provided by the Service Organization." Otherwise, the communication of recommended control improvements would be most effective if it took place within a short timeframe of issuance of the service auditor's report.

Management's Responsibilities During Engagement Completion

5.88 The responsibilities of management of the service organization towards the end of the engagement include

- modifying the description of the service organization's system, if appropriate (Chapter 4 describes a number of situations in which the service auditor would recommend that management of the service organization modify the description of the service organization's system.);
- modifying management's written assertion, if appropriate;
- providing written representations;
- informing the service auditor of subsequent events; and
- distributing the report to appropriate parties.

Modifying Management's Written Assertion

5.89 Paragraph 3.75 of this guide indicates that in order for the service auditor to express an unqualified opinion, management's written assertion generally would be expected to align with the service auditor's report, including modification of the assertion to reflect the deviations identified in the service auditor's report.

5.90 In some situations management of the service organization may choose not to revise its assertion, for example, because management disagrees with the service auditor's recommendation, for example, to revise or delete information in the description of the service organization's system. In other situations, management may agree with the service auditor's recommendation, but may prefer not to delay the issuance of the type 1 or type 2 report while modifications to the description are made or additional testing is performed. In such circumstances, management of the service organization would be more likely to modify its written assertion.

5.91 The following is an illustrative explanatory paragraph that the service auditor has added to the service auditor's report because of a deviation in the fairness of the presentation of management's description of the service organization's system:

> Explanatory Paragraph in Service Auditor' Report
>
> Example Service Organization has not included the following control objective and related controls in its description, which we believe are relevant to user entities internal control over financial reporting—"Controls provide reasonable assurance that logical access to system resources (for example, programs, data, table, and parameters) is restricted to authorized and appropriate individuals."

The following is a modification to the illustrative assertion presented in paragraph A71, example 1, of SSAE No. 16 to reflect the deviation in the description of the service organization's system identified in the service auditor's report. New language is shown in boldface italics

> Modified Assertion Regarding the Fairness of the Presentation of the Description
>
> a. *Except for the matter described in the following paragraph,* the description fairly presents the [*type or name of*] system made available to user entities of the system during some or all of the period [*date*] to [*date*] for processing their transactions [*or identification of the*

Reporting and Completing the Engagement 121

function performed by the system]. The criteria we used in making this assertion were that the description. . . .

(At the end of the portion of management's written assertion that addresses the fairness of the presentation of management's description of the service organization's system, management would add a paragraph such as the following:)

> ***The description of Example Service Organization's system does not include the control objective "Controls provide reasonable assurance that logical access to system resources (for example, programs, data, table, and parameters) is restricted to authorized and appropriate individuals;" nor, have we included the controls designed to achieve that control objective. That control objective is relevant to user entities internal control over financial reporting. As a result, the description is not fairly presented***

5.92 If the service auditor's report is modified because controls are not suitability designed or operating effectively, it would be expected that management's written assertion would also be modified.

5.93 The following is an example of a modification to the illustrative management assertion presented in paragraph A71, example 1, of SSAE No. 16 that would be used when controls were not operating effectively. New language is shown in boldface italics:

> c. ***Except for the matter described in the following paragraph,*** the controls related to the control objectives stated in the description were suitably designed and operating effectively throughout the period December 1, 20X0, to November 30, 20X1, to achieve those control objectives. The criteria we used in making this assertion were that:
>
> 1. The risks that threaten the achievement of the control objectives stated in the description have been identified;
>
> 2. The controls identified in the description would, if operating as described, provide reasonable assurance that those risks would not prevent the control objectives stated in the description from being achieved; and
>
> 3. The controls were consistently applied as designed, and manual controls were applied by individuals who have the appropriate competence and authority.

As noted on page [mn], controls related to reconciliations and annual physical counts were not performed from [date] to [date]. As a result, controls were not operating effectively to achieve the control objective "Controls provide reasonable assurance that securities account master files are properly reconciled to subsidiary ledgers and surprise physical counts are performed."

AAG-ASO 5.93

Distribution of the Report by Management

5.94 When engaged by the service organization, the service auditor provides the report to management of the service organization, and management distributes the report to the parties to whom use of the report is restricted.

5.95 In most cases, the service auditor is engaged by the service organization to perform the service auditor's engagement. However, in some cases the service auditor may be engaged by one or more user entities. A service auditor should distribute the service auditor's report only to the party that engaged the service auditor.

5.96 Paragraph 70 of AT section 101 states that "A practitioner should consider informing his or her client that restricted-use reports are not intended for distribution to nonspecified parties, regardless of whether they are included in a document containing a separate general-use report." However, a practitioner is not responsible for controlling a client's distribution of restricted-use reports.

Appendix A

Statement on Standards for Attestation Engagements No. 16, Reporting on Controls at a Service Organization

TABLE OF CONTENTS

	Paragraph
Statement on Standards for Attestation Engagements No. 16, *Reporting on Controls at a Service Organization*	.01-.A72
Introduction	.01-.05
Scope of This Section	.01-.04
Effective Date	.05
Objectives	.06
Definitions	.07
Requirements	.08-.58
Management and Those Charged With Governance	.08
Acceptance and Continuance	.09-.12
Assessing the Suitability of the Criteria (Ref: par. .A6 and .A22—.A23)	.13-.16
Materiality	.17
Obtaining an Understanding of the Service Organization's System (Ref: par. .A28—.A30)	.18
Obtaining Evidence Regarding Management's Description of the Service Organization's System (Ref: par. .A26 and .A31—.A35)	.19-.20
Obtaining Evidence Regarding the Design of Controls (Ref: par .A26 and .A36—.A39)	.21
Obtaining Evidence Regarding the Operating Effectiveness of Controls (Ref: par. .A26 and .A40—.A45)	.22-.27
Using the Work of the Internal Audit Function	.28-.35
Written Representations (Ref: par. .A51—.A55)	.36-.39
Other Information (Ref: par. .A56—.A57)	.40-.41
Subsequent Events	.42-.43
Documentation (Ref: par. .A58)	.44-.51
Preparing the Service Auditor's Report	.52-.57
Other Communication Responsibilities	.58
Application and Other Explanatory Material	.A1-.A72
Scope of This Section	.A1-.A4
Definitions	.A5-.A11
Management and Those Charged With Governance (Ref: par. 8)	.A12
Acceptance and Continuance	.A13-.A21
Assessing the Suitability of the Criteria (Ref: par. .13—.16)	.A22-.A24
Materiality (Ref: par. .17)	.A25-.A27
Obtaining an Understanding of the Service Organization's System (Ref: par. .18)	.A28-.A30
Obtaining Evidence Regarding Management's Description of the Service Organization's System (Ref: par. .19—.20)	.A31-.A35

Statement on Standards for Attestation Engagements No. 16, *Reporting on Controls at a Service Organization*—continued

  Obtaining Evidence Regarding the Design of Controls
    (Ref: par. .21) A36-.A39
  Obtaining Evidence Regarding the Operating Effectiveness
    of Controls (Ref: par. .22—.27) A40-.A45
  Using the Work of an Internal Audit Function A46-.A50
  Written Representations (Ref: par. .36—.39) A51-.A55
  Other Information A56-.A57
  Documentation A58
  Preparing the Service Auditor's Report A59-.A66
  Other Communication Responsibilities (Ref: par. .58) A67

Appendix A: Illustrative Service Auditor's Reports A68

Appendix B: Illustrative Modified Service Auditor's Reports A69

Appendix C: Illustrative Report Paragraphs for Service
  Organizations That Use a Subservice Organization A70

Exhibit A: Illustrative Assertions by Management of a
  Service Organization A71

Exhibit B: Comparison of Requirements of Section 801,
  Reporting On Controls at a Service Organization, With
  Requirements of International Standard on Assurance
  Engagements 3402, *Assurance Reports on Controls at
  a Service Organization* A72

Statement on Standards for Attestation Engagements No. 16 **127**

This section references the standard in its codified form as is appears in AICPA Professional Standards. Its supersedes the guidance for service auditors in AU section 324, **Service Organizations** *(AICPA, Professional Standards)*

Introduction

Scope of This Section

.01 This section addresses examination engagements undertaken by a service auditor to report on controls at organizations that provide services to user entities when those controls are likely to be relevant to user entities' internal control over financial reporting. It complements AU section 324, *Service Organizations,* in that reports prepared in accordance with this section may provide appropriate evidence under AU section 324. (Ref: par. .A1)

.02 The focus of this section is on controls at service organizations likely to be relevant to user entities' internal control over financial reporting. The guidance herein also may be helpful to a practitioner performing an engagement under section 101, *Attest Engagements,* to report on controls at a service organization

    a. other than those that are likely to be relevant to user entities' internal control over financial reporting (for example, controls that affect user entities' compliance with specified requirements of laws, regulations, rules, contracts, or grants, or controls that affect user entities' production or quality control). Section 601, *Compliance Attestation,* is applicable if a practitioner is reporting on an entity's own compliance with specified requirements or on its controls over compliance with specified requirements. (Ref: par. .A2–.A3)

    b. when management of the service organization is not responsible for the design of the system (for example, when the system has been designed by the user entity or the design is stipulated in a contract between the user entity and the service organization). (Ref: par. .A4)

.03 In addition to performing an examination of a service organization's controls, a service auditor may be engaged to (*a*) examine and report on a user entity's transactions or balances maintained by a service organization, or (*b*) perform and report the results of agreed upon procedures related to the controls of a service organization or to transactions or balances of a user entity maintained by a service organization. However, these engagements are not addressed in this section.

.04 The requirements and application material in this section are based on the premise that management of the service organization (also referred to as management) will provide the service auditor with a written assertion that is included in or attached to management's description of the service organization's system. Paragraph .10 of this section addresses the circumstance in which management refuses to provide such a written assertion. Section 101 indicates that when performing an attestation engagement, a practitioner may report directly on the subject matter or on management's assertion. For engagements conducted under this section, the service auditor is required to report directly on the subject matter.

AAG-ASO APP A

Effective Date

.05 This section is effective for service auditors' reports for periods ending on or after June 15, 2011. Earlier implementation is permitted.

Objectives

.06 The objectives of the service auditor are to

a. obtain reasonable assurance about whether, in all material respects, based on suitable criteria,
   i. management's description of the service organization's system fairly presents the system that was designed and implemented throughout the specified period (or in the case of a type 1 report, as of a specified date).
   ii. the controls related to the control objectives stated in management's description of the service organization's system were suitably designed throughout the specified period (or in the case of a type 1 report, as of a specified date).
   iii. when included in the scope of the engagement, the controls operated effectively to provide reasonable assurance that the control objectives stated in management's description of the service organization's system were achieved throughout the specified period.
b. report on the matters in 6(a) in accordance with the service auditor's findings.

Definitions

.07 For purposes of this section, the following terms have the meanings attributed in the subsequent text:

Carve-out method. Method of addressing the services provided by a subservice organization whereby management's description of the service organization's system identifies the nature of the services performed by the subservice organization and excludes from the description and from the scope of the service auditor's engagement, the subservice organization's relevant control objectives and related controls. Management's description of the service organization's system and the scope of the service auditor's engagement include controls at the service organization that monitor the effectiveness of controls at the subservice organization, which may include management of the service organization's review of a service auditor's report on controls at the subservice organization.

Complementary user entity controls. Controls that management of the service organization assumes, in the design of the service provided by the service organization, will be implemented by user entities, and which, if necessary to achieve the control objectives stated in management's description of the service organization's system, are identified as such in that description.

Control objectives. The aim or purpose of specified controls at the service organization. Control objectives address the risks that controls are intended to mitigate.

Controls at a service organization. The policies and procedures at a service organization likely to be relevant to user entities' internal control over financial reporting. These policies and procedures are designed, implemented, and documented by the service organization to provide reasonable assurance about the achievement of the control objectives relevant to the services covered by the service auditor's report. (Ref: par. .A5)

Controls at a subservice organization. The policies and procedures at a subservice organization likely to be relevant to internal control over financial reporting of user entities of the service organization. These policies and procedures are designed, implemented, and documented by a subservice organization to provide reasonable assurance about the achievement of control objectives that are relevant to the services covered by the service auditor's report.

Criteria. The standards or benchmarks used to measure and present the subject matter and against which the service auditor evaluates the subject matter. (Ref: par. .A6)

Inclusive method. Method of addressing the services provided by a subservice organization whereby management's description of the service organization's system includes a description of the nature of the services provided by the subservice organization as well as the subservice organization's relevant control objectives and related controls. (Ref: par. .A7–.A9)

Internal audit function. The service organization's internal auditors and others, for example, members of a compliance or risk department, who perform activities similar to those performed by internal auditors. (Ref: par. .A10)

Report on management's description of a service organization's system and the suitability of the design of controls (referred to in this section as a *type 1 report*). A report that comprises the following:

    a. Management's description of the service organization's system.

    b. A written assertion by management of the service organization about whether, in all material respects, and based on suitable criteria,

        i. management's description of the service organization's system fairly presents the service organization's system that was designed and implemented as of a specified date.

        ii. the controls related to the control objectives stated in management's description of the service organization's system were suitably designed to achieve those control objectives as of the specified date.

    c. A service auditor's report that expresses an opinion on the matters in (b)(i)–(b)(ii).

Report on management's description of a service organization's system and the suitability of the design and operating effectiveness of controls (referred to in this section as a *type 2 report*). A report that comprises the following:

    a. Management's description of the service organization's system.

  b. A written assertion by management of the service organization about whether in all material respects, and based on suitable criteria,

    i. management's description of the service organization's system fairly presents the service organization's system that was designed and implemented throughout the specified period.

    ii. the controls related to the control objectives stated in management's description of the service organization's system were suitably designed throughout the specified period to achieve those control objectives.

    iii. the controls related to the control objectives stated in management's description of the service organization's system operated effectively throughout the specified period to achieve those control objectives.

  c. A service auditor's report that

    i. expresses an opinion on the matters in (b)(i)–(b)(iii).

    ii. includes a description of the tests of controls and the results thereof.

Service auditor. A practitioner who reports on controls at a service organization.

Service organization. An organization or segment of an organization that provides services to user entities, which are likely to be relevant to those user entities' internal control over financial reporting.

Service organization's assertion. A written assertion about the matters referred to in part (b) of the definition of *Report on management's description of a service organization's system and the suitability of the design and operating effectiveness of controls,* for a type 2 report; and, for a type 1 report, the matters referred to in part (b) of the definition of *Report on management's description of a service organization's system and the suitability of the design of controls.*

Service organization's system. The policies and procedures designed, implemented, and documented, by management of the service organization to provide user entities with the services covered by the service auditor's report. Management's description of the service organization's system identifies the services covered, the period to which the description relates (or in the case of a type 1 report, the date to which the description relates), the control objectives specified by management or an outside party, the party specifying the control objectives (if not specified by management), and the related controls. (Ref: par. .A11)

Subservice organization. A service organization used by another service organization to perform some of the services provided to user entities that are likely to be relevant to those user entities' internal control over financial reporting.

Test of controls. A procedure designed to evaluate the operating effectiveness of controls in achieving the control objectives stated in management's description of the service organization's system.

User auditor. An auditor who audits and reports on the financial statements of a user entity.

User entity. An entity that uses a service organization.

Requirements

Management and Those Charged With Governance

.08 When this section requires the service auditor to inquire of, request representations from, communicate with, or otherwise interact with management of the service organization, the service auditor should determine the appropriate person(s) within the service organization's management or governance structure with whom to interact. This should include consideration of which person(s) have the appropriate responsibilities for and knowledge of the matters concerned. (Ref: par. .A12)

Acceptance and Continuance

.09 A service auditor should accept or continue an engagement to report on controls at a service organization only if (Ref: par. .A13)

    a. the service auditor has the capabilities and competence to perform the engagement. (Ref: par. .A14–.A15)

    b. the service auditor's preliminary knowledge of the engagement circumstances indicates that

        i. the criteria to be used will be suitable and available to the intended user entities and their auditors;

        ii. the service auditor will have access to sufficient appropriate evidence to the extent necessary; and

        iii. the scope of the engagement and management's description of the service organization's system will not be so limited that they are unlikely to be useful to user entities and their auditors.

    c. management agrees to the terms of the engagement by acknowledging and accepting its responsibility for the following:

        i. Preparing its description of the service organization's system and its assertion, including the completeness, accuracy, and method of presentation of the description and assertion. (Ref: par. .A16)

        ii. Having a reasonable basis for its assertion. (Ref: par. .A17)

        iii. Selecting the criteria to be used and stating them in the assertion.

        iv. Specifying the control objectives, stating them in the description of the service organization's system, and, if the control objectives are specified by law, regulation, or another party (for example, a user group or a professional body), identifying in the description the party specifying the control objectives.

        v. Identifying the risks that threaten the achievement of the control objectives stated in the description and designing, implementing, and documenting controls that are suitably designed and operating effectively to provide reasonable assurance that the control objectives stated in the description of the service organization's system will be achieved. (Ref: par. .A18)

vi. Providing the service auditor with

(1) access to all information, such as records and documentation, including service level agreements, of which management is aware that is relevant to the description of the service organization's system and the assertion;

(2) additional information that the service auditor may request from management for the purpose of the examination engagement;

(3) unrestricted access to personnel within the service organization from whom the service auditor determines it is necessary to obtain evidence relevant to the service auditor's engagement; and

(4) written representations at the conclusion of the engagement.

vii. Providing a written assertion that will be included in, or attached to management's description of the service organization's system, and provided to user entities.

.10 If management will not provide the service auditor with a written assertion, the service auditor should not circumvent the requirement to obtain an assertion by performing a service auditor's engagement under section 101. (Ref: par. .A19)

.11 Management's subsequent refusal to provide a written assertion represents a scope limitation and consequently, the service auditor should withdraw from the engagement. If law or regulation does not allow the service auditor to withdraw from the engagement, the service auditor should disclaim an opinion.

Request to Change the Scope of the Engagement

.12 If management requests a change in the scope of the engagement before the completion of the engagement, the service auditor should be satisfied, before agreeing to the change, that a reasonable justification for the change exists. (Ref: par. .A20–.A21)

Assessing the Suitability of the Criteria (Ref: par. .A6 and .A22–.A23)

.13 As required by paragraph .23 of section 101, the service auditor should assess whether management has used suitable criteria

a. in preparing its description of the service organization's system;

b. in evaluating whether controls were suitably designed to achieve the control objectives stated in the description; and

c. in the case of a type 2 report, in evaluating whether controls operated effectively throughout the specified period to achieve the control objectives stated in the description of the service organization's system.

AAG-ASO APP A

Statement on Standards for Attestation Engagements No. 16   **133**

.14 In assessing the suitability of the criteria to evaluate whether management's description of the service organization's system is fairly presented, the service auditor should determine if the criteria include, at a minimum,

    a. whether management's description of the service organization's system presents how the service organization's system was designed and implemented, including the following information about the service organization's system, if applicable:

        i. The types of services provided including, as appropriate, the classes of transactions processed.

        ii. The procedures, within both automated and manual systems, by which services are provided, including, as appropriate, procedures by which transactions are initiated, authorized, recorded, processed, corrected as necessary, and transferred to the reports and other information prepared for user entities.

        iii. The related accounting records, whether electronic or manual, and supporting information involved in initiating, authorizing, recording, processing, and reporting transactions; this includes the correction of incorrect information and how information is transferred to the reports and other information prepared for user entities.

        iv. How the service organization's system captures and addresses significant events and conditions other than transactions.

        v. The process used to prepare reports and other information for user entities.

        vi. The specified control objectives and controls designed to achieve those objectives, including as applicable, complementary user entity controls contemplated in the design of the service organization's controls.

        vii. Other aspects of the service organization's control environment, risk assessment process, information and communication systems (including the related business processes), control activities, and monitoring controls that are relevant to the services provided. (Ref: par. A17 and .A24)

    b. in the case of a type 2 report, whether management's description of the service organization's system includes relevant details of changes to the service organization's system during the period covered by the description. (Ref: par. .A44)

    c. whether management's description of the service organization's system does not omit or distort information relevant to the service organization's system, while acknowledging that management's description of the service organization's system is prepared to meet the common needs of a broad range of user entities and their user auditors, and may not, therefore, include every aspect of the service organization's system that each individual user entity and its user auditor may consider important in its own particular environment.

.15 In assessing the suitability of the criteria to evaluate whether the controls are suitably designed, the service auditor should determine if the criteria include, at a minimum, whether

AAG-ASO APP A

a. the risks that threaten the achievement of the control objectives stated in management's description of the service organization's system have been identified by management.
   b. the controls identified in management's description of the service organization's system would, if operating as described, provide reasonable assurance that those risks would not prevent the control objectives stated in the description from being achieved.

.16 In assessing the suitability of the criteria to evaluate whether controls operated effectively to provide reasonable assurance that the control objectives stated in management's description of the service organization's system were achieved, the service auditor should determine if the criteria include, at a minimum, whether the controls were consistently applied as designed throughout the specified period, including whether manual controls were applied by individuals who have the appropriate competence and authority.

Materiality

.17 When planning and performing the engagement, the service auditor should evaluate materiality with respect to the fair presentation of management's description of the service organization's system, the suitability of the design of controls to achieve the related control objectives stated in the description and, in the case of a type 2 report, the operating effectiveness of the controls to achieve the related control objectives stated in the description. (Ref: par. .A25–.A27)

Obtaining an Understanding of the Service Organization's System (Ref: par. .A28–.A30)

.18 The service auditor should obtain an understanding of the service organization's system, including controls that are included in the scope of the engagement.

Obtaining Evidence Regarding Management's Description of the Service Organization's System (Ref: par. .A26 and .A31–.A35)

.19 The service auditor should obtain and read management's description of the service organization's system and should evaluate whether those aspects of the description that are included in the scope of the engagement are presented fairly, including whether

   a. the control objectives stated in management's description of the service organization's system are reasonable in the circumstances. (Ref: par. .A34)
   b. controls identified in management's description of the service organization's system were implemented. (Ref: par. .A35)
   c. complementary user entity controls, if any, are adequately described. (Ref: par. .A32)
   d. services performed by a subservice organization, if any, are adequately described, including whether the inclusive method or the carve-out method has been used in relation to them.

.20 The service auditor should determine through inquiries made in combination with other procedures whether the service organization's system has

Statement on Standards for Attestation Engagements No. 16   **135**

been implemented. Such other procedures should include observation and inspection of records and other documentation of the manner in which the service organization's system operates and controls are applied. (Ref: par. .A35)

Obtaining Evidence Regarding the Design of Controls (Ref: par .A26 and .A36–.A39)

.21 The service auditor should determine which of the controls at the service organization are necessary to achieve the control objectives stated in management's description of the service organization's system and should assess whether those controls were suitably designed to achieve the control objectives by

 a. identifying the risks that threaten the achievement of the control objectives stated in management's description of the service organization's system, and (Ref: par. .A36)

 b. evaluating the linkage of the controls identified in management's description of the service organization's system with those risks.

Obtaining Evidence Regarding the Operating Effectiveness of Controls (Ref: par. .A26 and .A40–.A45)

Assessing Operating Effectiveness

.22 When performing a type 2 engagement, the service auditor should test those controls that the service auditor has determined are necessary to achieve the control objectives stated in management's description of the service organization's system and should assess their operating effectiveness throughout the period. Evidence obtained in prior engagements about the satisfactory operation of controls in prior periods does not provide a basis for a reduction in testing, even if it is supplemented with evidence obtained during the current period. (Ref: par. .A40–.A44)

.23 When performing a type 2 engagement, the service auditor should inquire about changes in the service organization's controls that were implemented during the period covered by the service auditor's report. If the service auditor believes the changes would be considered significant by user entities and their auditors, the service auditor should determine whether those changes are included in management's description of the service organization's system. If such changes are not included in the description, the service auditor should describe the changes in the service auditor's report and determine the effect on the service auditor's report. If the superseded controls are relevant to the achievement of the control objectives stated in the description, the service auditor should, if possible, test the superseded controls before the change. If the service auditor cannot test superseded controls relevant to the achievement of the control objectives stated in the description, the service auditor should determine the effect on the service auditor's report. (Ref: par. .A42(c) and .A45)

.24 When designing and performing tests of controls, the service auditor should

 a. perform other procedures in combination with inquiry to obtain evidence about the following:

  i. How the control was applied.

AAG-ASO APP A

>> ii. The consistency with which the control was applied.
>> iii. By whom or by what means the control was applied.
> b. determine whether the controls to be tested depend on other controls, and if so, whether it is necessary to obtain evidence supporting the operating effectiveness of those other controls.
> c. determine an effective method for selecting the items to be tested to meet the objectives of the procedure.

.25 When determining the extent of tests of controls and whether sampling is appropriate, the service auditor should consider the characteristics of the population of the controls to be tested, including the nature of the controls, the frequency of their application (for example, monthly, daily, many times per day), and the expected rate of deviation. AU section 350, *Audit Sampling*, addresses planning, performing, and evaluating audit samples. If the service auditor determines that sampling is appropriate, the service auditor should apply the requirements in paragraphs .31–.43 of AU section 350, which address sampling in tests of controls. Paragraphs .01–.14 and .45–.46 of AU section 350 provide additional guidance regarding the principles underlying those paragraphs.

Nature and Cause of Deviations

.26 The service auditor should investigate the nature and cause of any deviations identified, and should determine whether

> a. identified deviations are within the expected rate of deviation and are acceptable. If so, the testing that has been performed provides an appropriate basis for concluding that the control operated effectively throughout the specified period.
> b. additional testing of the control or of other controls is necessary to reach a conclusion about whether the controls related to the control objectives stated in management's description of the service organization's system operated effectively throughout the specified period.
> c. the testing that has been performed provides an appropriate basis for concluding that the control did not operate effectively throughout the specified period.

.27 If, as a result of performing the procedures in paragraph .26, the service auditor becomes aware that any identified deviations have resulted from intentional acts by service organization personnel, the service auditor should assess the risk that management's description of the service organization's system is not fairly presented, the controls are not suitably designed, and in a type 2 engagement, the controls are not operating effectively. (Ref: par. .A31)

Using the Work of the Internal Audit Function

Obtaining an Understanding of the Internal Audit Function
(Ref: par. .A46–.A47)

.28 If the service organization has an internal audit function, the service auditor should obtain an understanding of the nature of the responsibilities of the internal audit function and of the activities performed in order to determine whether the internal audit function is likely to be relevant to the engagement.

Planning to Use the Work of the Internal Audit Function

.29 When the service auditor intends to use the work of the internal audit function, the service auditor should determine whether the work of the internal audit function is likely to be adequate for the purposes of the engagement by evaluating the following:

    a. The objectivity and technical competence of the members of the internal audit function

    b. Whether the work of the internal audit function is likely to be carried out with due professional care

    c. Whether it is likely that effective communication will occur between the internal audit function and the service auditor, including consideration of the effect of any constraints or restrictions placed on the internal audit function by the service organization

.30 If the service auditor determines that the work of the internal audit function is likely to be adequate for the purposes of the engagement, in determining the planned effect of the work of the internal audit function on the nature, timing, or extent of the service auditor's procedures, the service auditor should evaluate the following:

    a. The nature and scope of specific work performed, or to be performed, by the internal audit function

    b. The significance of that work to the service auditor's conclusions

    c. The degree of subjectivity involved in the evaluation of the evidence gathered in support of those conclusions

Using the Work of the Internal Audit Function (Ref: par. .A48)

.31 In order for the service auditor to use specific work of the internal audit function, the service auditor should evaluate and perform procedures on that work to determine its adequacy for the service auditor's purposes.

.32 To determine the adequacy of specific work performed by the internal audit function for the service auditor's purposes, the service auditor should evaluate whether

    a. the work was performed by members of the internal audit function having adequate technical training and proficiency;

    b. the work was properly supervised, reviewed, and documented;

    c. sufficient appropriate evidence was obtained to enable the internal audit function to draw reasonable conclusions;

    d. conclusions reached are appropriate in the circumstances and any reports prepared by the internal audit function are consistent with the results of the work performed; and

    e. exceptions relevant to the engagement or unusual matters disclosed by the internal audit function are properly resolved.

Effect on the Service Auditor's Report

.33 If the work of the internal audit function has been used, the service auditor should not make reference to that work in the service auditor's opinion. Notwithstanding its degree of autonomy and objectivity, the internal audit function is not independent of the service organization. The service auditor has sole responsibility for the opinion expressed in the service auditor's report and, accordingly, that responsibility is not reduced by the service auditor's use of the work of the internal audit function. (Ref: par. .A49)

.34 In the case of a type 2 report, if the work of the internal audit function has been used in performing tests of controls, that part of the service auditor's report that describes the service auditor's tests of controls and results thereof should include a description of the internal auditor's work and of the service auditor's procedures with respect to that work. (Ref: par. .A50)

Direct Assistance

.35 When the service auditor uses members of the service organization's internal audit function to provide direct assistance, the service auditor should adapt and apply the requirements in paragraph .27 of AU section 322, *The Auditor's Consideration of the Internal Audit Function in an Audit of Financial Statements*.

Written Representations (Ref: par. .A51–.A55)

.36 The service auditor should request management to provide written representations that

a. reaffirm its assertion included in or attached to the description of the service organization's system;

b. it has provided the service auditor with all relevant information and access agreed to; and[1]

c. it has disclosed to the service auditor any of the following of which it is aware:

  i. Instances of noncompliance with laws and regulations or uncorrected errors attributable to the service organization that may affect one or more user entities.

  ii. Knowledge of any actual, suspected, or alleged intentional acts by management or the service organization's employees, that could adversely affect the fairness of the presentation of management's description of the service organization's system or the completeness or achievement of the control objectives stated in the description.

  iii. Design deficiencies in controls.

  iv. Instances when controls have not operated as described.

  v. Any events subsequent to the period covered by management's description of the service organization's system up to the date of the service auditor's report that could have a significant effect on management's assertion.

.37 If a service organization uses a subservice organization and management's description of the service organization's system uses the inclusive method, the service auditor also should obtain the written representations identified in paragraph .36 from management of the subservice organization.

.38 The written representations should be in the form of a representation letter addressed to the service auditor and should be as of the same date as the date of the service auditor's report.

---

[1] See paragraph .09(c)(vi)(1).

.39 If management does not provide one or more of the written representations requested by the service auditor, the service auditor should do the following:

  a. Discuss the matter with management
  b. Evaluate the effect of such refusal on the service auditor's assessment of the integrity of management and evaluate the effect that this may have on the reliability of management's representations and evidence in general
  c. Take appropriate actions, which may include disclaiming an opinion or withdrawing from the engagement

If management refuses to provide the representations in paragraphs .36(a)–.36(b) of this section, the service auditor should disclaim an opinion or withdraw from the engagement.

Other Information (Ref: par. .A56–.A57)

.40 The service auditor should read other information, if any, included in a document containing management's description of the service organization's system and the service auditor's report to identify material inconsistencies, if any, with that description. While reading the other information for the purpose of identifying material inconsistencies, the service auditor may become aware of an apparent misstatement of fact in the other information.

.41 If the service auditor becomes aware of a material inconsistency or an apparent misstatement of fact in the other information, the service auditor should discuss the matter with management. If the service auditor concludes that there is a material inconsistency or a misstatement of fact in the other information that management refuses to correct, the service auditor should take further appropriate action.[2]

Subsequent Events

.42 The service auditor should inquire whether management is aware of any events subsequent to the period covered by management's description of the service organization's system up to the date of the service auditor's report that could have a significant effect on management's assertion. If the service auditor becomes aware, through inquiry or otherwise, of such an event, or any other event that is of such a nature and significance that its disclosure is necessary to prevent users of a type 1 or type 2 report from being misled, and information about that event is not disclosed by management in its description, the service auditor should disclose such event in the service auditor's report.

.43 The service auditor has no responsibility to keep informed of events subsequent to the date of the service auditor's report; however, after the release of the service auditor's report, the service auditor may become aware of conditions that existed at the report date that might have affected management's assertion and the service auditor's report had the service auditor been aware of them. The evaluation of such subsequent information is similar to the evaluation of information discovered subsequent to the date of the report on an audit of financial statements, as described in AU section 561, *Subsequent*

---

[2] See paragraphs .91–.94 of section 101, *Attest Engagements*.

Discovery of Facts Existing at the Date of the Auditor's Report, and therefore, the service auditor should adapt and apply the guidance in AU section 561.

Documentation (Ref: par. .A58)

.44 The service auditor should prepare documentation that is sufficient to enable an experienced service auditor, having no previous connection with the engagement, to understand the following:

   a. The nature, timing, and extent of the procedures performed to comply with this section and with applicable legal and regulatory requirements

   b. The results of the procedures performed and the evidence obtained

   c. Significant findings or issues arising during the engagement, the conclusions reached thereon, and significant professional judgments made in reaching those conclusions

.45 In documenting the nature, timing, and extent of procedures performed, the service auditor should record the following:

   a. Identifying characteristics of the specific items or matters being tested

   b. Who performed the work and the date such work was completed

   c. Who reviewed the work performed and the date and extent of such review

.46 If the service auditor uses specific work of the internal audit function, the service auditor should document the conclusions reached regarding the evaluation of the adequacy of the work of the internal audit function and the procedures performed by the service auditor on that work.

.47 The service auditor should document discussions of significant findings or issues with management and others, including the nature of the significant findings or issues, when the discussions took place, and with whom.

.48 If the service auditor has identified information that is inconsistent with the service auditor's final conclusion regarding a significant finding or issue, the service auditor should document how the service auditor addressed the inconsistency.

.49 The service auditor should assemble the engagement documentation in an engagement file and complete the administrative process of assembling the final engagement file on a timely basis, no later than 60 days following the service auditor's report release date.

.50 After the assembly of the final engagement file has been completed, the service auditor should not delete or discard documentation before the end of its retention period.

.51 If the service auditor finds it necessary to modify existing engagement documentation or add new documentation after the assembly of the final engagement file has been completed, the service auditor should, regardless of the nature of the modifications or additions, document the following:

   a. The specific reasons for making them

   b. When and by whom they were made and reviewed

Statement on Standards for Attestation Engagements No. 16   141

Preparing the Service Auditor's Report

Content of the Service Auditor's Report (Ref: par. .A59)

.52 A service auditor's type 2 report should include the following elements:
- a. A title that includes the word *independent*.
- b. An addressee.
- c. Identification of
    - i. management's description of the service organization's system and the function performed by the system.
    - ii. any parts of management's description of the service organization's system that are not covered by the service auditor's report. (Ref: par. .A56)
    - iii. any information included in a document containing the service auditor's report that is not covered by the service auditor's report. (Ref: par. .A56)
    - iv. the criteria.
    - v. any services performed by a subservice organization and whether the carve-out method or the inclusive method was used in relation to them. Depending on which method is used, the following should be included:
        - (1) If the carve-out method was used, a statement that management's description of the service organization's system excludes the control objectives and related controls at relevant subservice organizations, and that the service auditor's procedures do not extend to the subservice organization.
        - (2) If the inclusive method was used, a statement that management's description of the service organization's system includes the subservice organization's specified control objectives and related controls, and that the service auditor's procedures included procedures related to the subservice organization.
- d. If management's description of the service organization's system refers to the need for complementary user entity controls, a statement that the service auditor has not evaluated the suitability of the design or operating effectiveness of complementary user entity controls, and that the control objectives stated in the description can be achieved only if complementary user entity controls are suitably designed and operating effectively, along with the controls at the service organization.
- e. A reference to management's assertion and a statement that management is responsible for (Ref: par. .A60)
    - i. preparing the description of the service organization's system and the assertion, including the completeness, accuracy, and method of presentation of the description and assertion;

AAG-ASO APP A

ii. providing the services covered by the description of the service organization's system;

iii. specifying the control objectives unless the control objectives are specified by law, regulation, or another party, and stating them in the description of the service organization's system;

iv. identifying the risks that threaten the achievement of the control objectives;

v. selecting the criteria; and

vi. designing, implementing, and documenting controls that are suitably designed and operating effectively to achieve the related control objectives stated in the description of the service organization's system.

f. A statement that the service auditor's responsibility is to express an opinion on the fairness of the presentation of management's description of the service organization's system and on the suitability of the design and operating effectiveness of the controls to achieve the related control objectives stated in the description, based on the service auditor's examination.

g. A statement that the examination was conducted in accordance with attestation standards established by the American Institute of Certified Public Accountants and that those standards require the service auditor to plan and perform the examination to obtain reasonable assurance about whether management's description of the service organization's system is fairly presented and the controls are suitably designed and operating effectively throughout the specified period to achieve the related control objectives.

h. A statement that an examination of management's description of a service organization's system and the suitability of the design and operating effectiveness of the service organization's controls to achieve the related control objectives stated in the description involves performing procedures to obtain evidence about the fairness of the presentation of the description and the suitability of the design and operating effectiveness of those controls to achieve the related control objectives stated in the description.

i. A statement that the examination included assessing the risks that management's description of the service organization's system is not fairly presented and that the controls were not suitably designed or operating effectively to achieve the related control objectives.

j. A statement that the examination also included testing the operating effectiveness of those controls that the service auditor considers necessary to provide reasonable assurance that the related control objectives stated in management's description of the service organization's system were achieved.

k. A statement that an examination engagement of this type also includes evaluating the overall presentation of management's description of the service organization's system and suitability of the control objectives stated in the description.

Statement on Standards for Attestation Engagements No. 16

l. A statement that the service auditor believes the examination provides a reasonable basis for his or her opinion.

m. A statement about the inherent limitations of controls, including the risk of projecting to future periods any evaluation of the fairness of the presentation of management's description of the service organization's system or conclusions about the suitability of the design or operating effectiveness of controls.

n. The service auditor's opinion on whether, in all material respects, based on the criteria described in management's assertion,

    i. management's description of the service organization's system fairly presents the service organization's system that was designed and implemented throughout the specified period.

    ii. the controls related to the control objectives stated in management's description of the service organization's system were suitably designed to provide reasonable assurance that those control objectives would be achieved if the controls operated effectively throughout the specified period.

    iii. the controls the service auditor tested, which were those necessary to provide reasonable assurance that the control objectives stated in management's description of the service organization's system were achieved, operated effectively throughout the specified period.

    iv. if the application of complementary user entity controls is necessary to achieve the related control objectives stated in management's description of the service organization's system, a reference to this condition.

o. A reference to a description of the service auditor's tests of controls and the results thereof, that includes

    i. identification of the controls that were tested, whether the items tested represent all or a selection of the items in the population, and the nature of the tests in sufficient detail to enable user auditors to determine the effect of such tests on their risk assessments. (Ref: par. .A50)

    ii. if deviations have been identified in the operation of controls included in the description, the extent of testing performed by the service auditor that led to the identification of the deviations (including the number of items tested), and the number and nature of the deviations noted (even if, on the basis of tests performed, the service auditor concludes that the related control objective was achieved). (Ref: par. .A65)

p. A statement restricting the use of the service auditor's report to management of the service organization, user entities of the service organization's system during some or all of the period covered by the service auditor's report, and the independent auditors of such user entities. (Ref: par. .A61–.A64)

q. The date of the service auditor's report.

r. The name of the service auditor and the city and state where the service auditor maintains the office that has responsibility for the engagement.

.53 A service auditor's type 1 report should include the following elements:
   a. A title that includes the word *independent*.
   b. An addressee.
   c. Identification of
      i. management's description of the service organization's system and the function performed by the system.
      ii. any parts of management's description of the service organization's system that are not covered by the service auditor's report. (Ref: par. .A56)
      iii. any information included in a document containing the service auditor report that is not covered by the service auditor's report. (Ref: par. .A56)
      iv. the criteria.
      v. any services performed by a subservice organization and whether the carve-out method or the inclusive method was used in relation to them. Depending on which method is used, the following should be included:
         (1) If the carve-out method was used, a statement that management's description of the service organization's system excludes the control objectives and related controls at relevant subservice organizations, and that the service auditor's procedures do not extend to the subservice organization.
         (2) If the inclusive method was used, a statement that management's description of the service organization's system includes the subservice organization's specified control objectives and related controls, and that the service auditor's procedures included procedures related to the subservice organization.
   d. If management's description of the service organization's system refers to the need for complementary user entity controls, a statement that the service auditor has not evaluated the suitability of the design or operating effectiveness of complementary user entity controls, and that the control objectives stated in the description can be achieved only if complementary user entity controls are suitably designed and operating effectively, along with the controls at the service organization.
   e. A reference to management's assertion and a statement that management is responsible for (Ref: par. .A60)
      i. preparing the description of the service organization's system and assertion, including the completeness, accuracy, and method of presentation of the description and assertion;

Statement on Standards for Attestation Engagements No. 16 145

        ii. providing the services covered by the description of the service organization's system;

       iii. specifying the control objectives, unless the control objectives are specified by law, regulation, or another party, and stating them in the description of the service organization's system;

       iv. identifying the risks that threaten the achievement of the control objectives,

       v. selecting the criteria; and

       vi. designing, implementing, and documenting controls that are suitably designed and operating effectively to achieve the related control objectives stated in the description of the service organization's system.

f. A statement that the service auditor's responsibility is to express an opinion on the fairness of the presentation of management's description of the service organization's system and on the suitability of the design of the controls to achieve the related control objectives stated in the description, based on the service auditor's examination.

g. A statement that the examination was conducted in accordance with attestation standards established by the American Institute of Certified Public Accountants, and that those standards require the service auditor to plan and perform the examination to obtain reasonable assurance about whether management's description of the service organization's system is fairly presented and the controls are suitably designed as of the specified date to achieve the related control objectives.

h. A statement that the service auditor has not performed any procedures regarding the operating effectiveness of controls and, therefore, expresses no opinion thereon.

i. A statement that an examination of management's description of a service organization's system and the suitability of the design of the service organization's controls to achieve the related control objectives stated in the description involves performing procedures to obtain evidence about the fairness of the presentation of the description and the suitability of the design of those controls to achieve the related control objectives stated in the description.

j. A statement that the examination included assessing the risks that management's description of the service organization's system is not fairly presented and that the controls were not suitably designed to achieve the related control objectives.

k. A statement that an examination engagement of this type also includes evaluating the overall presentation of management's description of the service organization's system and suitability of the control objectives stated in the description.

l. A statement that the service auditor believes the examination provides a reasonable basis for his or her opinion.

m. A statement about the inherent limitations of controls, including the risk of projecting to future periods any evaluation of the fairness of the presentation of management's description of the service

AAG-ASO APP A

organization's system or conclusions about the suitability of the design of the controls to achieve the related control objectives.

n. The service auditor's opinion on whether, in all material respects, based on the criteria described in management's assertion,

   i. management's description of the service organization's system fairly presents the service organization's system that was designed and implemented as of the specified date.

   ii. the controls related to the control objectives stated in management's description of the service organization's system were suitably designed to provide reasonable assurance that those control objectives would be achieved if the controls operated effectively as of the specified date.

   iii. if the application of complementary user entity controls is necessary to achieve the related control objectives stated in management's description of the service organization's system, a reference to this condition.

o. A statement restricting the use of the service auditor's report to management of the service organization, user entities of the service organization's system as of the end of the period covered by the service auditor's report, and the independent auditors of such user entities. (Ref: par. .A61–.A64)

p. The date of the service auditor's report.

q. The name of the service auditor and the city and state where the service auditor maintains the office that has responsibility for the engagement.

Report Date

.54 The service auditor should date the service auditor's report no earlier than the date on which the service auditor has obtained sufficient appropriate evidence to support the service auditor's opinion.

Modified Opinions (Ref: par. .A66)

.55 The service auditor's opinion should be modified and the service auditor's report should contain a clear description of all the reasons for the modification, if the service auditor concludes that

a. management's description of the service organization's system is not fairly presented, in all material respects;

b. the controls are not suitably designed to provide reasonable assurance that the control objectives stated in management's description of the service organization's system would be achieved if the controls operated as described;

c. in the case of a type 2 report, the controls did not operate effectively throughout the specified period to achieve the related control objectives stated in management's description of the service organization's system; or

d. the service auditor is unable to obtain sufficient appropriate evidence

Statement on Standards for Attestation Engagements No. 16 **147**

.56 If the service auditor plans to disclaim an opinion because of the inability to obtain sufficient appropriate evidence, and, based on the limited procedures performed, has concluded that,

   a. certain aspects of management's description of the service organization's system are not fairly presented, in all material respects;
   b. certain controls were not suitably designed to provide reasonable assurance that the control objectives stated in management's description of the service organization's system would be achieved if the controls operated as described; or
   c. in the case of a type 2 report, certain controls did not operate effectively throughout the specified period to achieve the related control objectives stated in management's description of the service organization's system,

the service auditor should identify these findings in his or her report.

.57 If the service auditor plans to disclaim an opinion, the service auditor should not identify the procedures that were performed nor include statements describing the characteristics of a service auditor's engagement in the service auditor's report; to do so might overshadow the disclaimer.

Other Communication Responsibilities

.58 If the service auditor becomes aware of incidents of noncompliance with laws and regulations, fraud, or uncorrected errors attributable to management or other service organization personnel that are not clearly trivial and that may affect one or more user entities, the service auditor should determine the effect of such incidents on management's description of the service organization's system, the achievement of the control objectives, and the service auditor's report. Additionally, the service auditor should determine whether this information has been communicated appropriately to affected user entities. If the information has not been so communicated, and management of the service organization is unwilling to do so, the service auditor should take appropriate action. (Ref: par. .A67)

AAG-ASO APP A

Application and Other Explanatory Material

Scope of This Section

.A1 *Internal control* is a process designed to provide reasonable assurance regarding the achievement of objectives related to the reliability of financial reporting, effectiveness and efficiency of operations, and compliance with applicable laws and regulations. Controls related to a service organization's operations and compliance objectives may be relevant to a user entity's internal control over financial reporting. Such controls may pertain to assertions about presentation and disclosure relating to account balances, classes of transactions or disclosures, or may pertain to evidence that the user auditor evaluates or uses in applying auditing procedures. For example, a payroll processing service organization's controls related to the timely remittance of payroll deductions to government authorities may be relevant to a user entity because late remittances could incur interest and penalties that would result in a liability for the user entity. Similarly, a service organization's controls over the acceptability of investment transactions from a regulatory perspective may be considered relevant to a user entity's presentation and disclosure of transactions and account balances in its financial statements. (Ref: par. .01)

.A2 Paragraph .02 of this section refers to other engagements that the practitioner may perform and report on under section 101 to report on controls at a service organization. Paragraph .02 is not, however, intended to

- provide for the alteration of the definitions of *service organization* and *service organization's system* in paragraph .07 to permit reports issued under this section to include in the description of the service organization's system aspects of their services (including relevant control objectives and related controls) not likely to be relevant to user entities' internal control over financial reporting, or

- permit a report to be issued that combines reporting under this section on a service organization's controls that are likely to be relevant to user entities' internal control over financial reporting, with reporting under section 101 on controls that are not likely to be relevant to user entities' internal control over financial reporting. (Ref: par. .02(a))

.A3 When a service auditor conducts an engagement under section 101 to report on controls at a service organization other than those controls likely to be relevant to user entities' internal control over financial reporting, and the service auditor intends to use the guidance in this section in planning and performing that engagement, the service auditor may encounter issues that differ significantly from those associated with engagements to report on a service organization's controls likely to be relevant to user entities' internal control over financial reporting. For example,

- identification of suitable and available criteria, as prescribed in paragraphs .23–.34 of section 101, for evaluating the fairness of presentation of management's description of the service organization's system and the suitability of the design and the operating effectiveness of the controls.

Statement on Standards for Attestation Engagements No. 16   **149**

- identification of appropriate control objectives, and the basis for evaluating the reasonableness of the control objectives in the circumstances of the particular engagement.
- identification of the intended users of the report and the manner in which they intend to use the report.
- relevance and appropriateness of the definitions in paragraph .07 of this section, many of which specifically relate to internal control over financial reporting.
- application of references to auditing standards (AU sections) that are intended to provide the service auditor with guidance relevant to internal control over financial reporting.
- application of the concept of materiality in the circumstances of the particular engagement.
- developing the language to be used in the practitioner's report, including addressing paragraphs .84–.87 of section 101, which identify the elements to be included in an examination report. (Ref: par. .02(a))

.A4   When management of the service organization is not responsible for the design of the system, it is unlikely that management of the service organization will be in a position to assert that the system is suitably designed. Controls cannot operate effectively unless they are suitably designed. Because of the inextricable link between the suitability of the design of controls and their operating effectiveness, the absence of an assertion with respect to the suitability of design will likely preclude the service auditor from opining on the operating effectiveness of controls. As an alternative, the practitioner may perform tests of controls in either an agreed-upon procedures engagement under section 201, *Agreed Upon Procedures Engagements*, or an examination of the operating effectiveness of the controls under section 101. (Ref: par. .02(b))

Definitions

Controls at a Service Organization (Ref: par. .07)

.A5   The policies and procedures referred to in the definition of *controls at a service organization* in paragraph .07 include aspects of user entities' information systems maintained by the service organization and may also include aspects of one or more of the other components of internal control at a service organization. For example, the definition of *controls at a service organization* may include aspects of the service organization's control environment, monitoring, and control activities when they relate to the services provided. Such definition does not, however, include controls at a service organization that are not related to the achievement of the control objectives stated in management's description of the service organization's system; for example, controls related to the preparation of the service organization's own financial statements.

Criteria (Ref: par. .07 and .14–.16)

.A6   For the purposes of engagements performed in accordance with this section, criteria need to be available to user entities and their auditors to enable them to understand the basis for the service organization's assertion about the fair presentation of management's description of the service organization's system, the suitability of the design of controls that address control

AAG-ASO APP A

objectives stated in the description of the system and, in the case of a type 2 report, the operating effectiveness of such controls. Information about suitable criteria is provided in paragraphs .23–.34 of section 101. Paragraphs .14–.16 of this section discuss the criteria for evaluating the fairness of the presentation of management's description of the service organization's system and the suitability of the design and operating effectiveness of the controls.

Inclusive Method (Ref: par. .07)

.A7 As indicated in the definition of *inclusive method* in paragraph .07, a service organization that uses a subservice organization presents management's description of the service organization's system to include a description of the services provided by the subservice organization as well as the subservice organization's relevant control objectives and related controls. When the inclusive method is used, the requirements of this section also apply to the services provided by the subservice organization, including the requirement to obtain management's acknowledgement and acceptance of responsibility for the matters in paragraph .09(c)(i)–(vii) as they relate to the subservice organization.

.A8 Performing procedures at the subservice organization entails coordination and communication between the service organization, the subservice organization, and the service auditor. The inclusive method generally is feasible if, for example, the service organization and the subservice organization are related, or if the contract between the service organization and the subservice organization provides for issuance of a service auditor's report. If the service auditor is unable to obtain an assertion from the subservice organization regarding management's description of the service organization's system provided, including the relevant control objectives and related controls at the subservice organization, the service auditor is unable to use the inclusive method but may instead use the carve-out method.

.A9 There may be instances when the service organization's controls, such as monitoring controls, permit the service organization to include in its assertion the relevant aspects of the subservice organization's system, including the relevant control objectives and related controls of the subservice organization. In such instances, the service auditor is basing his or her opinion solely on the controls at the service organization, and hence, the inclusive method is not applicable.

Internal Audit Function (Ref: par. .07)

.A10 The "others" referenced in the definition of *internal audit function* may be individuals who perform activities similar to those performed by internal auditors and include service organization personnel (in addition to internal auditors), and third parties working under the direction of management or those charged with governance.

Service Organization's System (Ref: par. .07)

.A11 The policies and procedures referred to in the definition of *service organization's system* refer to the guidelines and activities for providing transaction processing and other services to user entities and include the infrastructure, software, people, and data that support the policies and procedures.

Management and Those Charged With Governance (Ref: par. .08)

.A12 Management and governance structures vary by entity, reflecting influences such as size and ownership characteristics. Such diversity means that it is not possible for this section to specify for all engagements the person(s) with whom the service auditor is to interact regarding particular matters. For example, the service organization may be a segment of an organization and not a separate legal entity. In such cases, identifying the appropriate management personnel or those charged with governance from whom to request written representations may require the exercise of professional judgment.

Acceptance and Continuance

.A13 If one or more of the conditions in paragraph .09 are not met and the service auditor is nevertheless required by law or regulation to accept or continue an engagement to report on controls at a service organization, the service auditor is required, in accordance with the requirements in paragraphs .55–.56, to determine the effect on the service auditor's report of one or more of such conditions not being met. (Ref: par. .09)

Capabilities and Competence to Perform the Engagement (Ref: par. .09a)

.A14 Relevant capabilities and competence to perform the engagement include matters such as the following:

- Knowledge of the relevant industry
- An understanding of information technology and systems
- Experience in evaluating risks as they relate to the suitable design of controls
- Experience in the design and execution of tests of controls and the evaluation of the results

.A15 In performing a service auditor's engagement, the service auditor need not be independent of each user entity. (Ref: par. .09a)

Management's Responsibility for Documenting the Service Organization's System (Ref: par. .09(c)(i))

.A16 Management of the service organization is responsible for documenting the service organization's system. No one particular form of documentation is prescribed and the extent of documentation may vary depending on the size and complexity of the service organization and its monitoring activities.

Reasonable Basis for Management's Assertion (Ref: par. .07, definition of service organization's system; par. .09(c)(ii) and .14(a)(vii))

.A17 Management's monitoring activities may provide evidence of the design and operating effectiveness of controls in support of management's assertion. *Monitoring of controls* is a process to assess the effectiveness of internal control performance over time. It involves assessing the effectiveness of controls on a timely basis, identifying and reporting deficiencies to appropriate individuals within the service organization, and taking necessary corrective actions. Management accomplishes monitoring of controls through ongoing activities, separate evaluations, or a combination of the two. Ongoing monitoring activities are often built into the normal recurring activities of an entity and include regular management and supervisory activities. Internal auditors or personnel performing similar functions may contribute to the monitoring of a service organization's activities. Monitoring activities may also include using information communicated by external parties, such as customer complaints and regulator comments, which may indicate problems or highlight areas in need of improvement. The greater the degree and effectiveness of ongoing monitoring, the less need for separate evaluations. Usually, some combination of ongoing monitoring and separate evaluations will ensure that internal control maintains its effectiveness over time. The service auditor's report on controls is not a substitute for the service organization's own processes to provide a reasonable basis for its assertion.

Identification of Risks (Ref: par. .09(c)(v))

.A18 Control objectives relate to risks that controls seek to mitigate. For example, the risk that a transaction is recorded at the wrong amount or in the wrong period can be expressed as a control objective that transactions are recorded at the correct amount and in the correct period. Management is responsible for identifying the risks that threaten achievement of the control objectives stated in management's description of the service organization's system. Management may have a formal or informal process for identifying relevant risks. A formal process may include estimating the significance of identified risks, assessing the likelihood of their occurrence, and deciding about actions to address them. However, because control objectives relate to risks that controls seek to mitigate, thoughtful identification by management of control objectives when designing, implementing, and documenting the service organization's system may itself comprise an informal process for identifying relevant risks.

Management's Refusal to Provide a Written Assertion

.A19 A recent change in service organization management or the appointment of the service auditor by a party other than management are examples of situations that may cause management to be unwilling to provide the service auditor with a written assertion. However, other members of management may be in a position to, and will agree to, sign the assertion so that the service auditor can meet the requirement of paragraph .09(c)(vii). (Ref: par. .10)

Request to Change the Scope of the Engagement (Ref: par. .12)

.A20 A request to change the scope of the engagement may not have a reasonable justification if, for example, the request is made

- to exclude certain control objectives at the service organization from the scope of the engagement because of the likelihood that the service auditor's opinion would be modified with respect to those control objectives.
- to prevent the disclosure of deviations identified at a subservice organization by requesting a change from the inclusive method to the carve-out method.

.A21 A request to change the scope of the engagement may have a reasonable justification when, for example, the request is made to exclude from the engagement a subservice organization because the service organization cannot arrange for access by the service auditor, and the method used for addressing

Statement on Standards for Attestation Engagements No. 16 153

the services provided by that subservice organization is changed from the inclusive method to the carve-out method.

Assessing the Suitability of the Criteria (Ref: par. .13–.16)

.A22 Section 101 requires a practitioner, among other things, to determine whether the subject matter is capable of evaluation against criteria that are suitable and available to users. As indicated in paragraph .27 of section 101, regardless of who establishes or develops the criteria, management is responsible for selecting the criteria and for determining whether the criteria are appropriate. The subject matter is the underlying condition of interest to intended users of an attestation report. The following table identifies the subject matter and minimum criteria for each of the opinions in type 2 and type 1 reports.

	Subject Matter	*Criteria*	*Comment*
Opinion on the fair presentation of management's description of the service organization's system (type 1 and type 2 reports).	Management's description of the service organization's system that is likely to be relevant to user entities' internal control over financial reporting and is covered by the service auditor's report, and management's assertion about whether the description is fairly presented.	Management's description of the service organization's system is fairly presented if it a. presents how the service organization's system was designed and implemented including, as appropriate, the matters identified in paragraph .14(a) and, in the case of a type 2 report, includes relevant details of changes to the service organization's system during the period covered by the description. b. does not omit or distort information relevant to the service organization's system, while acknowledging that management's description of the service organization's system is prepared to meet the common needs of a broad range of user entities and may not, therefore, include every aspect of the service organization's system that each individual user entity may consider important in its own particular environment.	The specific wording of the criteria for this opinion may need to be tailored to be consistent with criteria established by, for example, law, regulation, user groups, or a professional body. Criteria for evaluating management's description of the service organization's system are provided in paragraph .14. Paragraphs .19–.20 and .A31–.A33 offer further guidance on determining whether these criteria are met.

(continued)

AAG-ASO APP A

	Subject Matter	Criteria	Comment
Opinion on suitability of design and operating effectiveness (type 2 reports).	The design and operating effectiveness of the controls that are necessary to achieve the control objectives stated in management's description of the service organization's system.	The controls are suitably designed and operating effectively to achieve the control objectives stated in management's description of the service organization's system if a. management has identified the risks that threaten the achievement of the control objectives stated in management's description of the service organization's system. b. the controls identified in management's description of the service organization's system would, if operating as described, provide reasonable assurance that those risks would not prevent the control objectives stated in the description from being achieved. c. the controls were consistently applied as designed throughout the specified period. This includes whether manual controls were applied by individuals who have the appropriate competence and authority.	When the criteria for this opinion are met, controls will have provided reasonable assurance that the related control objectives stated in management's description of the service organization's system were achieved throughout the specified period.	The control objectives stated in management's description of the service organization's system are part of the criteria for these opinions. The control objectives stated in the description will differ from engagement to engagement. If the service auditor concludes that the control objectives stated in the description are not fairly presented, then those control objectives would not be suitable as part of the criteria for forming an opinion on the design and operating effectiveness of the controls.
Opinion on suitability of design (type 1 reports).	The suitability of the design of the controls necessary to achieve the control objectives stated in management's description of the service organization's system and relevant to the services covered by the service auditor's report.	The controls are suitably designed to achieve the control objectives stated in management's description of the service organization's system if a. management has identified the risks that threaten the achievement of the control objectives stated in its description of the service organization's system.	Meeting these criteria does not, of itself, provide any assurance that the control objectives stated in management's description of the service organization's system were achieved because no evidence has been obtained about the operating effectiveness of the controls.

Statement on Standards for Attestation Engagements No. 16

Subject Matter	Criteria	Comment
	b. the controls identified in management's description of the service organization's system would, if operating as described, provide reasonable assurance that those risks would not prevent the control objectives stated in the description from being achieved.	

.A23 Paragraph .14(a) identifies a number of elements that are included in management's description of the service organization's system as appropriate. These elements may not be appropriate if the system being described is not a system that processes transactions; for example, if the system relates to general controls over the hosting of an IT application but not the controls embedded in the application itself. (Ref: par. .14)

.A24 The requirement to include in management's description of the service organization's system "other aspects of the service organization's control environment, risk assessment process, information and communication systems (including the related business processes), control activities, and monitoring controls, that are relevant to the services provided" is also applicable to the internal control components of subservice organizations used by the service organization when the inclusive method is used. See AU section 314, *Understanding the Entity and Its Environment and Assessing the Risks of Material Misstatement*, for a discussion of these components. (Ref: par. .14(a)(vii))

Materiality (Ref: par. .17)

.A25 In an engagement to report on controls at a service organization, the concept of materiality relates to the information being reported on, not the financial statements of user entities. The service auditor plans and performs procedures to determine whether management's description of the service organization's system is fairly presented, in all material respects; whether controls at the service organization are suitably designed in all material respects to achieve the control objectives stated in the description; and in the case of a type 2 report, whether controls at the service organization operated effectively throughout the specified period in all material respects to achieve the control objectives stated in the description. The concept of materiality takes into account that the service auditor's report provides information about the service organization's system to meet the common information needs of a broad range of user entities and their auditors who have an understanding of the manner in which the system is being used by a particular user entity for financial reporting.

.A26 Materiality with respect to the fair presentation of management's description of the service organization's system and with respect to the design of controls primarily includes the consideration of qualitative factors; for example, whether

- management's description of the service organization's system includes the significant aspects of the processing of significant transactions.

AAG-ASO APP A

- management's description of the service organization's system omits or distorts relevant information.
- the controls have the ability, as designed, to provide reasonable assurance that the control objectives stated in management's description of the service organization's system would be achieved.

Materiality with respect to the operating effectiveness of controls includes the consideration of both quantitative and qualitative factors; for example, the tolerable rate and observed rate of deviation (a quantitative matter) and the nature and cause of any observed deviations (a qualitative matter).

.A27 The concept of materiality is not applied when disclosing, in the description of the tests of controls, the results of those tests when deviations have been identified. This is because, in the particular circumstances of a specific user entity or user auditor, a deviation may have significance beyond whether or not, in the opinion of the service auditor, it prevents a control from operating effectively. For example, the control to which the deviation relates may be particularly significant in preventing a certain type of error that may be material in the particular circumstances of a user entity's financial statements.

Obtaining an Understanding of the Service Organization's System (Ref: par. .18)

.A28 Obtaining an understanding of the service organization's system, including related controls, assists the service auditor in the following:

- Identifying the boundaries of the system and how it interfaces with other systems
- Assessing whether management's description of the service organization's system fairly presents the service organization's system that has been designed and implemented
- Determining which controls are necessary to achieve the control objectives stated in management's description of the service organization's system, whether controls were suitably designed to achieve those control objectives, and, in the case of a type 2 report, whether controls were operating effectively throughout the period to achieve those control objectives

.A29 Management's description of the service organization's system includes "aspects of the service organization's control environment, risk assessment process, information and communication systems (including relevant business processes), control activities and monitoring activities that are relevant to the services provided." Although aspects of the service organization's control environment, risk assessment process, and monitoring activities may not be presented in the description in the context of control objectives, they may nevertheless be necessary to achieve the specified control objectives stated in the description. Likewise, deficiencies in these controls may have an effect on the service auditor's assessment of whether the controls, taken as a whole, were suitably designed or operating effectively to achieve the specified control objectives. See AU section 314 for a discussion of these components of internal control.

.A30 The service auditor's procedures to obtain the understanding referred to in paragraph .A28 may include the following:

Statement on Standards for Attestation Engagements No. 16   **157**

- Inquiring of management and others within the service organization who, in the service auditor's judgment, may have relevant information
- Observing operations and inspecting documents, reports, and printed and electronic records of transaction processing
- Inspecting a selection of agreements between the service organization and user entities to identify their common terms
- Reperforming the application of a control

One or more of the preceding procedures may be accomplished through the performance of a walkthrough.

Obtaining Evidence Regarding Management's Description of the Service Organization's System (Ref: par. .19–.20)

.A31 In a service auditor's examination engagement, the service auditor plans and performs the engagement to obtain reasonable assurance of detecting errors or omissions in management's description of the service organization's system and instances in which control objectives were not achieved. Absolute assurance is not attainable because of factors such as the need for judgment, the use of sampling, and the inherent limitations of controls at the service organization that affect whether the description is fairly presented and the controls are suitably designed and operating effectively to achieve the control objectives, and because much of the evidence available to the service auditor is persuasive rather than conclusive in nature. Also, procedures that are effective for detecting unintentional errors or omissions in the description, and instances in which control objectives were not achieved, may be ineffective for detecting intentional errors or omissions in the description and instances in which the control objectives were not achieved that are concealed through collusion between service organization personnel and a third party or among management or employees of the service organization. Therefore, the subsequent discovery of the existence of material omissions or errors in the description or instances in which control objectives were not achieved does not, in and of itself, evidence inadequate planning, performance, or judgment on the part of the service auditor. (Ref: par. .27)

.A32 Considering the following questions may assist the service auditor in determining whether management's description of the service organization's system is fairly presented, in all material respects:

- Does management's description address the major aspects of the service provided and included in the scope of the engagement that could reasonably be expected to be relevant to the common needs of a broad range of user auditors in planning their audits of user entities' financial statements?
- Is the description prepared at a level of detail that could reasonably be expected to provide a broad range of user auditors with sufficient information to obtain an understanding of internal control in accordance with AU section 314? The description need not address every aspect of the service organization's processing or the services provided to user entities and need not be so detailed that it would potentially enable a reader to compromise security or other controls at the service organization.

AAG-ASO APP A

- Is the description prepared in a manner that does not omit or distort information that might affect the decisions of a broad range of user auditors; for example, does the description contain any significant omissions or inaccuracies regarding processing of which the service auditor is aware?
- Does the description include relevant details of changes to the service organization's system during the period covered by the description when the description covers a period of time?
- Have the controls identified in the description actually been implemented?
- Are complementary user entity controls, if any, adequately described? In most cases, the control objectives stated in the description are worded so that they are capable of being achieved through the effective operation of controls implemented by the service organization alone. In some cases, however, the control objectives stated in the description cannot be achieved by the service organization alone because their achievement requires particular controls to be implemented by user entities. This may be the case when, for example, the control objectives are specified by a regulatory authority. When the description does include complementary user entity controls, the description separately identifies those controls along with the specific control objectives that cannot be achieved by the service organization alone. (Ref: par. .19(c))
- If the inclusive method has been used, does the description separately identify controls at the service organization and controls at the subservice organization? If the carve-out method is used, does the description identify the functions that are performed by the subservice organization? When the carve-out method is used, the description need not describe the detailed processing or controls at the subservice organization.

.A33 The service auditor's procedures to evaluate the fair presentation of management's description of the service organization's system may include the following:

- Considering the nature of the user entities and how the services provided by the service organization are likely to affect them; for example, the predominant types of user entities, and whether the user entities are regulated by government agencies
- Reading contracts with user entities to gain an understanding of the service organization's contractual obligations
- Observing procedures performed by service organization personnel
- Reviewing the service organization's policy and procedure manuals and other documentation of the system; for example, flowcharts and narratives
- Performing walkthroughs of transactions through the service organization's system

.A34 Paragraph .19(a) requires the service auditor to evaluate whether the control objectives stated in management's description of the service organization's system are reasonable in the circumstances. Considering the following questions may assist the service auditor in this evaluation:

- Have the control objectives stated in the description been specified by the service organization or by outside parties, such as regulatory authorities, a user group, a professional body, or others?

- Do the control objectives stated in the description and specified by the service organization relate to the types of assertions commonly embodied in the broad range of user entities' financial statements to which controls at the service organization could reasonably be expected to relate (for example, assertions about existence and accuracy that are affected by access controls that prevent or detect unauthorized access to the system)? Although the service auditor ordinarily will not be able to determine how controls at a service organization specifically relate to the assertions embodied in individual user entities' financial statements, the service auditor's understanding of the nature of the service organization's system, including controls, and the services being provided is used to identify the types of assertions to which those controls are likely to relate.

- Are the control objectives stated in the description and specified by the service organization complete? Although a complete set of control objectives can provide a broad range of user auditors with a framework to assess the effect of controls at the service organization on assertions commonly embodied in user entities' financial statements, the service auditor ordinarily will not be able to determine how controls at a service organization specifically relate to the assertions embodied in individual user entities' financial statements and cannot, therefore, determine whether control objectives are complete from the viewpoint of individual user entities or user auditors. It is the responsibility of individual user entities or user auditors to assess whether the service organization's description addresses the particular control objectives that are relevant to their needs. If the control objectives are specified by an outside party, including control objectives specified by law or regulation, the outside party is responsible for their completeness and reasonableness. (Ref: par. .19(a))

.A35 The service auditor's procedures to determine whether the system described by the service organization has been implemented may be similar to, and performed in conjunction with, procedures to obtain an understanding of that system. Other procedures that the service auditor may use in combination with inquiry of management and other service organization personnel include observation, inspection of records and other documentation, as well as reperformance of the manner in which transactions are processed through the system and controls are applied. (Ref: par. .19(b) and .20)

Obtaining Evidence Regarding the Design of Controls (Ref: par. .21)

.A36 The risks and control objectives identified in paragraph .21(a) encompass intentional and unintentional acts that threaten the achievement of the control objectives. (Ref: par. .21(a))

.A37 From the viewpoint of a user auditor, a control is suitably designed to achieve the control objectives stated in management's description of the service organization's system if individually or in combination with other controls, it would, when complied with satisfactorily, provide reasonable assurance that material misstatements are prevented, or detected and corrected. A service auditor, however, is not aware of the circumstances at individual user entities that would affect whether or not a misstatement resulting from a control deficiency is material to those user entities. Therefore, from the viewpoint of a service auditor, a control is suitably designed if individually or in combination with other controls, it would, when complied with satisfactorily, provide reasonable assurance that the control objective(s) stated in the description of the service organization's system are achieved.

.A38 A service auditor may consider using flowcharts, questionnaires, or decision tables to facilitate understanding the design of the controls.

.A39 Controls may consist of a number of activities directed at the achievement of various control objectives. Consequently, if the service auditor evaluates certain activities as being ineffective in achieving a particular control objective, the existence of other activities may allow the service auditor to conclude that controls related to the control objective are suitably designed to achieve the control objective.

Obtaining Evidence Regarding the Operating Effectiveness of Controls (Ref: par. .22–.27)

.A40 From the viewpoint of a user auditor, a control is operating effectively if individually or in combination with other controls, it provides reasonable assurance that material misstatements whether due to fraud or error are prevented, or detected and corrected. A service auditor, however, is not aware of the circumstances at individual user entities that would affect whether or not a misstatement resulting from a control deviation is material to those user entities. Therefore, from the viewpoint of a service auditor, a control is operating effectively if individually or in combination with other controls, it provides reasonable assurance that the control objectives stated in management's description of the service organization's system are achieved. Similarly, a service auditor is not in a position to determine whether any observed control deviation would result in a material misstatement from the viewpoint of an individual user entity. (Ref: par. .22)

.A41 Obtaining an understanding of controls sufficient to opine on the suitability of their design is not sufficient evidence regarding their operating effectiveness unless some automation provides for the consistent operation of the controls as they were designed and implemented. For example, obtaining information about the implementation of a manual control at a point in time does not provide evidence about operation of the control at other times. However, because of the inherent consistency of IT processing, performing procedures to determine the design of an automated control and whether it has been implemented may serve as evidence of that control's operating effectiveness, depending on the service auditor's assessment and testing of controls such as those over program changes. (Ref: par. .22)

.A42 A type 2 report that covers a period that is less than six months is unlikely to be useful to user entities and their auditors. If management's description of the service organization's system covers a period that is less than six months, the description may describe the reasons for the shorter period and the service auditor's report may include that information as well. Circumstances that may result in a report covering a period of less than six months include the following:

- The service auditor was engaged close to the date by which the report on controls is to be issued, and controls cannot be tested for operating effectiveness for a six month period.
- The service organization or a particular system or application has been in operation for less than six months.
- Significant changes have been made to the controls, and it is not practicable either to wait six months before issuing a report or to issue a report covering the system both before and after the changes. (Ref: par. .23)

.A43 Evidence about the satisfactory operation of controls in prior periods does not provide evidence of the operating effectiveness of controls during the current period. The service auditor expresses an opinion on the effectiveness of controls throughout each period; therefore, sufficient appropriate evidence about the operating effectiveness of controls throughout the current period is required for the service auditor to express that opinion for the current period. Knowledge of deviations observed in prior engagements may, however, lead the service auditor to increase the extent of testing during the current period. (Ref: par. .22)

.A44 Determining the effect of changes in the service organization's controls that were implemented during the period covered by the service auditor's report involves gathering information about the nature and extent of such changes, how they affect processing at the service organization, and how they might affect assertions in the user entities' financial statements. (Ref: par. .14(b) and .23)

.A45 Certain controls may not leave evidence of their operation that can be tested at a later date and, accordingly, the service auditor may find it appropriate to test the operating effectiveness of such controls at various times throughout the reporting period. (Ref: par. .22)

Using the Work of an Internal Audit Function

Obtaining an Understanding of the Internal Audit Function (Ref: par. .28)

.A46 An internal audit function may be responsible for providing analyses, evaluations, assurances, recommendations, and other information to management and those charged with governance. An internal audit function at a service organization may perform activities related to the service organization's internal control or activities related to the services and systems, including controls that the service organization provides to user entities.

.A47 The scope and objectives of an internal audit function vary widely and depend on the size and structure of the service organization and the requirements of management and those charged with governance. Internal audit function activities may include one or more of the following:

- Monitoring the service organization's internal control or the application processing systems. This may include controls relevant to the services provided to user entities. The internal audit function may be assigned specific responsibility for reviewing controls, monitoring their operation, and recommending improvements thereto.

- Examination of financial and operating information. The internal audit function may be assigned to review the means by which the service organization identifies, measures, classifies, and reports financial and operating information; to make inquiries about specific matters; and to perform other procedures including detailed testing of transactions, balances, and procedures.
- Evaluation of the economy, efficiency, and effectiveness of operating activities including nonfinancial activities of the service organization.
- Evaluation of compliance with laws, regulations, and other external requirements and with management policies, directives, and other internal requirements.

Using the Work of the Internal Audit Function (Ref: par .31–.32)

.A48 The nature, timing, and extent of the service auditor's procedures on specific work of the internal auditors will depend on the service auditor's assessment of the significance of that work to the service auditor's conclusions (for example, the significance of the risks that the controls tend to mitigate), the evaluation of the internal audit function, and the evaluation of the specific work of the internal auditors. Such procedures may include the following:

- Examination of items already examined by the internal auditors
- Examination of other similar items
- Observation of procedures performed by the internal auditors

Effect on the Service Auditor's Report (Ref: par. .33–.34)

.A49 The responsibility to report on management's description of the service organization's system and the suitability of the design and operating effectiveness of controls rests solely with the service auditor and cannot be shared with the internal audit function. Therefore, the judgments about the significance of deviations in the design or operating effectiveness of controls, the sufficiency of tests performed, the evaluation of identified deficiencies, and other matters affecting the service auditor's report are those of the service auditor. In making judgments about the extent of the effect of the work of the internal audit function on the service auditor's procedures, the service auditor may determine, based on risk associated with the controls and the significance of the judgments relating to them, that the service auditor will perform the work relating to some or all of the controls rather than using the work performed by the internal audit function.

.A50 In the case of a type 2 report, when the work of the internal audit function has been used in performing tests of controls, the service auditor's description of that work and of the service auditor's procedures with respect to that work may be presented in a number of ways, for example, (Ref: par. .34 and .52(o)(i))

- by including introductory material to the description of tests of controls indicating that certain work of the internal audit function was used in performing tests of controls.

- attribution of individual tests to internal audit.

Written Representations (Ref: par. .36–.39)

.A51 Written representations reaffirming the service organization's assertion about the effective operation of controls may be based on ongoing monitoring activities, separate evaluations, or a combination of the two. (Ref: par. .A12)

.A52 In certain circumstances, a service auditor may obtain written representations from parties in addition to management of the service organization, such as those charged with governance.

.A53 The written representations required by paragraph .36 are separate from and in addition to the assertion included in or attached to management's description of the service organization's system required by paragraph .09(c)(vii).

.A54 If the service auditor is unable to obtain written representations regarding relevant control objectives and related controls at the subservice organization, management of the service organization would be unable to use the inclusive method but could use the carve-out method.

.A55 In addition to the written representations required by paragraph .36, the service auditor may consider it necessary to request other written representations.

Other Information

.A56 The "other information" referred to in paragraphs .40–.41 may be the following:

- Information provided by the service organization and included in a section of the service auditor's type 1 or type 2 report, or
- Information outside the service auditor's type 1 or type 2 report included in a document that contains the service auditor's report. This other information may be provided by the service organization or by another party. (Ref: par. .40, .52(c)(ii)–(iii), and .53(c)(ii)–(iii))

.A57 If other information included in a document containing management's description of the service organization's system and the service auditor's report contains future-oriented information that cannot be reasonably substantiated, the service auditor may request that the information be removed or revised. (Ref: par. .41)

Documentation

.A58 Paragraph 57 of Statement on Quality Control Standards No. 7, *A Firm's System of Quality Control* (QC sec. 10A), requires the firm to establish policies and procedures that address engagement performance, supervision responsibilities, and review responsibilities. The requirement to document who reviewed the work performed and the extent of the review, in accordance with the firm's policies and procedures addressing review responsibilities, does not imply a need for each specific working paper to include evidence of review. The requirement, however, means documenting what work was reviewed, who reviewed such work, and when it was reviewed. (Ref: par. .44)

AAG-ASO APP A

Preparing the Service Auditor's Report

Content of the Service Auditor's Report (Ref: par. .52–.53)

.A59 Examples of service auditors' reports are presented in appendixes A–C and illustrative assertions by management of the service organization are presented in exhibit A.

.A60 The service organization's assertion may be presented in management's description of the service organization's system or may be attached to the description. (Ref: par. .52(e) and .53(e))

Use of the Service Auditor's Report (Ref: par. .52(p) and .53(o))

.A61 Paragraph .79 of section 101 requires that the use of a practitioner's report be restricted to specified parties when the criteria used to evaluate or measure the subject matter are available only to specified parties or appropriate only for a limited number of parties who either participated in their establishment or can be presumed to have an adequate understanding of the criteria. The criteria used for engagements to report on controls at a service organization are relevant only for the purpose of providing information about the service organization's system, including controls, to those who have an understanding of how the system is used for financial reporting by user entities and, accordingly, the service auditor's report states that the report and the description of tests of controls are intended only for use by management of the service organization, user entities of the service organization ("during some or all of the period covered by the report" for a type 2 report, and "as of the ending date of the period covered by the report" for a type 1 report), and their user auditors. (The illustrative service auditor's reports in appendix A illustrate language for a paragraph restricting the use of a service auditor's report.)

.A62 Paragraph .79 of section 101 indicates that the need for restriction on the use of a report may result from a number of circumstances, including the potential for the report to be misunderstood when taken out of the context in which it was intended to be used, and the extent to which the procedures performed are known or understood.

.A63 Although a service auditor is not responsible for controlling a service organization's distribution of a service auditor's report, a service auditor may inform the service organization of the following:

- A service auditor's type 1 report is not intended for distribution to parties other than the service organization, user entities of the service organization's system as of the end of the period covered by the service auditor's report, and their user auditors.

- A service auditor's type 2 report is not intended for distribution to parties other than the service organization, user entities of the service organization's system during some or all of the period covered by the service auditor's report, and their user auditors.

.A64 A user entity is also considered a user entity of the service organization's subservice organizations if controls at subservice organizations are relevant to internal control over financial reporting of the user entity. In such case, the user entity is referred to as an indirect or downstream user entity of the subservice organization. Consequently, an indirect or downstream user entity may be included in the group to whom use of the service auditor's report is

Statement on Standards for Attestation Engagements No. 16 **165**

restricted if controls at the service organization are relevant to internal control over financial reporting of such indirect or downstream user entity.

Description of the Service Auditor's Tests of Controls and the Results Thereof (Ref: par. .52(o)(ii))

.A65 In describing the service auditor's tests of controls for a type 2 report, it assists readers if the service auditor's report includes information about causative factors for identified deviations, to the extent the service auditor has identified such factors.

Modified Opinions (Ref: par. .55–.57)

.A66 Examples of elements of modified service auditor's reports are presented in appendix B.

Other Communication Responsibilities (Ref: par. .58)

.A67 Actions that a service auditor may take when he or she becomes aware of noncompliance with laws and regulations, fraud, or uncorrected errors at the service organization (after giving additional consideration to instances in which the service organization has not appropriately communicated this information to affected user entities, and the service organization is unwilling to do so) include the following:

- Obtaining legal advice about the consequences of different courses of action
- Communicating with those charged with governance of the service organization
- Disclaiming an opinion, modifying the service auditor's opinion, or adding an emphasis paragraph
- Communicating with third parties, for example, a regulator, when required to do so
- Withdrawing from the engagement

Appendix A: Illustrative Service Auditor's Reports

The following illustrative reports are for guidance only and are not intended to be exhaustive or applicable to all situations.

Example 1: Type 2 Service Auditor's Report

Independent Service Auditor's Report on a Description of a Service Organization's System and the Suitability of the Design and Operating Effectiveness of Controls

To: XYZ Service Organization

Scope

We have examined XYZ Service Organization's description of its [*type or name of*] system for processing user entities' transactions [*or identification of the function performed by the system*] throughout the period [*date*] to [*date*] (description) and the suitability of the design and operating effectiveness of controls to achieve the related control objectives stated in the description.

Service organization's responsibilities

On page XX of the description, XYZ Service Organization has provided an assertion about the fairness of the presentation of the description and suitability of the design and operating effectiveness of the controls to achieve the related control objectives stated in the description. XYZ Service Organization is responsible for preparing the description and for the assertion, including the completeness, accuracy, and method of presentation of the description and the assertion, providing the services covered by the description, specifying the control objectives and stating them in the description, identifying the risks that threaten the achievement of the control objectives, selecting the criteria, and designing, implementing, and documenting controls to achieve the related control objectives stated in the description.

Service auditor's responsibilities

Our responsibility is to express an opinion on the fairness of the presentation of the description and on the suitability of the design and operating effectiveness of the controls to achieve the related control objectives stated in the description, based on our examination. We conducted our examination in accordance with attestation standards established by the American Institute of Certified Public Accountants. Those standards require that we plan and perform our examination to obtain reasonable assurance about whether, in all material respects, the description is fairly presented and the controls were suitably designed and operating effectively to achieve the related control objectives stated in the description throughout the period [*date*] to [*date*].

An examination of a description of a service organization's system and the suitability of the design and operating effectiveness of the service organization's controls to achieve the related control objectives stated in the description involves performing procedures to obtain evidence about the fairness of the presentation of the description and the suitability of the design and operating effectiveness of those controls to achieve the related control objectives stated in the description. Our procedures included assessing the risks that the description is not fairly presented and that the controls were not suitably designed or operating effectively to achieve the related control objectives stated in the description. Our procedures also included testing the operating effectiveness of those controls that we consider necessary to provide reasonable assurance that the related control objectives stated in the description were achieved. An examination engagement of this type also includes evaluating the overall presentation of the description and the suitability of the control objectives stated therein, and the suitability of the criteria specified by the service organization and described at page *[aa]*. We believe that the evidence we obtained is sufficient and appropriate to provide a reasonable basis for our opinion.

Inherent limitations

Because of their nature, controls at a service organization may not prevent, or detect and correct, all errors or omissions in processing or reporting transactions [*or identification of the function performed by the system*]. Also, the projection to the future of any evaluation of the fairness of the presentation of the description, or conclusions about the suitability of the design or operating effectiveness of the controls to achieve the related control objectives is subject to the risk that controls at a service organization may become inadequate or fail.

Opinion

In our opinion, in all material respects, based on the criteria described in XYZ Service Organization's assertion on page [*aa*],

a. the description fairly presents the [*type or name of*] system that was designed and implemented throughout the period [*date*] to [*date*].

b. the controls related to the control objectives stated in the description were suitably designed to provide reasonable assurance that the control objectives would be achieved if the controls operated effectively throughout the period [*date*] to [*date*].

c. the controls tested, which were those necessary to provide reasonable assurance that the control objectives stated in the description were achieved, operated effectively throughout the period [*date*] to [*date*].

Description of tests of controls

The specific controls tested and the nature, timing, and results of those tests are listed on pages [*yy–zz*].

Restricted use

This report, including the description of tests of controls and results thereof on pages [*yy–zz*], is intended solely for the information and use of XYZ Service Organization, user entities of XYZ Service Organization's [*type or name of*] system during some or all of the period [*date*] to [*date*], and the independent auditors of such user entities, who have a sufficient understanding to consider it, along with other information including information about controls implemented by user entities themselves, when assessing the risks of material misstatements of user entities' financial statements. This report is not intended to be and should not be used by anyone other than these specified parties.

[*Service auditor's signature*]

[*Date of the service auditor's report*]

[*Service auditor's city and state*]

Following is a modification of the scope paragraph in a type 2 service auditor's report if the description refers to the need for complementary user entity controls. (New language is shown in boldface italics):

> We have examined XYZ Service Organization's description of its [*type or name of*] system for processing user entities' transactions [*or identification of the function performed by the system*] throughout the period [*date*] to [*date*] (description) and the suitability of the design and operating effectiveness of controls to achieve the related control objectives stated in the description. ***The description indicates that certain control objectives specified in the description can be achieved only if complementary user entity controls contemplated in the design of XYZ Service Organization's controls are suitably designed and operating effectively, along with related controls at the service organization. We have not evaluated the suitability of the design or operating effectiveness of such complementary user entity controls.***

Following is a modification of the applicable subparagraphs of the opinion paragraph of a type 2 service auditor's report if the application of complementary user entity controls is necessary to achieve the related control objectives stated in the description of the service organization's system (New language is shown in boldface italics):

> b. The controls related to the control objectives stated in the description were suitably designed to provide reasonable assurance that those control objectives would be achieved if the controls operated effectively throughout the period [*date*] to [*date*] ***and user entities applied the complementary user entity controls contemplated in the design of XYZ Service Organization's controls throughout the period [date] to [date]***.
>
> c. The controls tested, which ***together with the complementary user entity controls referred to in the scope paragraph of this report, if operating effectively,*** were those necessary to provide reasonable assurance that the control objectives stated in the description were achieved, operated effectively throughout the period [*date*] to [*date*].

Following is a modification of the paragraph that describes the responsibilities of management of the service organization for use in a type 2 service auditor's report when the control objectives have been specified by an outside party. (New language is shown in boldface italics):

> On page XX of the description, XYZ Service Organization has provided an assertion about the fairness of the presentation of the description and suitability of the design and operating effectiveness of the controls to achieve the related control objectives stated in the description. XYZ Service Organization is responsible for preparing the description and for its assertion], including the completeness, accuracy, and method of presentation of the description and assertion, providing the services covered by the description, selecting the criteria, and designing, implementing, and documenting controls to achieve the related control objectives stated in the description. ***The control objectives have been specified by [name of party specifying the control objectives] and are stated on page [aa] of the description***.

Example 2: Type 1 Service Auditor's Report

Independent Service Auditor's Report on a Description of a Service Organization's System and the Suitability of the Design of Controls

To: XYZ Service Organization

Scope

We have examined XYZ Service Organization's description of its [*type or name of*] system for processing user entities' transactions [*or identification of the function performed by the system*] as of [*date*], and the suitability of the design of controls to achieve the related control objectives stated in the description.

Service organization's responsibilities

On page XX of the description, XYZ Service Organization has provided an assertion about the fairness of the presentation of the description and suitability of the design of the controls to achieve the related controls objectives stated in the description. XYZ Service Organization is responsible for preparing the description and for its assertion, including the completeness, accuracy, and method of presentation of the description and the assertion, providing the services covered by the description, specifying the control objectives and stating them in the description, identifying the risks that threaten the achievement of the control objectives, selecting the criteria, and designing, implementing, and documenting controls to achieve the related control objectives stated in the description.

Service auditor's responsibilities

Our responsibility is to express an opinion on the fairness of the presentation of the description and on the suitability of the design of the controls to achieve the related control objectives stated in the description, based on our examination. We conducted our examination in accordance with attestation standards established by the American Institute of Certified Public Accountants. Those standards require that we plan and perform our examination to obtain reasonable assurance, in all material respects, about whether the description is fairly presented and the controls were suitably designed to achieve the related control objectives stated in the description as of [*date*].

An examination of a description of a service organization's system and the suitability of the design of the service organization's controls to achieve the related control objectives stated in the description involves performing procedures to obtain evidence about the fairness of the presentation of the description of the system and the suitability of the design of the controls to achieve the related control objectives stated in the description. Our procedures included assessing the risks that the description is not fairly presented and that the controls were not suitably designed to achieve the related control objectives stated in the description. An examination engagement of this type also includes evaluating the overall presentation of the description and the suitability of the control objectives stated therein, and the suitability of the criteria specified by the service organization and described at page [*aa*].

We did not perform any procedures regarding the operating effectiveness of the controls stated in the description and, accordingly, do not express an opinion thereon.

We believe that the evidence we obtained is sufficient and appropriate to provide a reasonable basis for our opinion.

Inherent limitations

Because of their nature, controls at a service organization may not prevent, or detect and correct, all errors or omissions in processing or reporting transactions [*or identification of the function performed by the system*]. The projection to the future of any evaluation of the fairness of the presentation of the description, or any conclusions about the suitability of the design of the controls to achieve the related control objectives is subject to the risk that controls at a service organization may become ineffective or fail.

Opinion

In our opinion, in all material respects, based on the criteria described in XYZ Service Organization's assertion,

    a. the description fairly presents the [*type or name of*] system that was designed and implemented as of [*date*], and

    b. the controls related to the control objectives stated in the description were suitably designed to provide reasonable assurance that the control objectives would be achieved if the controls operated effectively as of [*date*].

Restricted use

This report is intended solely for the information and use of XYZ Service Organization, user entities of XYZ Service Organization's [*type or name of*] system as of [*date*], and the independent auditors of such user entities, who have a sufficient understanding to consider it, along with other information including information about controls implemented by user entities themselves, when obtaining an understanding of user entities information and communication systems relevant to financial reporting. This report is not intended to be and should not be used by anyone other than these specified parties.

[*Service auditor's signature*]

[*Date of the service auditor's report*]

[*Service auditor's city and state*]

Following is a modification of the scope paragraph in a type 1 report if the description of the service organization's system refers to the need for complementary user entity controls. (New language is shown in boldface italics)

    We have examined XYZ Service Organization's description of its [type or name of] system (description) made available to user entities of the system for processing their transactions [or identification of the function performed by the system] as of [date], and the suitability of the design of controls to achieve the related control objectives stated in the description. ***The description indicates that certain complementary user entity controls must be suitably designed and implemented at user entities for related controls at the service organization to be considered suitably designed to achieve the related control objectives. We have not evaluated the suitability of the design or operating effectiveness of such complementary user entity controls.***

Following is a modification of the applicable subparagraph in the opinion paragraph of a type 1 report if the application of complementary user entity controls is necessary to achieve the related control objectives stated in management's

Statement on Standards for Attestation Engagements No. 16

description of the service organization's system (New language is shown in boldface italics):

> b. The controls related to the control objectives stated in the description were suitably designed to provide reasonable assurance that those control objectives would be achieved if the controls operated effectively as of [date] ***and user entities applied the complementary user entity controls contemplated in the design of XYZ Service Organization's controls as of [date].***

Following is a modification of the paragraph that describes management of XYZ Service Organization's responsibilities to be used in a type 1 report when the control objectives have been specified by an outside party. (New language is shown in boldface italics):

> On page XX of the description, XYZ Service Organization has provided an assertion about the fairness of the presentation of the description and suitability of the design of the controls to achieve the related control objectives stated in the description. XYZ Service Organization is responsible for preparing the description and assertion, including the completeness, accuracy, and method of presentation of the description and assertion, providing the services covered by the description, selecting the criteria, and designing, implementing, and documenting controls to achieve the related control objectives stated in the description. ***The control objectives have been specified by [name of party specifying the control objectives] and are stated on page [aa] of the description.***

.A69

Appendix B: Illustrative Modified Service Auditor's Reports

The following examples of modified service auditor's reports are for guidance only and are not intended to be exhaustive or applicable to all situations. They are based on the illustrative reports in appendix A.

Example 1: Qualified Opinion for a Type 2 Report—The Description of the Service Organization's System is Not Fairly Presented in All Material Respects

The following is an illustrative paragraph describing the basis for the qualified opinion. The paragraph would be inserted before the modified opinion paragraph. All other report paragraphs are unchanged.

Basis for qualified opinion

The accompanying description states on page [*mn*] that XYZ Service Organization uses operator identification numbers and passwords to prevent unauthorized access to the system. Based on inquiries of staff personnel and observation of activities, we have determined that operator identification numbers and passwords are employed in applications A and B but are not required to access the system in applications C and D.

Opinion

In our opinion, except for the matter described in the preceding paragraph, and based on the criteria described in XYZ Service Organization's assertion on page *[aa]*, in all material respects . . .

Example 2: Qualified Opinion—The Controls are Not Suitably Designed to Provide Reasonable Assurance That the Control Objectives Stated in the Description of the Service Organization's System Would be Achieved if the Controls Operated Effectively

The following is an illustrative paragraph describing the basis for the qualified opinion. The paragraph would be inserted before the modified opinion paragraph. All other report paragraphs are unchanged.

Basis for qualified opinion

As discussed on page [*mn*] of the accompanying description, from time to time, XYZ Service Organization makes changes in application programs to correct deficiencies or to enhance capabilities. The procedures followed in determining whether to make changes, in designing the changes, and in implementing them do not include review and approval by authorized individuals who are independent from those involved in making the changes. There also are no specified requirements to test such changes or provide test results to an authorized reviewer prior to implementing the changes. As a result the controls are not suitably designed to achieve the control objective, "Controls provide reasonable assurance that changes to existing applications are authorized, tested, approved, properly implemented, and documented."

AAG-ASO APP A

Opinion

In our opinion, except for the matter described in the preceding paragraph, and based on the criteria described in XYZ Service Organization's assertion on page *[aa]*, in all material respects . . .

Example 3: Qualified Opinion for a Type 2 Report—The Controls Did Not Operate Effectively Throughout the Specified Period to Achieve the Control Objectives Stated in the Description of the Service Organization's System

The following is an illustrative paragraph describing the basis for the qualified opinion. The paragraph would be inserted before the modified opinion paragraph. All other report paragraphs are unchanged.

Basis for qualified opinion

XYZ Service Organization states in its description that it has automated controls in place to reconcile loan payments received with the various output reports. However, as noted on page [*mn*] of the description of tests of controls and results thereof, this control was not operating effectively throughout the period [*date*] to [*date*] due to a programming error. This resulted in the nonachievement of the control objective, "Controls provide reasonable assurance that loan payments received are properly recorded" throughout the period January 1, 20X1, to April 30, 20X1. XYZ Service Organization implemented a change to the program performing the calculation as of May 1, 20X1, and our tests indicate that it was operating effectively throughout the period May 1, 20X1, to December 31, 20X1.

Opinion

In our opinion, except for the matter described in the preceding paragraph, and based on the criteria described in XYZ Service Organization's assertion on page [*aa*], in all material respects. . . .

Example 4: Qualified Opinion—The Service Auditor is Unable to Obtain Sufficient Appropriate Evidence

The following is an illustrative paragraph describing the basis for the qualified opinion. The paragraph would be inserted before the modified opinion paragraph. All other report paragraphs are unchanged.

Basis for qualified opinion

XYZ Service Organization states in its description that it has automated controls in place to reconcile loan payments received with the output generated. However, electronic records of the performance of this reconciliation for the period from [*date*] to [*date*] were deleted as a result of a computer processing error and, therefore, we were unable to test the operation of this control for that period. Consequently, we were unable to determine whether the control objective, "Controls provide reasonable assurance that loan payments received are properly recorded" was achieved throughout the period [*date*] to [*date*].

Opinion

In our opinion, except for the matter described in the preceding paragraph, and based on the criteria described in XYZ Service Organization's assertion on page [*aa*], in all material respects . . .

.A70

Appendix C: Illustrative Report Paragraphs for Service Organizations That Use a Subservice Organization

Following are modifications of the illustrative type 2 report in example 1 of appendix A for use in engagements in which the service organization uses a subservice organization. (New language is shown in boldface italics; deleted language is shown by strikethrough.)

Example 1: Carve-Out Method

Scope

We have examined XYZ Service Organization's description of its system for processing user entities' transactions [or *identification of the function performed by the system*] throughout the period [*date*] to [*date*] (description) and the suitability of the design and operating effectiveness of controls to achieve the related control objectives stated in the description.

XYZ Service Organization uses a computer processing service organization for all of its computerized application processing. The description on pages [bb–cc] includes only the controls and related control objectives of XYZ Service Organization and excludes the control objectives and related controls of the computer processing service organization. Our examination did not extend to controls of the computer processing service organization.

All other report paragraphs are unchanged.

Example 2: Inclusive Method

Scope

We have examined XYZ Service Organization's **and ABC Subservice Organization's** description of ~~its~~ ***their*** [*type or name of*] system for processing user entities' transactions [or *identification of the function performed by the system*] throughout the period [*date*] to [*date*] (description) and the suitability of the design and operating effectiveness of ***XYZ Service Organization's and ABC Subservice Organization's*** controls to achieve the related control objectives stated in the description. ***ABC Subservice Organization is an independent service organization that provides computer processing services to XYZ Service Organization. XYZ Service Organization's description includes a description of ABC Subservice Organization's [type or name of] system used by XYZ Service Organization to process transactions for its user entities, as well as relevant control objectives and controls of ABC Subservice Organization.***

XYZ Service Organization's responsibilities

On page XX of the description, XYZ Service Organization ***and ABC Subservice Organization*** ~~has~~ ***have*** provided ~~an~~ ***their*** assertions about the fairness of the presentation of the description and suitability of the design and operating effectiveness of the controls to achieve the related control objectives stated in the description. XYZ Service Organization ***and ABC Subservice Organization are*** ~~is~~ responsible for preparing the description and assertions, including the completeness, accuracy, and method of presentation of the description and assertions, providing the services covered by the description, specifying the control objectives and stating them in the description, identifying the risks that threaten the achievement of the control objectives, selecting the criteria, and designing, implementing, and documenting controls to achieve the related control objectives stated in the description.

Inherent limitations

Because of their nature, controls at a service organization *or subservice organization* may not prevent, or detect and correct, all errors or omissions in processing or reporting transactions. Also, the projection to the future of any evaluation of the fairness of the presentation of the description or any conclusions about the suitability of the design or operating effectiveness of the controls to achieve the related control objectives is subject to the risk that controls at a service organization *or subservice organization* may become ineffective or fail.

Opinion

In our opinion, in all material respects, based on the criteria specified in XYZ Service Organization's **and ABC Subservice Organization's** assertions on page [*aa*],

    a. the description fairly presents *XYZ Service Organization's* the [*type or name of*] system *and ABC Subservice Organization's* [*type or name of*] *system used by XYZ Service Organization to process transactions for its user entities* [*or identification of the function performed by the service organization's system*] that *were* was designed and implemented throughout the period [*date*] to [*date*].

    b. the controls related to the control objectives *of XYZ Service Organization and ABC Subservice Organization* stated in the description were suitably designed to provide reasonable assurance that the control objectives would be achieved if the controls operated effectively throughout the period [*date*] to [*date*].

    c. the controls *of XYZ Service Organization and ABC Subservice Organization that* we tested, which were those necessary to provide reasonable assurance that the control objectives stated in the description were achieved, operated effectively throughout the period [*date*] to [*date*].

All other report paragraphs are unchanged.

.A71

Exhibit A: Illustrative Assertions by Management of a Service Organization

The assertion by management of the service organization may be included in management's description of the service organization's system or may be attached to the description. The following illustrative assertions are intended for assertions that are included in the description.

The following illustrative management assertions are for guidance only and are not intended to be exhaustive or applicable to all situations.

Example 1: Assertion by Management of a Service Organization for a Type 2 Report

XYZ Service Organization's Assertion

We have prepared the description of XYZ Service Organization's [*type or name of*] system (description) for user entities of the system during some or all of the period [*date*] to [*date*], and their user auditors who have a sufficient understanding to consider it, along with other information, including information about controls implemented by user entities of the system themselves, when assessing the risks of material misstatements of user entities' financial statements. We confirm, to the best of our knowledge and belief, that

   a. the description fairly presents the [*type or name of*] system made available to user entities of the system during some or all of the period [*date*] to [*date*] for processing their transactions [*or identification of the function performed by the system*]. The criteria we used in making this assertion were that the description
      i. presents how the system made available to user entities of the system was designed and implemented to process relevant transactions, including
         (1) the classes of transactions processed.
         (2) the procedures, within both automated and manual systems, by which those transactions are initiated, authorized, recorded, processed, corrected as necessary, and transferred to the reports presented to user entities of the system.
         (3) the related accounting records, supporting information, and specific accounts that are used to initiate, authorize, record, process, and report transactions; this includes the correction of incorrect information and how information is transferred to the reports presented to user entities of the system.
         (4) how the system captures and addresses significant events and conditions, other than transactions.
         (5) the process used to prepare reports or other information provided to user entities' of the system.
         (6) specified control objectives and controls designed to achieve those objectives.

(7) other aspects of our control environment, risk assessment process, information and communication systems (including the related business processes), control activities, and monitoring controls that are relevant to processing and reporting transactions of user entities of the system.

    ii. does not omit or distort information relevant to the scope of the [*type or name of*] system, while acknowledging that the description is prepared to meet the common needs of a broad range of user entities of the system and the independent auditors of those user entities, and may not, therefore, include every aspect of the [*type or name of*] system that each individual user entity of the system and its auditor may consider important in its own particular environment.

b. the description includes relevant details of changes to the service organization's system during the period covered by the description when the description covers a period of time.

c. the controls related to the control objectives stated in the description were suitably designed and operated effectively throughout the period [*date*] to [*date*] to achieve those control objectives. The criteria we used in making this assertion were that

    i. the risks that threaten the achievement of the control objectives stated in the description have been identified by the service organization;

    ii. the controls identified in the description would, if operating as described, provide reasonable assurance that those risks would not prevent the control objectives stated in the description from being achieved; and

    iii. the controls were consistently applied as designed, including whether manual controls were applied by individuals who have the appropriate competence and authority.

Example 2: Assertion by Management of a Service Organization for a Type 1 Report

XYZ Service Organization's Assertion

We have prepared the description of XYZ Service Organization's [*type or name of*] system (description) for user entities of the system as of [*date*], and their user auditors who have a sufficient understanding to consider it, along with other information including information about controls implemented by user entities themselves, when obtaining an understanding of user entities' information and communication systems relevant to financial reporting. We confirm, to the best of our knowledge and belief, that

a. the description fairly presents the [*type or name of*] system made available to user entities of the system as of [*date*] for processing their transactions [*or identification of the function performed by the system*]. The criteria we used in making this assertion were that the description

i. presents how the system made available to user entities of the system was designed and implemented to process relevant transactions, including
   (1) the classes of transactions processed.
   (2) the procedures, within both automated and manual systems, by which those transactions are initiated, authorized, recorded, processed, corrected as necessary, and transferred to the reports presented to user entities of the system.
   (3) the related accounting records, supporting information, and specific accounts that are used to initiate, authorize, record, process, and report transactions; this includes the correction of incorrect information and how information is transferred to the reports provided to user entities of the system.
   (4) how the system captures and addresses significant events and conditions, other than transactions.
   (5) the process used to prepare reports or other information provided to user entities of the system.
   (6) specified control objectives and controls designed to achieve those objectives.
   (7) other aspects of our control environment, risk assessment process, information and communication systems (including the related business processes), control activities, and monitoring controls that are relevant to processing and reporting transactions of user entities of the system.
ii. does not omit or distort information relevant to the scope of the [*type or name of*] system, while acknowledging that the description is prepared to meet the common needs of a broad range of user entities of the system and the independent auditors of those user entities, and may not, therefore, include every aspect of the [*type or name of*] system that each individual user entity of the system and its auditor may consider important in its own particular environment.

b. the controls related to the control objectives stated in the description were suitably designed as of [*date*] to achieve those control objectives. The criteria we used in making this assertion were that
   i. the risks that threaten the achievement of the control objectives stated in the description have been identified by the service organization.
   ii. the controls identified in the description would, if operating as described, provide reasonable assurance that those risks would not prevent the control objectives stated in the description from being achieved.

.A72

Exhibit B: Comparison of Requirements of Section 801, *Reporting On Controls at a Service Organization*, With Requirements of International Standard on Assurance Engagements 3402, *Assurance Reports on Controls at a Service Organization*

This analysis was prepared by the AICPA Audit and Attest Standards staff to highlight substantive differences between section 801, *Reporting on Controls at a Service Organization*, and International Standard on Assurance Engagements (ISAE) 3402, *Assurance Reports on Controls at a Service Organization*, and to explain the rationale for those differences. This analysis is not authoritative and is prepared for informational purposes only.

1. Intentional Acts by Service Organization Personnel

Paragraph .26 of this section requires the service auditor to investigate the nature and cause of any deviations identified, as does paragraph 28 of ISAE 3402. Paragraph .27 of this section indicates that if the service auditor becomes aware that the deviations resulted from intentional acts by service organization personnel, the service auditor should assess the risk that the description of the service organization's system is not fairly presented and that the controls are not suitably designed or operating effectively. The ISAE does not contain the requirement included in paragraph .27 of this section. The Auditing Standards Board (ASB) believes that information about intentional acts affects the nature, timing, and extent of the service auditor's procedures. Therefore, paragraph .27 provides follow-up action for the service auditor when he or she obtains information about intentional acts as a result of performing the procedures in paragraph .26 of this section.

Paragraph .36(c)(ii) of this section, which is not included in ISAE 3402, also requires the service auditor to request written representations from management that it has disclosed to the service auditor knowledge of any actual, suspected, or alleged intentional acts by management or the service organization's employees, of which it is aware, that could adversely affect the fairness of the presentation of management's description of the service organization's system or the completeness or achievement of the control objectives stated in the description.

2. Anomalies

Paragraph 29 of ISAE 3402 contains a requirement that enables a service auditor to conclude that a deviation identified in tests of controls involving sampling is not representative of the population from which the sample was drawn. This section does not include this requirement because of concerns about use of terms such as, "in the extremely rare circumstances" and "a high degree of certainty." These terms are not used in U.S professional standards and the ASB believes their introduction in this section could have unintended consequences. The ASB also believes that the deletion of this requirement will enhance examination quality because deviations identified by the service auditor in tests of controls involving sampling will be treated in the same manner as any other deviation identified by the practitioner, rather than as an anomaly.

3. Direct Assistance

Paragraph .35 of this section requires the service auditor to adapt and apply the requirements in paragraph .27 of AU section 322, *The Auditor's Consideration of the Internal Audit Function in an Audit of Financial Statements*, when the service auditor uses members of the service organization's internal audit function to provide direct assistance. Because AU section 322 provides for an auditor to use the work of the internal audit function in a direct assistance capacity, paragraph .35 of this section also provides for this. The International Standards on Auditing and the ISAEs do not provide for use of the internal audit function for direct assistance.

4. Subsequent Events

With respect to events that occur subsequent to the period covered by the description of the service organization's system up to the date of the service auditor's report, paragraph .42 of this section requires the service auditor to disclose in the service auditor's report, if not disclosed by management in its description, any event that is of such a nature and significance that its disclosure is necessary to prevent users of a type 1 or type 2 report from being misled. The ASB believes that information about such events could be important to user entities and their auditors. ISAE 3402 limits the types of subsequent events that would need to be disclosed in the service auditor's report to those that could have a significant effect on the service auditor's report.

Paragraph .43 of this section requires the service auditor to adapt and apply the guidance in AU section 561, *Subsequent Discovery of Facts Existing at the Date of the Auditor's Report*, if, after the release of the service auditor's report, the service auditor becomes aware of conditions that existed at the report date that might have affected management's assertion and the service auditor's report had the service auditor been aware of them. The ISAE does not include a similar requirement. The ASB believes that, by analogy, AU section 561 provides needed guidance to a service auditor by presenting the various circumstances that could occur during the subsequent events period and the actions a service auditor should take.

5. Statement Restricting Use of the Service Auditor's Report

This section requires the service auditor's report to include a statement restricting the use of the report to management of the service organization, user entities of the service organization's system, and user auditors. The ASB believes that the unambiguous language in the restricted use statement prevents misunderstanding regarding who the report is intended for. Paragraphs .A61–.A62 of this section explain the reasons for restricting the use of the report. ISAE 3402 requires the service auditor's report to include a statement indicating that the report is intended only for user entities and their auditors, However, the ISAE does not require the inclusion of a statement restricting the use of the report to specified parties, although it does not prohibit the inclusion of restricted use language in the report.

6. Documentation Completion

Paragraph 50 of the ISAE requires the service auditor to assemble the documentation in an engagement file and complete the administrative process of assembling the final engagement file on a timely basis after the date of the service auditor's assurance report. Paragraph .49 of this section also requires the service auditor to assemble the engagement documentation in an engagement file and complete the administrative process of assembling the final engagement file on a timely basis, but also indicates that a timely basis is no later than 60 days following the service auditor's report release date. The ASB made this change to parallel the definition of *documentation completion date* in paragraph .27 of AU section 339, *Audit Documentation*.

7. Engagement Acceptance and Continuance

Paragraph .09 of this section establishes conditions for the acceptance and continuance of an engagement to report on controls at a service organization. One of the conditions is that management acknowledge and accept responsibility for providing the service auditor with written representations at the conclusion of the engagement. ISAE 3402 does not include this requirement as a condition of engagement acceptance and continuance.

8. Disclaimer of Opinion

If management does not provide the service auditor with certain written representations, paragraph 40 of ISAE 3402 requires the service auditor, after discussing the matter with management, to disclaim an opinion. In the same circumstances, paragraph .39 of this section requires the service auditor to take appropriate action, which may include disclaiming an opinion or withdrawing from the engagement.

Paragraphs .56–.57 of this section contain certain incremental requirements when the service auditor plans to disclaim an opinion.

9. Elements of the Section 801 Report That Are Not Required in the ISAE 3402 Report.

Paragraphs .52–.53 of this section contain certain requirements regarding the content of the service auditor's report, which are incremental to those in ISAE 3402. These incremental requirements are included in paragraphs .52(c)(iii); .52(e)(iv); .52(i); and .52(k) for type 2 reports, and in paragraphs .53(c)(iii); .53(e)(iv); .53(j); and .53(k) for type 1 reports.

Appendix B

Illustrative Type 2 Reports

Although Statement on Standards for Attestation Engagements (SSAE) No. 16, *Reporting on Controls at a Service Organization* (AICPA, *Professional Standards*, AT sec. 801), specifies the components of a type 1 or type 2 report and the information to be included in each component, it does not specify how the components should be organized within the type 1 or type 2 report. Service organizations and service auditors may organize and present the required information in a variety of formats. The formats presented in this appendix are not meant to be prescriptive but rather illustrative. This appendix contains four illustrative type 2 reports. The reports are for Example Service Organization and Example Trust Organization. The examples illustrate different methods of organizing a type 2 report. These illustrative reports contain all of the sections of a type 2 report; however, for brevity, the illustrative reports do not include everything that might be described in a type 2 report. Ellipses (...) or notes to readers indicate places at which detail has been omitted from the illustrative reports.

The control objectives and controls specified by the service organizations in examples 1–4, as well as the tests performed by the service auditors, are presented for illustrative purposes only. They are not intended to represent a complete or standard set of control objectives, controls, or tests of controls that would be appropriate for all service organizations. The determination of the appropriate control objectives, controls, and tests of controls for a specific service organization can be made only in the context of specific facts and circumstances. Accordingly, it is expected that actual type 2 reports will contain differing control objectives, controls, and tests of controls that are tailored to the service organization that is the subject of the engagement.

In examples 1, 3, and 4 of this appendix, the components of the illustrative type 2 reports are referred to as "sections," for example, section 2 contains management's assertion. The components of the illustrative type 2 report in example 3 are identified by specifying the page numbers at which the component is found.

The following chart identifies features of each illustrative type 2 report included in this appendix.

Summary of Features of Illustrative Type 2 Reports in Appendix B

Example Number and Name of Service Organization	*Type of System Provided by Service Organization*	*Name of Subservice Organization and Method of Presentation*	*Service Provided by the Subservice Organization(s)*	*Are Complementary User Entity Controls Required by the Service Organization or Subservice Organization?*	*Format of the Type 2 Report*
1. Example Service Organization	Savings system	N/A	N/A	Service organization requires complementary user entity controls	Narrative containing four report components referred to as sections 1, 2, 3, and 4

(continued)

Example Number and Name of Service Organization	Type of System Provided by Service Organization	Name of Subservice Organization and Method of Presentation	Service Provided by the Subservice Organization(s)	Are Complementary User Entity Controls Required by the Service Organization or Subservice Organization?	Format of the Type 2 Report
2. Example Service Organization	Savings system	Computer Subservice Organization Inclusive method	Computer processing	No	Narrative containing five report components designated by page numbers (additional component is the subservice organization's assertion)
3. Example Service Organization	Savings system	Computer Subservice Organization Carve-out method	Computer processing	Service organization does not require complementary user entity controls Subservice organization requires complementary user entity controls	Narrative containing four report components referred to as sections 1, 2, 3, and 4
4. Example Trust Organization	System for processing transactions for user entities of its Institutional Trust Division	DTC, DTC/MBS, the FED, XYZ Bank, DEF Bank, ABC Pricing Service Org., BLB Inc., xTRA, RTR, BRD Inc., NR Trust, and Carve-out method	Depository, subcustodial, pricing, and corporate action services	Yes	Four report components referred to as sections 1, 2, 3, and 4 Sections 1, 2, and 3 are in narrative format. Section 3 omits the service organization's control objectives and related controls; that information is included in section 4 in which each control objective is followed by a three-column table describing the service organization's controls, the service auditor's tests, and the results of the tests.

Example 1—Service Organization Presents Subservice Organization Using the Carve-Out Method; Service Organization Requires Complementary User Entity Controls

Example Service Organization

Report on Example Service Organization's Description of its Savings System and on the Suitability of the Design and Operating Effectiveness of Its Controls

In example 1, Example Service Organization informs report users that complementary user entity controls are required to achieve control objective 11. Changes to the report related to the need for complementary user entity controls are shown in boldface italics. This report is written in narrative format and includes the following four sections:

> Section 1. The service auditor's report
>
> Section 2. Management of Example Service Organization's assertion, which is attached to Example Service Organization's description of its system
>
> Section 3. Example Service Organization's description of its system
>
> Section 4. The service auditor's description of tests of controls and results

Table of Contents

Section	Description of Section
1.	Independent Service Auditor's Report
2.	Example Service Organization's Assertion
3.	Description of Example Service Organization's Savings System Overview of Operations Relevant Aspects of the Control Environment, Risk Assessment Process, Information and Communication Systems, and Monitoring Controls Control Objectives and Related Controls
4.	Independent Service Auditor's Description of Tests of Controls and Results

In the following illustrative service auditor's report, required elements of a type 2 report are immediately followed by a parenthetical identifying the SSAE No. 16 paragraph that contains the requirement.

1
Independent (52[a]) Service Auditor's Report[1]

To Management of Example Service Organization (52[b]):

Scope

We have examined Example Service Organization's description of its savings system for processing user entities' transactions (52[c][i]) throughout the period December 1, 20X0, to November 30, 20X1 (description), and the suitability of design and operating effectiveness of controls to achieve the related control objectives stated in the description. *The description indicates that certain control objectives specified in the description can be achieved only if complementary user entity controls contemplated in the design of Example Service Organization's controls are suitably designed and operating effectively, along with related controls at the service organization. We have not evaluated the suitability of the design and operating effectiveness of such complementary user entity controls* (52[d]).

Service organization's responsibilities

In section 2 of this report, Example Service Organization has provided an assertion (52[e]) about the fair presentation of the description and the suitability of design and operating effectiveness of the controls to achieve the related control objectives stated in the description. Example Service Organization is responsible for preparing the description and for the assertion, including the completeness, accuracy, and method of presentation of the description and the assertion, providing the services covered by the description, specifying the control objectives and stating them in the description, identifying the risks that threaten the achievement of the control objectives, selecting the criteria, and designing, implementing, and documenting controls to achieve the related control objectives stated in the description (52[e]).

Service auditor's responsibilities

Our responsibility is to express an opinion on the fairness of presentation of the description and the suitability of the design and operating effectiveness of the controls to achieve the control objectives stated in the description, based on our examination (52[f]). We conducted our examination in accordance with attestation standards established by the American Institute of Certified Public Accountants. Those standards require that we plan and perform our examination to obtain reasonable assurance about whether, in all material respects, the description is fairly presented and the controls were suitably designed and operating effectively to achieve the related control objectives stated in the description throughout the period from December 1, 20X0, to November 30, 20X1 (52[g]).

An examination of a description of a service organization's system and the suitability of the design and operating effectiveness of the service organization's controls to achieve the related control objectives stated in the description involves performing procedures to obtain evidence about the fairness of presentation of the description of the system and the suitability of the design and operating effectiveness of those controls to achieve the related control objectives stated in the description (52[h]). Our procedures included assessing the

---

[1] The parenthetical references refer to the required elements in a type 2 report listed in paragraph 52 of Statement on Standards for Attestation Engagements No. 16, *Reporting on Controls at a Service Organization* (AICPA, *Professional Standards*, AT sec. 801).

risks that the description is not fairly presented and that the controls were not suitably designed or operating effectively to achieve the related control objectives stated in the description (52[i]). Our procedures also included testing the operating effectiveness of those controls that we consider necessary to provide reasonable assurance that the related controls objectives stated in the description were achieved (52)[j]). An examination engagement of this type also includes evaluating the overall presentation of the description and the suitability of the control objectives stated therein, and the suitability of the criteria specified by the service organization and described in management's assertion in section 2 of this report (52[k]). We believe that the evidence we obtained is sufficient and appropriate to provide a reasonable basis for our opinion (52[l]).

Inherent limitations

Because of their nature, controls at a service organization may not prevent, or detect and correct, all errors or omissions in processing or reporting transactions. Also, the projection to the future of any evaluation of the fairness of the presentation of the description, or conclusions about the suitability of design or operating effectiveness of the controls to achieve the related control objectives, is subject to the risk that controls at a service organization may become inadequate or fail (52[m]).

Opinion

In our opinion, in all material respects, based on the criteria described in Example Service Organization's assertion in section 2 of this report

    a. The description fairly presents the savings system that was designed and implemented throughout the period December 1, 20X0, to November 30, 20X1 (52[n][i]).

    b. The controls related to the control objectives stated in the description of were suitably designed to provide reasonable assurance that the control objectives would be achieved if the controls operated effectively throughout the period December 1, 20X0, to November 30, 20X1 (52[n][ii]), **and user entities applied the complementary user entity controls contemplated in the design of Example Service Organization's controls throughout the period December 1, 20X0, to November 30, 20X1** (52[n][iv]).

    c. The controls tested, which **together with the complementary user entity controls referred to in the scope paragraph of this report, if operating effectively,** were those necessary to provide reasonable assurance that the control objectives stated in the description were achieved, operated effectively through the period December 1, 20X0, to November 30, 20X1 (52[n][iii]).

Description of tests of controls

The specific controls tested and the nature, timing, and results of those tests are listed in section 4 of this report (52[o]).

Restricted use

This report and the description of tests of controls and results thereof in section 4 of this report are intended solely for the information and use of Example Service Organization, user entities of Example Service Organization's savings system during some or all of the period December 1, 20X0, to November 30, 20X1, and the independent auditors of such user entities, who have a sufficient understanding to consider it, along with other information including information about the controls implemented by user entities themselves, when assessing the risks of material misstatements of user entities' financial statements. This report is not intended to be and should not be used by anyone other than those specified parties (52[p]).

[*Service auditor's signature*] (52[r])

December 15, 20X1 (52[q])

Los Angeles, CA (52[r])

2
Example Service Organization's Assertion[2]

We have prepared the description of Example Service Organization's savings system (description) for user entities of the system during some or all of the period December 1, 20X0, to November 30, 20X1, and their user auditors who have a sufficient understanding to consider it, along with other information, including information about controls implemented by user entities of the system themselves, when assessing the risks of material misstatements of user entities' financial statements. We confirm, to the best of our knowledge and belief, that:

    a. The description fairly presents the savings system made available to user entities of the system during some or all of the period December 1, 20X0, to November 30, 20X1, for processing their transactions. The criteria we used in making this assertion were that the description (52[c][iv])

        1. presents how the system made available to user entities of the system was designed and implemented to process relevant transactions, including, if applicable:

- the types of services provided including, as appropriate, the classes of transactions processed.
- the procedures, within both automated and manual systems, by which services are provided, including, as appropriate, procedures by which transactions are initiated, authorized, recorded, processed, corrected as necessary, and transferred to reports and other information prepared for user entities.
- the related accounting records, supporting information, and specific accounts that are used to initiate, authorize, record, process, and report transactions; this includes the correction of incorrect information and how information is transferred to the reports and other information prepared for user entities.
- how the system captures significant events and conditions, other than transactions.
- the process used to prepare reports and other information for user entities.

---

[2] Management's assertion should be placed on the service organization's letterhead.

Illustrative Type 2 Reports

- the specified control objectives and controls designed to achieve those objectives, including as applicable, complementary user entity controls contemplated in the design of the service organization's controls.
- other aspects of our control environment, risk assessment process, information and communication systems (including related business processes), control activities, and monitoring controls that are relevant to processing and reporting transactions of user entities of the system.

2. does not omit or distort information relevant to the scope of the savings system, while acknowledging that the description is presented to meet the common needs of a broad range of user entities of the systems and their financial statement auditors, and may not, therefore, include every aspect of the savings system that each individual user entity of the system and its auditor may consider important in its own particular environment.
3. includes relevant details of the changes to the savings system during the period covered by the description.

b. The controls related to the control objectives stated in the description were suitably designed and operating effectively throughout the period December 1, 20X0, to November 30, 20X1, to achieve those control objectives. The criteria we used in making this assertion were that

1. the risks that threaten the achievement of the control objectives stated in the description have been identified by management;
2. the controls identified in the description would, if operating as described, provide reasonable assurance that those risks would not prevent the control objectives stated in the description from being achieved; and
3. the controls were consistently applied as designed, and manual controls were applied by individuals who have the appropriate competence and authority.

3

Description of Example Service Organization's Savings System
Overview of Operations

Example Service Organization is located in Los Angeles, California, and provides computer services primarily to user entities in the financial services industry. Applications enable user entities to process savings, mortgage loan, consumer loan, commercial loan, and general ledger transactions. This description addresses only controls related to the savings application.

Numerous terminals located at user entities are connected to Example Service Organization through leased lines that provide online, real-time access to the applications. Example Service Organization processes transactions using one ABC central processor under the control of Operating System Release 2.1. . . .

Relevant Aspects of the Control Environment, Risk Assessment Process, and Monitoring Controls

Operations are under the direction of the president and the board of directors of Example Service Organization. The board of directors has established an audit committee that oversees the internal audit function. The organization employs a staff of approximately 35 people and is supported by the following functional areas:

- *Administration and systems development.* Coordinates all aspects of Example Service Organization's operations, including service billing. Identifies areas requiring controls and implements those controls. Performs systems planning, development, and implementation. Reviews network operations and telecommunications and performs disaster-recovery planning and database administration.

- *Customer support.* Supports end users in all aspects of their use of the application system including research and resolution of identified problems. Administers application security (including passwords), changes to application parameters, and the distribution of user documentation.

- *Application programming.* Performs regular maintenance programming, programming for user-requested enhancements, and updates the systems documentation.

- *Terminal support.* Performs end-user terminal training. Researches and resolves terminal and network problems and performs timely installations of enhancements to terminal and network software.

- *Operations.* Manages daily computer operations, nightly production processing, report production and distribution, and system utilization and capacities.

- *Marketing.* Provides analysis for new business prospects and new product planning.

The managers of each of the functional areas report to the director of information systems. Example Service Organizations employees are not authorized to initiate or authorize transactions, to change or modify user files except through normal production procedures, or to correct user errors. All shifts at Example Service Organization are managed by shift supervisors and the director of information systems. Incident reports, processing logs, job schedules, and equipment activity reports are monitored by the director of information systems. These reports track daily processing activities and identify hardware and software problems and system usage.

Weekly management meetings are held to discuss special processing requests, operational performance, and the development and maintenance of projects in process.

Written position descriptions for employees are maintained by the director of information systems and the personnel department. The descriptions are reviewed annually and revised as necessary.

References are sought and background, credit, and security checks are conducted for all Example Service Organization personnel hired. The confidentiality of user information is stressed during the new-employee orientation program and is emphasized in the personnel manual issued to each employee. The organization provides a mandatory orientation program to all full-time employees which includes Example Service Organization Ethical Values training and orientation to Example Service Organization's Ethics Hotline. All employees participate in an annual update program and confirm their understanding of Example Service Organization's ethical values. Example Service Organization encourages employees to attend other formal outside training. An internal supervisory training program was recently initiated.

Employees are required to take vacation in accordance with Example Service Organization's policy, which requires that all employees who are eligible for two or more weeks of vacation take off five consecutive business days during each calendar year. No employee may take vacation during the last week or first ten days of each quarter. Vacation must be taken in the calendar year in which it is earned.

Example Service Organization's policy requires that after three months of employment, new employees receive a written performance evaluation from their supervisors, and that all employees receive an annual written performance evaluation and salary review. These reviews are based on employee-stated goals and objectives that are prepared and reviewed with the employee's supervisor. Completed appraisals are reviewed by senior management and become a permanent part of the employee's personnel file.

The internal auditors provide the audit committee with an assessment of controls. The internal auditors execute an information technology internal audit program and follow up on any operational exceptions or concerns that may arise. The internal auditors use audit software to perform various recalculations and analyses using actual production data in an offline mode.

Example Service Organization has placed into operation a risk assessment process to identify and manage risks that could affect its ability to provide reliable transaction processing for users. This process requires management to identify significant risks in their areas of responsibility and to implement appropriate measures to address those risks. The agenda for each quarterly management meeting includes a discussion of these matters. This process has identified risks resulting from the nature of the services the organization provides, and management has implemented various measures to manage those risks.

Example Service Organization's management and supervisory personnel monitor the quality of control performance as a routine part of their activities. To assist them in this monitoring, Example Service Organization has implemented a series of "key indicator" management reports that measure the results of various processes involved in processing transactions for users. Key indicator reports include reports of actual transaction processing volumes compared with anticipated volumes, actual processing times compared with scheduled times, and actual system availability and response times compared with established service level goals and standards. All exceptions to normal or scheduled processing related to hardware, software, or procedural problems are logged, reported, and resolved daily. Key indicator reports are reviewed daily and weekly by appropriate levels of management, and action is taken as necessary.

Information and Communication

Example Service Organization's savings application is part of an integrated software system. This system provides online, real-time processing of monetary and nonmonetary transactions and provides batch and memo post processing capabilities. Processing activities are divided into online and off-line processing segments. During ordinary business hours, users may make inquiries and enter monetary and nonmonetary transactions through various terminals, including teller terminals. Additional transactions are transmitted from automatic teller machines, the Federal Reserve Bank (FED), and user banks. Such transactions are received via electronic data transmission or via tape delivered by courier.

Each application uses the standard operating system and related systems software to interact with terminals, to accept data, to apply prescribed processes to data, to maintain an audit trail, and to respond to inquiries.

Online daily processing occurs during pre-established hours when users are open. Monetary, nonmonetary, and inquiry transactions are entered at teller terminals located at users' branch offices serviced by Example Service Organization. Nonmonetary and inquiry transactions are entered at other terminals designated as administrative terminals in user branch offices and other user offices. Terminals are linked to the online data communications network through leased telephone lines.

Telecommunications software polls the terminals in the network for available input transactions. . . .

Off-line daily processing is performed in accordance with daily schedules and generally occurs when the online system is not running. These programs determine whether control totals agree with the totals of related detail accounts, and produce daily and special request reports.

Example Service Organization has implemented various methods of communication to inform all employees of their individual roles and responsibilities related to transaction processing and controls and of significant events. These methods include orientation and training programs for newly hired employees, a monthly organization newsletter that summarizes significant events and changes occurring during the month and planned for the following month, and the use of electronic mail messages to communicate time sensitive messages and information.

Managers also hold periodic staff meetings as appropriate. Every employee has a written position description, and every position description includes the responsibility to communicate significant issues and exceptions to an appropriate higher level of authority within the organization in a timely manner.

Example Service Organization also has implemented various methods of communication to inform users of the role and responsibilities of Example Service Organization in processing their transactions, and to communicate significant events to users in a timely manner. These methods include Example Service Organization's active participation in quarterly user group meetings, the monthly Example Service Organization newsletter, which summarizes the significant events and changes during the month and planned for the following month, and the user liaison who maintains contact with designated user representatives to inform them of new issues and developments. Users also are encouraged to communicate questions and problems to their liaison, and such matters are logged and tracked until resolved, with the resolution also reported to the user entity.

Personnel in Example Service Organization's customer support unit provide ongoing communication with customers. The customer support unit maintains records of problems reported by customers, as well as problems or incidents noted during processing, and monitors such items until they are resolved. The customer support unit also communicates information regarding changes in processing schedules, system enhancements, and other information to customers.

Following is a description of the savings application.

Savings Application

The savings application maintains account balances based on deposits, withdrawals, earnings postings, journal debits and credits, and other transactions. The application provides for online data entry and inquiry functions and online, real-time posting of monetary and nonmonetary transactions entered through teller terminals. . . .

> *Note to Readers:* For brevity, the remainder of the description of the savings application is not presented in this illustrative type 2 report.

Control Objectives and Related Controls

> *Note to Readers:* In this illustrative report, the control objectives and related controls are stated in management's description of the service organization's system and are then repeated in the section of this type 2 report that contains the service auditor's tests of controls and results. An alternative presentation is to include the service organization's control objectives and related controls in the service auditor's description of tests of controls and results. This avoids the need to repeat the control objectives and related controls in two sections. When this presentation is used, the service auditor typically includes an introductory note in the section containing the service auditor's description of tests and controls and results to inform readers that the control objectives and related controls are an integral part of management's description of the service organization's system.

General Computer Control Objectives and Related Controls

Control Objective 1

Program change controls provide reasonable assurance that changes to existing applications are authorized, tested, documented, approved, and implemented to result in complete, accurate, and timely transactions and balances.

Description of controls that address control objective 1. Each user designates the individuals who are authorized to request program changes. All program change requests are submitted in writing to the manager of customer support. The manager of customer support maintains a log of all program change requests received.

After a program change request has been received and logged, it is reviewed by personnel in the customer support department to determine whether the requested change is an enhancement of a program or the correction of a programming error and to develop an estimate of the number of hours that will be required to make and implement the program change.

Biweekly management meetings are held with the director of information systems, the manager of application programming, and representatives of the user entities to consider program change requests and the status of active projects. Based on these discussions, the director of information systems approves or disapproves the change request. Upon approval, the director of information systems signs off on the program change request and forwards it to the manager of application programming.

The manager of application programming receives approved program change requests and prepares a customer work request (CWR) form. Information listed on the form includes the name of the originator, the name of the bank, the bank's user code, the program affected, and a description of the requested program change. A log of all CWRs is maintained and monitored by the manager of application programming.

The director of information systems must authorize change control personnel to release production-program source code to the programmer. The programming staff does not have direct access to production program source code. The programmer makes changes to program code using a program development library. The programmer does not have the ability to compile a changed program into executable form in the production environment. Programming changes are made using an online programming utility, and changes to source code are generated and annotated with the date of the change. Depending on the change, program unit tests and system tests are performed by the programmer and reviewed by the manager of application programming.

Acceptance tests are performed using test files and the resulting output is verified by the requesting party. Recently processed production data is used as the test data, without updating any live files. If the program change involves a new function, test data is jointly developed by the programmer and the requesting party. All test results are verified by the programmer, the manager of application programming, and the requesting party. At the completion of all testing, the programmer, manager of application programming, and the requesting party sign off on the CWR.

After acceptance tests are completed, the director of information systems reviews all test results and documentation. If the director is satisfied with the program change, he or she authorizes change control personnel to compile the new source code in the production environment and sign off on the CWR.

Updates to the production libraries are performed by change control personnel after authorization by the director of information systems. Each time a program is compiled in the production environment, an entry is electronically recorded in a log that is printed and reviewed daily for any unauthorized activity.

Documentation is updated by the programmer, reviewed by the manager of application programming, and distributed to the appropriate parties.

> **Note to Readers:** For brevity, the controls for control objectives 2–10 and 12–14 are not presented in this illustrative report.

Control Objective 2

Program change controls provide reasonable assurance that new applications being developed are authorized, tested, documented, approved, and implemented to result in complete, accurate, and timely transactions and balances.

Control Objective 3

Program change controls provide reasonable assurance that network infrastructure is configured as authorized to (1) support the effective functioning of application controls during the period to result in valid, complete, accurate, and timely processing and reporting of transactions and balances and (2) protect data from unauthorized changes.

Control Objective 4

Controls provide reasonable assurance that physical access to computer and other resources is restricted to properly authorized and appropriate individuals.

Control Objective 5

Controls provide reasonable assurance that logical access to programs, data, and computer resources (for example, programs, tables, and parameters) is restricted to properly authorized and appropriate individuals for authorized users.

Control Objective 6

Controls provide reasonable assurance that applications and system processing are appropriately authorized and executed in a complete, accurate, and timely manner, and deviations, problems, and errors are identified, tracked, recorded, and resolved in a complete, accurate, and timely manner.

Control Objective 7

Controls provide reasonable assurance that data transmissions between Example Computer Service Organization and its users and other entities are from authorized sources and are complete, accurate, secure, and timely.

Control Objective 8

Controls provide reasonable assurance that data is backed up regularly and available for restoration in the event of processing errors, unexpected processing interruptions, or both.

Savings Application Control Objectives and Related Controls

Control Objective 9

Controls provide reasonable assurance that savings deposit and withdrawal transactions are received from authorized sources.

Control Objective 10

Controls provide reasonable assurance that savings deposit and withdrawal transactions received from the user entities are recorded completely, accurately, and in a timely manner.

Control Objective 11

Controls provide reasonable assurance that programmed interest and penalties are calculated in accordance with user specified business rules.

Note to Readers: Control objective 11 illustrates a situation in which the application of complementary user entity controls is necessary to achieve the control objective.

Description of controls that address control objective 11. Application security restricts update access to user defined indexes used to calculate interest and penalties to the appropriate user. Each user entity assigns passwords to user entity personnel authorized to update or change the indexes.

Programs used to calculate interest and penalties are subject to the controls described for control objective 1, "Controls provide reasonable assurance that changes to existing applications are authorized, tested, documented, approved, and implemented in a complete, accurate, and timely manner."

Complementary user entity controls. User entities are responsible for establishing controls to restrict access to user defined indexes to authorized user entity personnel. Any index can be selected and changed online at any time by user entities with an appropriate password. The balances applicable to each rate are established by the user entities in account type parameters. A report can be generated that shows the current content of the indexes and the date they were last changed.

Control Objective 12

Controls provide reasonable assurance that processing is performed timely and in accordance with user specified business rules.

Control Objective 13

Controls provide reasonable assurance that data maintained on files remains complete and accurate and the current versions of data files are used.

Control Objective 14

Controls provide reasonable assurance that output data and documents are complete and accurate and distributed to authorized recipients in a timely manner.

4

In the following illustrative service auditor's description of tests of controls and results, the required elements of the description of tests of controls and results are immediately followed by a parenthetical identifying the SSAE No. 16 paragraph that contains the requirement.

Independent Service Auditor's Description of Tests of Controls and Results

Example Service Organization's control objectives are repeated in this section so that readers can easily relate the tests of controls and results to the control objectives.

General Computer Control Objectives and Related Controls

Control Objective 1

Controls provide reasonable assurance that changes to existing applications are authorized, tested, documented, approved, and implemented in a complete, accurate, and timely manner.

Tests of controls that address control objective 1.

- Inspected a sample of documents evidencing the processing of program change requests to determine whether requests are logged, reviewed by appropriate management personnel, and submitted in writing.
- Inspected the log of CWRs and traced a sample of entries to the CWR form and the corresponding program change request. Inspected each CWR form and program change request in the sample for completeness and proper approval. For the program

Illustrative Type 2 Reports

changes in the sample that were completed and implemented during the period, inspected the test results for proper documentation and approval. Inspected the CWR forms for proper authorization of the program change to be compiled in the production environment.

- Selected a sample of program changes implemented during the period from a report generated by the program-change software and inspected the CWR form and program-change request for completeness and proper approval.
- Determined through review of security tables and reports and observation that the programming staff does not have direct access to program source code.
- Inspected a sample of the daily logs of compiled programs for evidence of review.
- Inquired of management and staff as to procedures and controls (52[o][i]).

Results of tests. No exceptions noted.

Note to Readers: For brevity, the control objectives and tests of controls for control objectives 2–10 and 12–14 are not presented in this illustrative report.

Savings Application Control Objectives and Related Controls

Control Objective 11

Controls provide reasonable assurance that programmed interest and penalties are calculated in accordance with user specified business rules.

Note to Readers: Control objective 11 illustrates a situation in which the application of complementary user entity controls is required to achieve the control objective.

Example Service Organization's description of controls that address control objective 11. Application security restricts update access to user-defined indexes, used to calculate interest and penalties, to the appropriate user entity. Within each user entity, passwords are required to update or change the indexes.

Programs used to calculate interest and penalties are subject to the controls described for control objective 1, "Controls provide reasonable assurance that changes to existing applications are authorized, tested, documented, approved, and implemented in a complete, accurate, and timely manner."

Complementary user entity controls. User entities are responsible for establishing controls at the user entity to restrict access to and change of user defined indexes to authorized user entity personnel. Any index can be selected and changed online at any time by user entities with an appropriate password. The balances applicable to each rate are established by the user entities in account type parameters. A report can be generated that shows the current content of the indexes and the date they were last changed.

Tests of controls.
- Selected a sample of tables containing user-defined indexes for interest and penalty calculations. Inspected the application security tables to determine whether access to change entries in the indexes was restricted to the appropriate user entities.
- Observed the process of changing indexes (using a test facility), noting that passwords are required.
- Inquired of programming staff as to changes to the interest and penalty calculation programs.
- Included changes to interest and penalty calculations in the population of changes tested for control objective 1.

Results of tests. No exceptions were noted.

> ***Note to Readers:*** The service auditor performs procedures to test the fairness of the presentation of the description of how interest and penalties are calculated and also performs procedures to test the operating effectiveness of the controls that provide reasonable assurance that programmed interest and penalties are calculated in conformity with the description. The nature and objective of the procedures performed to evaluate the fairness of the presentation of the description are different from those performed to evaluate the operating effectiveness of the controls. The service auditor might recalculate interest and penalties to test the fairness of the description; however, recalculation alone generally would not provide evidence of the operating effectiveness of the controls related to the calculation of interest and penalties. In this example, the service auditor tested the general computer controls to obtain evidence related to the operating effectiveness of the controls because the service organization relies on the computer to calculate interest and penalties. The service auditor generally would not indicate that the only test of operating effectiveness performed for this control objective was recalculating interest and penalties.

Example 2—Service Organization Presents Subservice Organization Using the Inclusive Method

Example Service Organization

Report on Example Service Organization's Description of Its Savings System and Aspects of Computer Subservice Organization's Computer Processing and on the Suitability of Design and Operating Effectiveness of Controls

In this illustrative report, Example Service Organization outsources aspects of its computer processing to a subservice organization, Computer Subservice Organization, and elects to use the inclusive method of presentation for the subservice organization. Changes to the type 2 report related to the use of the inclusive method are shown in boldface italics. The parenthetical identifies the paragraph in SSAE No. 16 that contains the requirement related to the presentation of the subservice organization. The components of this type 2 report are identified by referring to the page numbers on which they are found. The report is written in narrative format and includes the following:

- The service auditor's report
- Management of Example Service Organization's assertion, which is attached to Example Service Organization's description of its system and aspects of Computer Subservice Organization's system
- Management of Computer Subservice Organization's assertion, which is attached to Example Service Organization's description of its system and aspects of Computer Subservice Organization's system
- Example Service Organization's description of its system and aspects of Computer Subservice Organization's system
- The service auditor's description of tests of controls and results

Table of Contents

	Page
Independent Service Auditor's Report	aa
Example Service Organization's Assertion	bb
Computer Subservice Organization's Assertion	cc
Description of Example Service Organization's Savings System **and Aspects of Computer Subservice Organization's Computer Processing** Overview of Operations Relevant Aspects of Example Service Organization's Control Environment, Risk Assessment Process, Information and Communication Systems, and Monitoring Controls ***Relevant Aspects of Computer Subservice Organization's Control Environment, Risk Assessment Process, Information and Communication Systems, and Monitoring Controls*** Control Objectives and Related Controls	dd
Independent Service Auditor's Description of Tests of Controls and Results	ii

AAG-ASO APP B

Independent Service Auditor's Report

To Management of Example Service Organization:

Scope

We have examined Example Service Organization's description of its savings system **and Computer Subservice Organization's description of relevant aspects of its computer processing services** (53[c][v][2]) for processing user entities' transactions throughout the period December 1, 20X0, to November 30, 20X1 (description), and the suitability of design and operating effectiveness of **Example Service Organization's and Computer Subservice Organization's** controls to achieve the related control objectives stated in the description. **Computer Subservice Organization is an independent service organization that provides computer processing services to Example Service Organization. Example Service Organization's description includes a description of Computer Subservice Organization's computer processing services used by Example Service Organization to process transactions for its user entities, as well as relevant control objectives and controls of Computer Subservice Organization** (53[c][v][2]).

Service organization's responsibilities

On pages [*bb*] **and [*cc*]**, Example Service Organization **and Computer Subservice Organization, respectively,** has **have** provided its **their** assertions about the fair presentation of the description and the suitability of the design and operating effectiveness of the controls to achieve the related control objectives stated in the description. Example Service Organization **and Computer Subservice Organization are** is responsible for preparing the description and for the assertions, including the completeness, accuracy, and method of presentation of the description and the assertions, providing the services covered by the description, specifying the control objectives and stating them in the description, identifying the risks that threaten the achievement of the control objectives, selecting the criteria, and designing, implementing, and documenting controls to achieve the related control objectives stated in the description.

Service auditor's responsibilities

Our responsibility is to express an opinion on the fairness of presentation of the description and on the suitability of the design and operating effectiveness of the controls to achieve the control objectives stated in the description, based on our examination. We conducted our examination in accordance with attestation standards established by the American Institute of Certified Public Accountants. Those standards require that we plan and perform our examination to obtain reasonable assurance about whether, in all material respects, the description is fairly presented and the controls were suitably designed and operating effectively to achieve the related control objectives stated in the description throughout the period from December 1, 20X0, to November 30, 20X1.

An examination of a description of a service organization's system and the suitability of the design and operating effectiveness of the service organization's controls to achieve the related control objectives stated in the description involves performing procedures to obtain evidence about the fairness of presentation of the description of the system and the suitability of the design and operating effectiveness of those controls to achieve the related control objectives stated in the description. Our procedures included assessing the risks that the description is not fairly presented and that the controls were not suitably designed or operating effectively to achieve the related control objectives stated in the description. Our procedures also included testing the operating effectiveness of those controls that we consider necessary to provide reasonable assurance that the related controls objectives stated in the description were achieved. An examination engagement of this type also includes evaluating the overall presentation of the description and the suitability of the control objectives stated therein, and the suitability of the criteria specified by the *service* organization and described in Example Service Organization's assertion **and Computer Subservice Organization's assertion,** at pages [bb] **and [cc], respectively.** We believe that the evidence we obtained is sufficient and appropriate to provide a reasonable basis for our opinion.

Inherent limitations

Because of their nature, controls at a service organization **or subservice organization** may not prevent, or detect and correct, all errors or omissions in processing or reporting transactions. Also, the projection to the future of any evaluation of the fairness of the presentation of the description, or conclusions about the suitability of the design or operating effectiveness of the controls to achieve the related control objectives is subject to the risk that controls at a service organization **or subservice organization** may become inadequate or fail.

Opinion

In our opinion, in all material respects, based on the criteria described in Example Service Organization's **and Computer Subservice Organization's** assertion**s on pages** [bb] **and [cc], respectively**

    a. The description fairly presents Example Service Organization's savings system **and Computer Subservice Organization's computer processing services used by Example Service Organization to process transactions for its user entities** that was **were** designed and implemented throughout the period December 1, 20X0, to November 30, 20X1.

    b. The controls related to the control objectives **of Example Service Organization and Computer Subservice Organization** stated in the description were suitably designed to provide reasonable assurance that the control objectives would be achieved if the controls operated effectively throughout the period December 1, 20X0, to November 30, 20X1.

    c. The controls **of Example Service Organization and Computer Subservice Organization that we** tested, which were those necessary to provide reasonable assurance that the control objectives stated in the description were achieved, operated effectively throughout the period December 1, 20X0, to November 30, 20X1.

Description of tests of controls

The specific controls tested and the nature, timing, and results of those tests are listed on pages [hh]–[rr].

Restricted use

This report and the description of tests of controls and results thereof on pages [hh–rr] are intended solely for the information and use of Example Service

Organization, user entities of Example Service Organization's savings system during some or all of the period December 1, 20X0, to November 30, 20X1, and the independent auditors of such user entities, who have a sufficient understanding to consider it, along with other information including information about the controls implemented by user entities themselves, when assessing the risks of material misstatements of user entities' financial statements. This report is not intended to be and should not be used by anyone other than those specified parties.

[*Service auditor's signature*]

December 15, 20X1

Los Angeles, CA

Example Service Organization's Assertion[3]

We have prepared the description of Example Service Organization's savings system (description) for user entities of the system during some or all of the period December 1, 20X0, to November 30, 20X1, and their user auditors who have a sufficient understanding to consider it, along with other information, including information about controls implemented by user entities of the systems themselves, when assessing the risks of material misstatements of user entities' financial statements. We confirm, to the best of our knowledge and belief, that:

    a. The description fairly presents the savings system made available to user entities of the system during some or all of the period December 1, 20X0, to November 30, 20X1, for processing their transactions. ***Example Service Organization uses a service organization, Computer Subservice Organization, to perform aspects of its computer processing.*** Pages [*hh–ii*] and [*mm-rr*] of the description present. Example Service Organization's control objectives (1–2 and 6–15) and related controls. ***Pages [jj–ll] of the description present Computer Subservice Organization's control objectives (3–5) and related controls. Computer Subservice Organization's assertion is presented on page [cc].*** The criteria we used in making *our* this assertion were that the description

        1. presents how the system made available to user entities of the system was designed and implemented to process relevant transactions, including, if applicable:

            • the types of services provided including, as appropriate, the classes of transactions processed.

            • the procedures, within both automated and manual systems, by which services are provided, including, as appropriate, procedures by which transactions are initiated, authorized, recorded, processed, corrected as necessary, and transferred to reports and other information prepared for user entities.

---

[3] Management's assertion should be placed on the service organization's letterhead.

- the related accounting records, supporting information, and specific accounts that are used to initiate, authorize, record, process, and report transactions; this includes the correction of incorrect information and how information is transferred to the reports and other information prepared for user entities.
- how the system captures significant events and conditions, other than transactions.
- the process used to prepare reports and other information for user entities.
- the specified control objectives and controls designed to achieve those objectives, including as applicable, complementary user entity controls contemplated in the design of the service organization's controls.
- other aspects of our control environment, risk assessment process, information and communication systems (including related business processes), control activities, and monitoring controls that are relevant to processing and reporting transactions of user entities of the system.

2. does not omit or distort information relevant to the scope of the savings system, while acknowledging that the description is presented to meet the common needs of a broad range of user entities of the systems and their financial statement auditors, and may not, therefore, include every aspect of the savings system that each individual user entity of the system and its auditor may consider important in its own particular environment.

3. includes relevant details of the changes to the savings system during the period covered by the description.

b. The controls related to the control objectives stated in the description were suitably designed and operating effectively throughout the period December 1, 20X0, to November 30, 20X1, to achieve those control objectives. The criteria we used in making this assertion were that

1. The risks that threaten the achievement of the control objectives stated in the description have been identified by management;

2. The controls identified in the description would, if operating as described provide reasonable assurance that those risks would not prevent the control objectives stated in the description from being achieved; and

3. The controls were consistently applied as designed, and manual controls were applied by individuals who have the appropriate competence and authority.

AAG-ASO APP B

Computer Subservice Organization's Assertion[4]

We have prepared the description of aspects of Computer Subservice Organization's computer processing system for Example Service Organization and user entities of Example Service Organization's savings system (description) during some or all of the period December 1, 20X0, to November 30, 20X1, and their user auditors who have a sufficient understanding to consider it, along with other information, including information about controls implemented by user entities of the systems themselves, when assessing the risks of material misstatements of user entities' financial statements. We confirm, to the best of our knowledge and belief, that:

1. The description fairly presents the aspects of Computer Subservice Organization's computer processing system made available to Example Service Organization and user entities of Example Service Organization's savings system during some or all of the period December 1, 20X0, to November 30, 20X1, for processing their transactions. The criteria we used in making this assertion were that the description

   a. presents how the system made available to Example Service Organization and user entities of Example Service Organization's savings system was designed and implemented to process relevant transactions, including, if applicable:

   - The types of services provided including, as appropriate, the classes of transactions processed.
   - The procedures, within both automated and manual systems, by which services are provided, including, as appropriate, procedures by which transactions are initiated, authorized, recorded, processed, corrected as necessary, and transferred to reports and other information prepared for user entities.
   - The related accounting records, supporting information, and specific accounts that are used to initiate, authorize, record, process, and report transactions; this includes the correction of incorrect information and how information is transferred to the reports and other information prepared for user entities.
   - How the system captures significant events and conditions, other than transactions.
   - The process used to prepare reports and other information for user entities.

---

[4] The assertion by management of the subservice organization should be placed on the subservice organization's letterhead.

AAG-ASO APP B

- *The specified control objectives and controls designed to achieve those objectives, including as applicable, complementary user entity controls contemplated in the design of the service organization's controls.*
- *Other aspects of our control environment, risk assessment process, information and communication systems (including related business processes), control activities, and monitoring controls that are relevant to processing and reporting transactions of user entities of the system.*

    b. *does not omit or distort information relevant to the scope of the savings system, while acknowledging that the description is presented to meet the common needs of a broad range of user entities of the systems and their financial statement auditors, and may not, therefore, include every aspect of the savings system that each individual user entity of the system and its auditor may consider important in its own particular environment.*

    c. *includes relevant details of the changes to the savings system during the period covered by the description.*

2. The controls related to the control objectives stated in the description that relate to aspects of Computer Subservice Organization's system made available to Example Service Organization were suitably designed and operating effectively throughout the period December 1, 20X0, to November 30, 20X1, to achieve those control objectives. The criteria we used in making this assertion were that

    a. *The risks that threaten the achievement of the control objectives stated in the description have been identified by management;*

    b. *The controls identified in the description would, if operating as described provide reasonable assurance that those risks would not prevent the control objectives stated in the description from being achieved; and*

    c. *The controls were consistently applied as designed, and manual controls were applied by individuals who have the appropriate competence and authority.*

Description of Example Service Organization's Savings System *and Aspects of Computer Subservice Organization's Computer Processing*

Overview of Operations

Example Service Organization is located in Los Angeles, California, and provides computer services primarily to user entities in the financial services industry. Applications enable user entities to process savings, mortgage loan, consumer loan, commercial loan, and general ledger transactions. This description addresses only controls related to the savings application.

Example Service Organization outsources aspects of computer processing to Computer Subservice Organization. This description includes relevant aspects of Computer Subservice Organization's processing, control objectives, and controls. Numerous terminals located at user entities are connected to Example Service Organization through leased lines that provide online, real-time access to the applications.

Relevant Aspects of Example Service Organization's Control Environment, Risk Assessment Process, and Monitoring Controls

> *Note to Readers:* The portion of the description entitled "Relevant Aspects of Example Service Organization's Control Environment, Risk Assessment Process, and Monitoring Controls" would be the same as it is in example 1. It is not repeated in this example.

Information and Communication Systems

> *Note to Readers:* The portion of the description entitled "Information and Communication Systems" would be the same as it is in example 1. It is not repeated in this example.

Savings Application

The savings application maintains account balances based on deposits, withdrawals, earnings postings, journal debits and credits, and other transactions. The application provides for online data entry and inquiry functions and online, real-time posting of monetary and nonmonetary transactions entered through teller terminals. . . .

> *Note to Readers:* For brevity, the remainder of the description of the savings application is not presented in this illustrative type 2 report.

Relevant Aspects of Computer Subservice Organization's Control Environment, Risk Assessment Process, Monitoring Controls, and Information and Communication Systems

> *Note to Readers:* Paragraph 19(d) of SSAE No. 16 requires the service auditor to determine whether the description of the service organization's system adequately describes services performed by a subservice organization, including whether the inclusive method or the carve-out method has been used in relation to them. Paragraph A32 of SSAE No. 16 indicates that when the inclusive method is used, one of the attributes of the description the service auditor may consider in determining whether the description is fairly presented is whether the description separately identifies controls at the service organization and controls at the subservice organization.

Illustrative Type 2 Reports

Computer Subservice Organization's operations are under the direction of the president and the board of directors of Computer Subservice Organization. The board of directors has an audit committee. The organization employs a staff of approximately 50 people and is supported by the following functional areas.

- *Administration.* Coordinates all aspects of Computer Subservice Organization's operations, including service billing.
- *Systems development.* Performs systems planning, development, and implementation. Reviews network operations and telecommunications and performs disaster-recovery planning and database administration.
- *User support.* Supports end users in all aspects of their use of the systems including research and resolution of identified problems. Administers application security (including passwords), changes to application parameters, and the distribution of user documentation.
- *Operations.* Manages daily computer operations, nightly production processing, report production and distribution, and system utilization and capacities.
- *Marketing.* Provides analysis for new business prospects and new product planning.

The managers of each of the functional areas report to the president and CEO.

All shifts at Computer Subservice Organization are managed by shift supervisors. Incident reports, processing logs, job schedules, and equipment activity reports track daily processing activities and identify hardware and software problems and system usage. They are monitored by the Operations manager.

Weekly management meetings are held to discuss special processing requests, operational performance, and the development and maintenance of projects in process.

Management also discusses significant risks that each manager has identified in his or her area of responsibility.

Written position descriptions for employees are maintained by human resources. The descriptions are reviewed annually and revised as necessary. Open positions are posted, and references are sought and background, credit, and security checks are conducted for all Computer Subservice Organization personnel hired. The confidentiality of information is stressed during mandatory new employee orientation.

Employees are required to take two or more weeks of vacation and at least five consecutive business days during each calendar year.

Computer Subservice Organization's policy requires annual performance evaluations by supervisors. Reviews are based on performance against role descriptions and employee stated goals and objectives that are prepared and reviewed with the employee's supervisor. Completed appraisals are reviewed by senior management and become a permanent part of the employee's personnel file.

Department managers and the internal control department monitor the quality of control performance as a routine part of their activities, using control management reports that measure the results of various processes involved in processing transactions for users. These reports include reports of actual transaction processing volumes compared with anticipated volumes, actual processing times compared with scheduled times, and actual system availability and response times compared with established service level goals and standards. All exceptions to normal or scheduled processing related to hardware, software, or procedural problems are logged, reported, and resolved daily. Key indicator reports are reviewed daily and weekly by appropriate levels of management and action is taken as necessary.

Computer Subservice Organization operates five ABC central processors under the control of Operating System Release 2.1. . . .

Control Objectives and Related Controls of Example Service Organization and Computer Subservice Organization

> *Note to Readers:* In this illustrative report, the control objectives and related controls are stated in management's description of the service organization's system and are then repeated in the service auditor's description of tests of controls and results. An alternative presentation is to include the service organization's control objectives and related controls in the service auditor's description of tests of controls and results. This avoids the need to repeat the control objectives and related controls in two places. When this presentation is used, the service auditor typically includes an introductory note to the service auditor's description of test of controls and results to inform readers that the control objectives and related controls are an integral part of management's description of the service organization's system.

General Computer Control Objectives and Related Controls

> *Note to Readers:* For brevity, Example Service Organization's controls related to its control objectives are not presented in this illustrative report. Control objectives 1–2 and 6–15 are Example Service Organization's control objectives. Control objectives 3–5 are Computer Subservice Organization's control objectives. Control objectives 3–5 and the controls designed to achieve those control objectives are solely related to the services provided by Computer Subservice Organization.

Example Service Organization's Control Objectives 1–2

Control objective 1. Controls provide reasonable assurance that changes to existing applications are authorized, tested, documented, approved, and implemented in a complete, accurate, and timely manner.

Control objective 2. Controls provide reasonable assurance that new applications being developed are authorized, tested, documented, approved, and implemented in a complete, accurate, and timely manner.

Computer Subservice Organization's Control Objectives 3–5

Control objective 3. Controls provide reasonable assurance that changes to the existing system software and implementation of new system software are

Illustrative Type 2 Reports

authorized, tested, documented, approved, and implemented in a complete, accurate, and timely manner.

Control objective 4. Controls provide reasonable assurance that physical access to computer resources is restricted to properly authorized and appropriate individuals.

Control objective 5. Controls provide reasonable assurance that logical access to system resources (for example, programs, data, tables, and parameters) is restricted to properly authorized and appropriate individuals at Computer Subservice Organization.

Example Service Organization's Control Objectives 6–15

Control objective 6. Controls provide reasonable assurance that logical access to system resources (for example, programs, data, tables, and parameters) is restricted to properly authorized and appropriate individuals at Example Service Organization.

Control objective 7. Controls provide reasonable assurance that job schedules are appropriately authorized and executed, and deviations, problems, and errors are identified, tracked, recorded, and resolved in a complete, accurate, and timely manner.

Control objective 8. Controls provide reasonable assurance that data transmissions between Example Computer Service Organization and its users and other entities are from authorized sources and are complete, accurate, secure, and timely.

Control objective 9. Controls provide reasonable assurance that data is backed up regularly and available for restoration in the event of processing errors, unexpected processing interruptions, or both.

Note to Readers: Paragraph 19(d) of SSAE No. 16 requires the service auditor to determine whether the description of the service organization's system adequately describes services performed by a subservice organization, including whether the inclusive method or the carve-out method has been used in relation to them. Paragraph A32 of SSAE No. 16 notes that when the inclusive method is used, one of the matters the service auditor may consider in determining whether the description is fairly presented is whether the description separately identifies controls at the service organization and controls at the subservice organization. In this example, descriptive headings are used to identify control objectives and related controls of the subservice organization.

Savings Application Control Objectives and Related Controls

Control objective 10. Controls provide reasonable assurance that savings deposit and withdrawal transactions are received from authorized sources.

Control objective 11. Controls provide reasonable assurance that savings deposit and withdrawal transactions received from the user entities are recorded in a complete, accurate, and timely manner.

Control objective 12. Controls provide reasonable assurance that programmed interest and penalties are calculated in accordance with user specified business rules.

Control objective 13. Controls provide reasonable assurance that processing is performed timely and in accordance with user specified business rules.

Control objective 14. Controls provide reasonable assurance that data maintained on files remains complete and accurate and the correct versions of data files are used.

Control objective 15. Controls provide reasonable assurance that output data and documents are complete and accurate and distributed to authorized recipients in a timely manner.

Independent Service Auditor's Description of Test of Controls and Results

> ***Note to Readers:*** The service auditor's description of tests of controls and results is essentially the same as section 4 in example 1. It is not repeated in this example.

Example 3—Service Organization Presents Subservice Organization Using the Carve-Out Method; Subservice Organization Requires Complementary User Entity Controls

Example Service Organization

Report on Example Service Organization's Description of Its Savings System and on the Suitability of the Design and Operating Effectiveness of Its Controls

In this illustrative report, Example Service Organization outsources aspects of its computer processing to a subservice organization, Computer Subservice Organization, and elects to use the carve-out method of presentation. Changes to the type 2 report related to the use of the carve-out method are shown in boldface italics. The parenthetical identifies the paragraph in SSAE No. 16 that contains the requirement related to the change. Computer Subservice Organization made its type 2 report available to Example Service Organization. The report indicates that complementary user entity controls are required. Because Example Service Organization is a user entity of Computer Subservice Organization, Example Service Organization has addressed that complementary user entity control in control objective 3 of its description. The illustrative type 2 report in this example is written in narrative format and includes the following four sections:

> *Section 1.* The service auditor's report
>
> *Section 2.* Management of Example Service Organization's assertion, which is attached to Example Service Organization's description of its system
>
> *Section 3.* Example Service Organization's description of its system
>
> *Section 4.* The service auditor's description of tests of controls and results

Table of Contents

Section	Description of Section
1.	Independent Service Auditor's Report
2.	Example Service Organization's Assertion
3.	Description of Example Service Organization's Savings System Overview of Operations Relevant Aspects of the Control Environment, Risk Assessment Process, Information and Communication Systems, and Monitoring Controls Control Objectives and Related Controls
4.	Independent Service Auditor's Description of Tests of Controls and Results

AAG-ASO APP B

1
Independent Service Auditor's Report

To Management of Example Service Organization:

Scope

We have examined Example Service Organization's description of its savings system for processing transactions for user entities throughout the period December 1, 20X0, to November 30, 20X1 (description), and the suitability of design and operating effectiveness of controls to achieve the related control objectives stated in the description.

Example Service Organization uses Computer Subservice Organization to perform aspects of its computer processing. The description of the system in section 3 of this report includes only the control objectives and related controls of Example Service Organization and excludes the control objectives and related controls at Computer Subservice Organization. Our examination did not extend to controls at Computer Subservice Organization (53[c][v][1]).

Service organization's responsibilities

In section 2 of this report, Example Service Organization has provided an assertion about the fair presentation of the description and the suitability of the design and operating effectiveness of the controls to achieve the related control objectives stated in the description. Example Service Organization is responsible for preparing the description and for the assertion, including the completeness, accuracy, and method of presentation of the description and the assertion, providing the services covered by the description, specifying the control objectives and stating them in the description, identifying the risks that threaten the achievement of the control objectives, selecting the criteria, and designing, implementing, and documenting controls to achieve the related control objectives stated in the description.

Service auditor's responsibilities

Our responsibility is to express an opinion on the fairness of presentation of the description and on the suitability of the design and operating effectiveness of the controls to achieve the control objectives stated in the description, based on our examination. We conducted our examination in accordance with attestation standards established by the American Institute of Certified Public Accountants. Those standards require that we plan and perform our examination to obtain reasonable assurance about whether, in all material respects, the description is fairly presented and the controls were suitably designed and operating effectively to achieve the related control objectives stated in the description throughout the period from December 1, 20X0, to November 30, 20X1.

An examination of a description of a service organization's system and the suitability of the design and operating effectiveness of the service organization's controls to achieve the related control objectives stated in the description involves performing procedures to obtain evidence about the fairness of presentation of the description of the system and the suitability of the design and operating effectiveness of those controls to achieve the related control objectives stated in the description. Our procedures included assessing the risks that the description is not fairly presented and that the controls were not suitably designed or operating effectively to achieve the related control objectives stated in the description. Our procedures also included testing the operating effectiveness of those controls that we consider necessary to provide reasonable assurance that the related controls objectives stated in the description were achieved. An examination engagement of this type also includes evaluating the overall presentation of the description and the suitability of the control objectives stated therein, and the suitability of the criteria specified by the service organization and described in management's assertion in section 2 of this report. We believe that the evidence we obtained is sufficient and appropriate to provide a reasonable basis for our opinion.

Inherent limitations

Because of their nature, controls at a service organization may not prevent or detect and correct all errors or omissions in processing or reporting transactions. Also, the projection to the future of any evaluation of the fairness of the presentation of the description, or conclusions about the suitability of design or operating effectiveness of the controls to achieve the related control objectives is subject to the risk that controls at a service organization may become inadequate or fail.

Opinion

In our opinion, in all material respects, based on the criteria described in Example Service Organization's assertion in section 2 of this report

   a. The description fairly presents the savings system that was designed and implemented throughout the period December 1, 20X0, to November 30, 20X1.
   b. The controls related to the control objectives stated in the description were suitably designed to provide reasonable assurance that the control objectives would be achieved if the controls operated effectively throughout the period December 1, 20X0, to November 30, 20X1.
   c. The controls tested, which were those necessary to provide reasonable assurance that the control objectives stated in the description were achieved, operated effectively throughout the period December 1, 20X0, to November 30, 20X1.

Description of tests of controls

The specific controls tested and the nature, timing, and results of those tests are listed in section 4 of this report.

Restricted use

This report and the description of tests of controls and results thereof in section 4 of this report are intended solely for the information and use of Example Service Organization, user entities of Example Service Organization's savings system during some or all of the period December 1, 20X0, to November 30, 20X1, and the independent auditors of such user entities, who have a sufficient understanding to consider it, along with other information including information about the controls implemented by user entities themselves, when assessing the risks of material misstatements of user entities' financial statements. This report is not intended to be and should not be used by anyone other than those specified parties.

[*Service auditor's signature*]

December 15, 20X1

Los Angeles, CA

AAG-ASO APP B

2

Example Service Organization's Assertion[5]

We have prepared the description of Example Service Organization's savings system (description) for user entities of the system during some or all of the period December 1, 20X0, to November 30, 20X1, and their user auditors who have a sufficient understanding to consider it, along with other information, including information about controls implemented by user entities of the systems themselves, when assessing the risks of material misstatements of user entities' financial statements. We confirm, to the best of our knowledge and belief, that:

1. The description fairly presents the savings system made available to user entities of the system during some or all of the period December 1, 20X0, to November 30, 20X1, for processing their transactions. *Example Service Organization uses Computer Subservice Organization to perform aspects of its computer processing. The description on pages [bb–cc] includes only the control objectives and related controls of Example Service Organization and excludes control objectives and related controls of Computer Subservice Organization.* The criteria we used in making this assertion were that the description

    a. presents how the system made available to user entities of the system was designed and implemented to process relevant transactions, including, if applicable:

    - The types of services provided including, as appropriate, the classes of transactions processed.
    - The procedures, within both automated and manual systems, by which services are provided, including, as appropriate, procedures by which transactions are initiated, authorized, recorded, processed, corrected as necessary, and transferred to reports and other information prepared for user entities.
    - The related accounting records, supporting information, and specific accounts that are used to initiate, authorize, record, process, and report transactions; this includes the correction of incorrect information and how information is transferred to the reports and other information prepared for user entities.
    - How the system captures significant events and conditions, other than transactions.
    - The process used to prepare reports and other information for user entities.
    - The specified control objectives and controls designed to achieve those objectives, including as applicable, complementary user entity controls

---

[5] Management's assertion should be placed on the service organization's letterhead.

contemplated in the design of the service organization's controls.

- Other aspects of our control environment, risk assessment process, information and communication systems (including related business processes), control activities, and monitoring controls that are relevant to processing and reporting transactions of user entities of the system.

    b. does not omit or distort information relevant to the scope of the savings system, while acknowledging that the description is presented to meet the common needs of a broad range of user entities of the systems and their financial statement auditors, and may not, therefore, include every aspect of the savings system that each individual user entity of the system and its auditor may consider important in its own particular environment.

    c. includes relevant details of the changes to the savings system during the period covered by the description.

2. The controls related to the control objectives stated in the description were suitably designed and operating effectively throughout the period December 1, 20X0, to November 30, 20X1, to achieve those control objectives. The criteria we used in making this assertion were that

    a. The risks that threaten the achievement of the control objectives stated in the description have been identified by management;

    b. The controls identified in the description would, if operating as described provide reasonable assurance that those risks would not prevent the control objectives stated in the description from being achieved; and

    c. The controls were consistently applied as designed, and manual controls were applied by individuals who have the appropriate competence and authority.

3

Description of Example Service Organization's Savings System

Overview of Operations

Example Service Organization is located in Los Angeles, California, and provides computer services primarily to user entities in the financial services industry. Applications enable user entities to process savings, mortgage loan, consumer loan, commercial loan, and general ledger transactions. This description addresses only controls related to the savings application. ***Example Service Organization has outsourced aspects of its computer processing to Computer Subservice Organization. This description does not include control objectives and related controls of Computer Subservice Organization.***

Numerous terminals located at user entities are connected to Example Service Organization through leased lines that provide online, real-time access to the applications. Example Service Organization processes transactions using one ABC central processor under the control of Operating System Release 2.1. . . .

Relevant Aspects of the Control Environment, Risk Assessment Process, and Monitoring Controls

> *Note to Readers:* The portion of the description entitled "Relevant Aspects of Example Service Organization's Control Environment, Risk Assessment Process, and Monitoring Controls," would be the same as it is in example 1 and is not repeated in this example.

Information and Communication Systems

> *Note to Readers:* The portion of the description entitled "Information and Communication Systems" would be the same as it is in example 1 and is not repeated in this example.

Savings Application

The savings application maintains account balances based on deposits, withdrawals, earnings postings, journal debits and credits, and other transactions. The application provides for online data entry and inquiry functions and online, real-time posting of monetary and nonmonetary transactions entered through teller terminals. . . .

> *Note to Readers:* For brevity, the remainder of the description of the savings application is not presented in this illustrative type 2 report.

Control Objectives and Related Controls

> *Note to Readers:* In this illustrative report, the control objectives and related controls are stated in management's description and are then repeated in the service auditor's tests of controls and results. An alternative presentation is to include the service organization's control objectives and related controls in the service auditor description of tests of controls and results. This avoids the need to repeat the control objectives and related controls in two sections. When this presentation is used, the service auditor typically includes an introductory note in the section containing the service auditor's tests of controls and results to inform readers that the control objectives and related controls are an integral part of management's description of the service organization's system.

General Computer Control Objectives and Related Controls

> *Note to Readers:* For brevity, the controls for the following control objectives are not presented in this illustrative report.

Control Objective 1

Controls provide reasonable assurance that changes to existing applications are authorized, tested, documented, approved, and implemented in a complete, accurate, and timely manner.

Control Objective 2

Controls provide reasonable assurance that new applications being developed are authorized, tested, documented, approved, and implemented in a complete, accurate, and timely manner.

Control Objective 3

Controls provide reasonable assurance that logical access to system resources (for example, programs, data, tables, and parameters) is restricted to properly authorized and appropriate individuals.

Computer Subservice Organization issued a type 2 report covering the period October 1, 20X0, to September 30, 20X1. The report included the following complementary user entity control: User entities should have controls in place to provide reasonable assurance that logical access to system resources is restricted to properly authorized and appropriate individuals. Example Service Organization has addressed this complementary user entity control in control objective 3.

Control Objective 4

Controls provide reasonable assurance that job schedules are appropriately authorized and executed, and deviations, problems, and errors are identified, tracked, recorded, and resolved in a complete, accurate, and timely manner.

Control Objective 5

Controls provide reasonable assurance that data transmissions between Example Service Organization and its users and other entities are from authorized sources and are complete, accurate, secure, and timely.

Savings Application Control Objectives and Related Controls

Control Objective 6

Controls provide reasonable assurance that savings deposit and withdrawal transactions are received from authorized sources.

Control Objective 7

Controls provide reasonable assurance that savings deposit and withdrawal transactions received from the user entities are initially recorded completely and accurately.

Control Objective 8

Controls provide reasonable assurance that programmed interest and penalties are calculated in conformity with the description.

Control Objective 9

Controls provide reasonable assurance that processing is performed in accordance with user specifications.

Control Objective 10

Controls provide reasonable assurance that data maintained on files remains authorized, complete, and accurate.

Control Objective 11

Controls provide reasonable assurance that output data and documents are complete and accurate and distributed to authorized recipients according to schedule.

AAG-ASO APP B

4
Independent Service Auditor's Description of Test of Controls and Results

Example Service Organization's control objectives are repeated in this section so that readers can easily relate the tests of controls and results to the control objectives.

General Computer Control Objectives and Related Controls

Control Objective 1

Controls provide reasonable assurance that changes to existing applications are authorized, tested, documented, approved, and implemented in a complete, accurate, and timely manner.

Tests of controls.

- Inspected a sample of documents evidencing the processing of program change requests to determine whether requests are logged, reviewed by appropriate management personnel, and submitted in writing.
- Inspected the log of customer work requests (CWRs) and traced a sample of entries to the CWR form and the corresponding program change request. Inspected each CWR form and program change request in the sample for completeness and proper approval. For the program changes in the sample that were completed and implemented during the period, inspected the test results for proper documentation and approval. Inspected the CWR forms for proper authorization of the program change to be compiled in the production environment.
- Selected a sample of program changes implemented during the period from a report generated by the program-change software and inspected the CWR form and program-change request for completeness and proper approval.
- Determined through review of various system reports, security tables, and observation that the programming staff does not have direct access to program-source code.
- Inspected a sample of the daily logs of compiled programs for reasonableness and evidence of review.
- Inquired of management and staff as to procedures and controls followed.

Results of tests. No exceptions noted.

Note to Readers: For brevity, the control objectives and tests of controls for control objectives 2–11 are not presented in this illustrative report.

Example 4—Service Organization Presents Subservice Organizations Using the Carve-Out Method; Service Organization Requires Complementary User Entity Controls

Report on Example Trust Organization's Description of Its Institutional Trust Division and on the Suitability of the Design and Operating Effectiveness of Its Controls

Example Trust Organization has outsourced various functions to subservice organizations and elects to use the carve-out method of presentation. In addition, complementary user entity controls are required to achieve certain control objectives. Changes to this type 2 report related to the need for complementary user entity controls are shown in boldface. Changes to the report related to the subservice organizations are shown in italics. The illustrative report in example 4 contains the following four sections:

Section 1. The service auditor's report.

Section 2. Management of Example Trust Organization's assertion, which is attached to Example Trust Organization's description of its system.

Section 3. Management of Example Trust Organization's description of its system. Example Trust Organization's control objectives and controls are not included in section 3. Instead, they are included in section 4 along with the service auditor's tests of controls and results.

Section 4. The service auditor's description of tests of controls and results are presented in a three-column table. Example Trust Organization's control objectives and controls are integrated in the description of tests of controls and results.

Table of Contents

Section	Description of Section
1.	Independent Service Auditor's Report
2.	Example Trust Organization's Assertion
3.	Example Trust Organization's Description Overview of Services Provided Control Environment, Risk Assessment Process, and Monitoring Information and Communication Subservice Organizations Complementary User Entity Controls
4.	Example Trust Organization's Control Objectives and Related Controls and Independent Service Auditor's Tests of Controls and Results of Tests

The service auditor's description of tests of controls and results are presented in section 4 of this type 2 report, which also contains the service organization's controls and control objectives. The service auditor's description of tests of controls and results are the responsibility of the service auditor and should be considered information provided by the service auditor.

1
Independent Service Auditor's Report

To Management of Example Trust Organization:

Scope

We have examined Example Trust Organization's description of its system for processing transactions for user entities of its Institutional Trust Division (system) throughout the period December 1, 20X0, to November 30, 20X1 (description), and the suitability of the design and operating effectiveness of controls to achieve the related control objectives stated in the description.

Example Trust Organization uses various subservice organizations including

- Depository Trust Company (DTC), the Federal Reserve Bank (FED), and XYZ Bank as depositories and DEF Bank and JKL Bank as custodians to settle and safe-keep customer assets.
- ABC Company, BLB Inc, xTRA, and RTR to obtain market data and to price securities.
- BRD Inc., NR Trust, and DEF Bank to obtain corporate action services.

Example Trust Organization's control objectives and related controls, which are listed in section 4 of this report, include only the control objectives and related controls of Example Trust Organization and exclude the control objectives and related controls of these subservice organizations. Our examination did not extend to controls at the subservice organizations.

The description indicates that certain control objectives specified in the description can be achieved only if complementary user entity controls contemplated in the design of Example Trust Organization's controls are suitably designed and operating effectively, along with related controls at the service organization. We have not evaluated the suitability of the design and operating effectiveness of such complementary user entity controls.

Service organization's responsibilities

In section 2 of this report, Example Trust Organization has provided an assertion about the fair presentation of the description and the suitability of the design and operating effectiveness of the controls to achieve the related control objectives stated in the description. Example Trust Organization is responsible for preparing the description and for its assertion, including the completeness, accuracy, and method of presentation of the description and assertion, providing the services covered by the description, specifying the control objectives and stating them in the description, identifying the risks that threaten the achievement of the control objectives, selecting the criteria, and designing, implementing, and documenting controls to achieve the related control objectives stated in the description.

Service auditor's responsibilities

Our responsibility is to express an opinion on the fairness of the presentation of the description and the suitability of the design and operating effectiveness of the controls to achieve the related control objectives stated in the description, based on our examination. We conducted our examination in accordance with attestation standards established by the American Institute of Certified Public Accountants. Those standards require that we plan and perform our examination to obtain reasonable assurance about whether, in all material respects, the description is fairly presented and the controls were suitably designed and operating effectively to achieve the related control objectives stated in the description throughout the period December 1, 20X0, to November 30, 20X1.

An examination of a description of a service organization's system and the suitability of the design and operating effectiveness of its controls to achieve the related control objectives stated in the description involves performing procedures to obtain evidence about the fairness of the presentation of the description of the system and the suitability of the design and operating effectiveness of those controls to achieve the related control objectives stated in the description. Our procedures included assessing the risks that the description is not fairly presented and that the controls were not suitably designed or operating effectively to achieve the related control objectives stated in the description. Our procedures also included testing the operating effectiveness of those controls that we consider necessary to provide reasonable assurance that the related controls objectives stated in the description were achieved. An examination engagement of this type also includes evaluating the overall presentation of the description, the suitability of the control objectives stated therein, and the suitability of the criteria specified by the service organization and described in management's assertion in section 2 of this report. We believe that the evidence we obtained is sufficient and appropriate to provide a reasonable basis for our opinion.

Inherent limitations

Because of their nature, controls at a service organization may not prevent, or detect and correct, all errors or omissions in processing or reporting transactions. Also, the projection to the future of any evaluation of the fairness of the presentation of the description, or conclusions about the suitability of the design or operating effectiveness of the controls to achieve the related control objectives is subject to the risk that controls at a service organization may become inadequate or fail.

Opinion

In our opinion, in all material respects, based on the criteria described in Example Trust Organization's assertion in section 2 of this report

    a. the description fairly presents the system that was designed and implemented throughout the period December 1, 20X0, to November 30, 20X1.

    b. the controls related to the control objectives stated in the description were suitably designed to provide reasonable assurance that the control objectives would be achieved if the controls operated effectively throughout the period December 1, 20X0, to November 30, 20X1, **and user entities applied the complementary user entity controls contemplated in the design of Example Trust Organization's controls throughout the period December 1, 20X0, to November 30, 20X1.**

c. The controls tested, which **together with the complementary user entity controls referred to in the scope paragraph of this report, if operating effectively,** were those necessary to provide reasonable assurance that the control objectives stated in the description were achieved, operated effectively throughout the period December 1, 20X0, to November 30, 20X1.

Description of tests of controls

The specific controls tested and the nature, timing, and results of those tests are listed in section 4 of this report.

Restricted use

This report and the description of tests of controls and results thereof in section 4 of this report are intended solely for the information and use of Example Trust Organization, user entities of Example Trust Organization's Institutional Trust Division during some or all of the period December 1, 20X0, to November 30, 20X1, and the independent auditors of such user entities, who have a sufficient understanding to consider it, along with other information including information about the controls implemented by user entities themselves, when assessing the risks of material misstatements of user entities' financial statements. This report is not intended to be and should not be used by anyone other than those specified parties.

[*Service auditor's signature*]

December 15, 20X1

New York, NY

2
Example Trust Organization's Assertion[6]

We have prepared the description of Example Trust Organization's system (description) for user entities of the Institutional Trust Division during some or all of the period December 1, 20X0, to November 30, 20X1, and their user auditors who have a sufficient understanding to consider it, along with other information, including information about controls implemented by user entities of the systems themselves, when assessing the risks of material misstatements of user entities' financial statements. We confirm, to the best of our knowledge and belief, that

a. The description fairly presents the system made available to user entities during some or all of the period December 1, 20X0, to November 30, 20X1, for processing their transactions. *Example Trust Organization uses various depository, subcustodian, pricing, and corporate action subservice organizations. The description includes only the control objectives and related controls of Example Trust Organization and excludes the control objectives and controls of these subservice organizations.* The criteria we used in making this assertion were that the description

　　i. presents how the system made available to user entities of the system was designed and implemented to process relevant transactions, including if applicable

---

[6] Management's assertion should be placed on the service organization's letterhead.

Illustrative Type 2 Reports

       (1) the types of services provided including, as appropriate, the classes of transactions processed.

       (2) the procedures, within both automated and manual systems, by which services are provided, including, as appropriate, procedures by which transactions are initiated, authorized, recorded, processed, corrected as necessary, and transferred to reports and other information prepared for user entities.

       (3) the related accounting records, supporting information, and specific accounts that are used to initiate, authorize, record, process, and report transactions; this includes the correction of incorrect information and how information is transferred to the reports and other information prepared for user entities.

       (4) how the system captures significant events and conditions, other than transactions.

       (5) the process used to prepare reports and other information for user entities.

       (6) the specified control objectives and controls designed to achieve those objectives, including as applicable, complementary user entity controls contemplated in the design of the service organization's controls.

       (7) other aspects of our control environment, risk assessment process, information and communication systems (including related business processes), control activities, and monitoring controls that are relevant to processing and reporting transactions of user entities of the system.

   ii. does not omit or distort information relevant to the scope of the system, while acknowledging that the description is presented to meet the common needs of a broad range of user entities of the system and their financial statement auditors, and may not, therefore, include every aspect of the system that each individual user entity of the system and its auditor may consider important in its own particular environment.

   iii. includes relevant details of the changes to the savings system during the period covered by the description

b. The controls related to the control objectives stated in the description were suitably designed and operating effectively throughout the period December 1, 20X0, to November 30, 20X1, to achieve those control objectives. The criteria we used in making this assertion were that

   i. the risks that threaten the achievement of the control objectives stated in the description have been identified by management;

   ii. the controls identified in the description would, if operating as described provide reasonable assurance that those risks would not prevent the control objectives stated in the description from being achieved; and

AAG-ASO APP B

iii. the controls were consistently applied as designed, and manual controls were applied by individuals who have the appropriate competence and authority.

3
Example Trust Organization's Description

Overview of Services Provided

Example Trust Organization is a full-service trust organization providing fiduciary services to corporate, personal, and institutional trust users. The organization provides services through the following five divisions:

- Corporate Trust Division. Serves as a trustee for securities issued by corporations. . . .

- Personal Trust Division. Services trusts established by individuals, foundations. . . .

- Institutional Trust Division. Services institutional users, including employee benefit plans, public funds, insurance companies, and other financial institutions. The Institutional Trust Division has ultimate responsibility for the administration of institutional trust accounts (accounts), including liaising with plan sponsors and investment managers. Account administration includes customer accounting and reporting, securities lending administration, participant loan administration, performance measurement, and compliance with the Employee Retirement Income Security Act (ERISA) of 1974. Each account has a designated administrator in the Institutional Trust Division. The administrator is supported by the Investment Management Division for accounts for which the organization has investment discretion. The Institutional Trust Division is organized along regional lines, with a senior executive responsible for oversight of each region's activities. The senior executives report to the executive vice president of the Institutional Trust Division, who reports to the president of the organization.

- Investment Management Division. Provides investment advisory services to accounts of the Corporate Trust, Personal Trust, and Investment Trust Divisions for which the organization is granted investment discretion.

- Trust Support Division. Serves as a central utility for the processing of transactions for users of the Corporate Trust, Personal Trust, and Institutional Trust Divisions. The Trust Support Division is organized along functional lines and includes the following groups:

    — Computerized information systems group (CISG). Provides data processing services to the five divisions of the organization. The CISG operates from a centralized processing site that provides numerous application-processing services to its users. The CISG's size and organization provide for separation of incompatible duties relating to computer operations, systems and programming, system software support, and data control. CISG

Illustrative Type 2 Reports 225

personnel are subject to the organization's personnel controls described on page [XXX].

— Securities processing group. Is responsible for securities movement and control, asset custody and control, securities lending, income accrual and collection, and corporate actions.

— Divisional support group. Is responsible for liaising with the Institutional Trust Division and the other divisions.

— Benefit payment, disbursement, and participant record-keeping group.

Control Environment, Risk Assessment Process, and Monitoring

Set forth in figure 1, "Organization Chart for Example Trust Organization," is the organization chart for Example Trust Organization at November 30, 20X1.

The organization's trust activities are overseen by the Trust Committee of the Board of Directors. The Trust Committee has established the following committees to oversee the organization's fiduciary activities relating to accounts: Trust Policy Committee, Investment Committee, Administrative and Investment Review Committee, and Trust Real Estate Investment Committee. Each committee is charged with monitoring and establishing policy for the fiduciary activities under its oversight.

This report addresses the Institutional Trust Division, which directly services accounts. It also addresses the Investment Management and Trust Support Divisions to the extent that these divisions support the activities of the Institutional Trust Division. Activities of the Corporate Trust and Personal Trust Divisions are beyond the scope of this report.

Trust activities are conducted in accordance with written policy and procedure guides that have been adopted by the trust policy committee. Policy and procedure guides are periodically updated. The responsibilities of the institutional trust and trust support divisions are allocated among personnel so as to segregate the following functions:

- Processing and recording transactions
- Maintaining custody of assets
- Reconciliation activities
- Compliance monitoring

AAG-ASO APP B

Figure 1
Organization Chart for Example Trust Organization

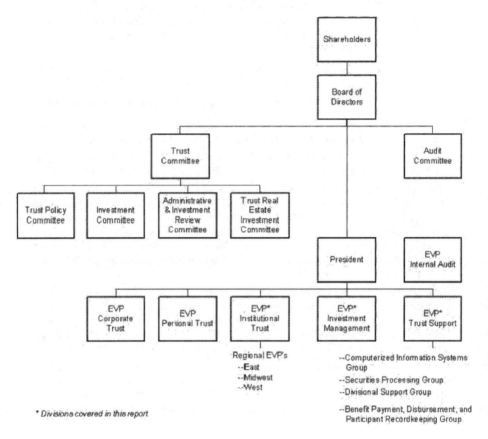

* *Divisions covered in this report*

Management Control

Example Trust Organization has a formal management information and reporting system that enables management to monitor key control and performance measurements.

Adherence to trust controls is monitored through a self-assessment program that is overseen by the compliance unit of the Institutional Trust Division. The assessment program has been designed to periodically evaluate account administration and support operations for compliance with the Institutional Trust Division's authorizing document, the organization's controls, and the applicable regulatory requirements. Results of the assessments are communicated to management and the trust committee.

Controls Related to Personnel

Example Trust Organization's formal hiring practices include verifying whether the qualifications of new employees meet their job responsibilities. Each new-position hiring must be jointly approved by the human resources department and the manager of the department requiring the employee. Hiring policies include requiring that employees have minimum education and experience requirements, that written references be submitted, and that employees execute confidentiality statements. The organization also performs background and credit investigations of potential employees.

Training of personnel is accomplished through supervised on-the-job training, outside seminars, and in-house classes. Certain positions require the completion of special training. For example, account administrators are trained in ERISA rules and regulations. Department managers are responsible to provide all account administrators such training. Department managers are also responsible for encouraging the training and development of employees so that all personnel continue to qualify for their functional responsibilities.

Formal performance reviews are conducted on a periodic basis. Employees are evaluated on objective criteria based on performance. An overall rating (unsatisfactory, satisfactory, or exceptional) is assigned.

Other Considerations

Example Trust Organization's controls are documented in its corporate compliance manual (CCM). The CCM is organized by product and business unit and sets forth the organization's controls, the laws and regulations to which the product or business unit is subject, and the compliance responsibilities of specific positions within the organization.

Example Trust Organization has a formal conflict-of-interest policy that, among other things, establishes rules of conduct for employees who service accounts. Employees and their immediate families are prohibited from divulging confidential information about client affairs, trading in securities of clients or their affiliates, and taking any action that is not in the best interest of clients. In addition, investment advisers in the Investment Management Division provide periodic brokerage statements to a compliance officer who reviews the statements for transactions proscribed by organization policy. Annually, each officer confirms in writing his or her compliance with the organization's conflict of interest policy.

Example Trust Organization is subject to regulation and supervision by the Office of the Comptroller of the Currency (OCC). Accordingly, the organization is required to file periodic reports with the OCC and is subject to periodic examination by the OCC.

The organization maintains insurance coverage against major risks. Insurance policies include an errors and omissions bond, employee fidelity bond, blanket-lost-original instruments bond, bankers' blanket bond, and trust-property-managers bond. Coverage is maintained at levels that the organization considers reasonable given the size and scope of its operations, and is provided by insurance companies that organization management believes are financially sound.

Internal Audit

Trust activities are monitored by the internal audit group, which reports to the audit committee of the board of directors. The internal audit program is designed to evaluate compliance with the organization's controls and the laws and regulations to which the organization is subject, including ERISA. The program also addresses the soundness and adequacy of accounting, operating, and administrative controls. Internal audits cover four broad areas of fiduciary services: account administration, regulatory compliance, transaction accounting, and asset custody. Internal audits of asset custody include periodic verification of assets held in trust through physical examination, confirmation, or review of reconciliations and underlying source documents. Formal reports of audit findings are prepared and submitted to management and to the audit committee.

Risk Assessment Process

Example Trust Organization has placed into operation a risk assessment process to identify and manage risks that could affect the organization's ability to provide reliable transaction processing to customers of the Institutional Trust Division. This process requires management to identify significant risks inherent in the processing of various types of transactions for customers and to implement appropriate measures to monitor and manage these risks.

This process has identified risks resulting from the nature of the services provided by the Institutional Trust Division, and management has implemented various measures designed to manage these risks. Risks identified in this process include the following:

- Operational risk associated with computerized information systems; manual processes involved in transaction processing; and external systems, for example, depository interfaces
- Credit risk associated with, among other things, securities settlement, securities loans, and investment of related cash collateral
- Market risk associated with the investment of cash collateral and the valuation of securities
- Fiduciary risk associated with acting on behalf of customers

Each of these risks is monitored as described under "Risk Monitoring," on page [XXX] of this report.

Monitoring

The management and supervisory personnel of the Institutional Trust Division monitor performance quality and control operation as a normal part of their activities. The organization has implemented a series of "key indicator" management reports that measure the results of various processes involved in providing transaction processing to customers. Key indicator reports include reports that identify

- The name, age, and cause of differences noted in various reconciliations, such as Securities Movement and Control System (SMAC) versus Depository Trust Company (DTC), the FED, and XYZ Bank; accrued income versus amounts actually collected.
- The number of failed settlement transactions.
- Variances (or absence thereof) in the price of securities held by customers.
- Various computerized information system events, such as failed access attempts, rejected items, deviations from scheduled processing, and program changes.

These reports are periodically reviewed (depending on the nature of the item being reported on) by appropriate levels of management, and action is taken as necessary. Depending on the nature, age, and amount (as applicable) of processing exceptions, they are referred to succeedingly higher levels of management for review.

Information and Communication

Description of Computerized Information Systems[7]

- Processing environment. The CISG operates a large-scale computer facility that has two mainframe computers. One computer is primarily used to support application processing and the other is primarily used to support application maintenance, development, testing, and systems software maintenance and testing. The computers are supported by the manufacturer's operating system and related components. . . .

- Security/access. The CISG has a centralized security administration department. This department is responsible for ensuring that the organization adheres to corporate security policy that. . . . Access to system resources and production information and program files is protected from unauthorized users by a global-access control system that. . . .

- Application development/maintenance. All requests for the development of new systems and changes to existing systems are submitted to the director of the CISG. All requests are processed within a software management system that includes the following processes: project request. . . .

Description of Transaction Processing

Basic Trust and Custody Services

Most of the transaction processing for accounts is automated. Controls over access and changes to the automated systems are described in the section titled "Description of Computerized Information Systems." Set forth in figure 2, "Transaction Processing of Accounts of Example Trust Organization," is an overview of the organization's applications, interfaces, and relationships to investment advisers, brokers, depositories, and custodians.

The application systems were developed by the organization and are operated on the organization's mainframe computer at its information center in New York City. The functions of each system are briefly described as follows:

- Institutional delivery system (IDS). Accepts automated trade inputs from terminals at outside investment advisers and investment management division advisers. Compares the trade inputs with broker trade notifications and interfaces with depositories or other custodians for trade delivery and settlement information, income collection, corporate actions, and security positions. Interfaces with the organization's wire transfer system for payments and receipts related to security purchase and sale transactions, income receipts, and other cash transactions.

- Security movement and control system (SMAC). Maintains inventory records of the organization's position in individual securities (including the physical location of such securities or the depository/custodian at which they are maintained) and the allocation of such positions to individual clients of the organization, including, but not limited to, accounts.

---

[7] In an actual report, there would be a more comprehensive description of the computer applications and the general computer controls. Such information is not included in this sample report.

- Automated income system (AIS). Receives transmissions of dividend declarations from outside pricing and corporate action services. Computes interest accruals on fixed-income securities. Tracks and processes the receipt of income. Allocates income to individual clients of the organization, including, but not limited to, accounts.

- Corporation action system (CAS). Receives transmissions of corporate actions, such as stock splits, reorganizations, and mergers. Supports the process of notification of security holders of actions and decision follow-ups (in the case of nonmandatory actions, such as tender offers).

- Trust accounting system (TAS). Obtains the prices of security holdings from outside sources. Performs analytical testing of the reasonableness of prices. Maintains records for accounts and generates accounting statements.

Figure 2

Transaction Processing of Accounts of Example Trust Organization

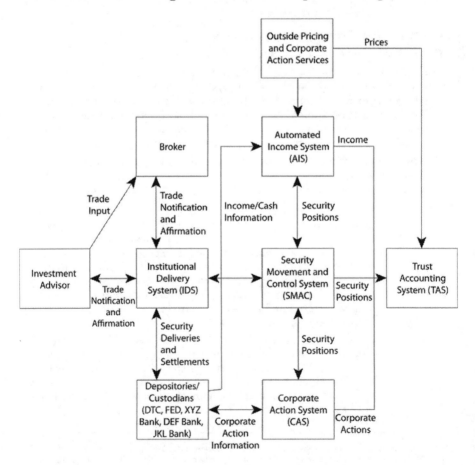

Trade Execution

Security trades are initiated by the Investment Management Division or by third-party advisers having investment discretion over particular accounts. Trade information is input into the IDS via a terminal at the investment adviser. Nonautomated trade execution instructions (received via facsimile transmission [fax] or telephone) are authenticated by signature verification or call-back procedure and are input into the IDS by authorized personnel in the securities processing group. Trade information is confirmed in writing by the organization with the broker or dealer who placed the trade.

Executed trades are affirmed through an automated process that compares the IDS trade information to trade depository information that the depository receives from the trade counterparty. The IDS provides for automated securities settlement on the prearranged date, which is typically three days after the trade date, or one day after the trade date for same day or next day settlements. Exceptions to the affirmation process are individually researched and resolved. Depositories include the DTC, the FED, and XYZ Bank. Trade positions for settlement with outside depositories are reconciled daily and a net settlement is made with each depository.

Deliveries of securities (via depositories or via physical delivery of securities in the organization's vault) in connection with security sale transactions are affected only upon the receipt of cash. Similarly, cash is paid for security-purchase transactions only upon receipt of the securities. If the securities are not received or delivered on the settlement date, the settlement "fails." In that case, the purchase or sale of the security is reflected in the customer's portfolio, and a payable or receivable, respectively, is recorded for the future cash payment or receipt. The organization monitors such fails through the IDS and the SMAC to ensure that they are resolved on a timely basis.

Free deliveries of securities are sometimes required for securities pledged as collateral or for re-registration. Free deliveries of collateral are initiated by the investment manager through ordinary trade input. Free deliveries for re-registration are typically physical (that is, not via a depository).

The Security Movement and Control Department of the Trust Support Division is responsible for the receipt and delivery of physical securities (other than purchase and sale transactions), the processing of maintenance entries, securities re-registration, and the transfer of securities between accounts, as instructed by the account administrator. Securities are received via certified or registered mail. Hand-delivered securities are received under dual control. Securities being processed are maintained in a fireproof file that is secured in a vault during nonbusiness hours. Securities that must be delivered to external custodians are sent by insured courier. Receipt of the security is confirmed directly with the custodian. A log is maintained of all securities sent to a transfer agent for change of the nominee name. Follow-up is required if the security is not returned in 30 days. Mail loss affidavits are prepared if the security is lost in transit to or from the transfer agent.

Asset Custody and Control

The organization maintains trust assets at three depositories, one custodian bank, and in the organization's vault in New York City. Custodial relationships are reviewed on a periodic basis to ensure that the quality and extent of services are adequate for the organization's needs.

Assets are recorded on the SMAC by location code. Asset holding lists can be provided on an asset, account, or location code level. Asset-holding lists are used by the organization to prepare custodian reconciliations and to resolve any out-of-balance positions. Assets are recorded on the SMAC and identified to individual accounts. Physical holdings of securities or book entry holdings at depositories are held in aggregate under Example Trust Organization's name as trustee or nominee. Asset holding lists provide detailed information by account to permit the reconciliation of aggregate positions by security to the individual account positions.

Reconciliations of asset positions between the DTC, and the FED and the organization's SMAC are performed on a daily basis. Reconciliations of asset positions between XYZ Bank and the organization's SMAC are performed on a daily basis. The reconciliations are produced by comparing the custodian's position, per custodian-provided computer tapes, to the SMAC's asset-position listing. An aged exception report is produced that is used for follow-up. Reconciling items aged over 30 days are reported to senior management.

The trust vaults are maintained under dual control at all times. Securities placed into or removed from the vaults are recorded in vault logs. Any security removed from the vaults must be returned to the main vault or placed in a night vault at the end of each business day. Annual vault counts are performed by internal auditors on a surprise basis.

Income Accrual, Collections, and Corporate Actions

The Income Accrual and Collection Department of the Securities Processing Group is responsible for processing and recording income accruals, collecting dividends and interest due on the payable date, processing income received, investigating underpayments and overpayments, and processing due bills and claims for income. Interest income is recorded to accounts on an accrual basis. Discounts are accreted and premiums are amortized in accordance with customer instructions. Dividend income is recorded to accounts on the ex-dividend date, as directed by the corporate actions department of the securities processing group.

Income collections, accruals, and cash dividends are processed using the AIS. Other corporate actions, such as tender offers and stock splits, are processed using the CAS. Both the AIS and the CAS receive data regarding corporate actions by independent sources. Information about trust asset holdings of the organization is obtained by the AIS and the CAS through an automated interface with the SMAC. The AIS reads the security holdings files of the SMAC daily to identify securities for which dividends have been declared and to ensure that AIS files of fixed income securities are complete and accurate. The AIS then prepares, by user, a file of expected income collections or an "income map." These maps are matched against the paying agent's records before the expected payment date to research and correct any discrepancies before the payment date. For securities held at depositories, information on expected payments is received from the depositories and from an automated interface with the AIS. For securities held in the vault, a printout of the income map is generated by the AIS and manually compared to the paying agent's advice. Similarly, income collections are subsequently reconciled to the income maps in the AIS. Differences between actual and expected receipts are identified by the AIS, and an exception report is generated and used for investigation. Once differences are resolved, the income maps are adjusted, if necessary, and then released to the TAS. This release causes the collection to be reflected in each user's account.

On a daily basis, the AIS provides information on income accruals to the SMAC so that the customer accounting records can be automatically updated.

On a daily basis, the CAS prepares a list of new and pending corporate actions. For mandatory actions, such as bond calls or stock splits, CAS updates the SMAC, the TAS, and the AIS for subsequent security pricings, income payments, and other items. Nonmandatory actions, such as tender offers, are assigned to a client service representative by the area supervisor. The client service representative contacts the customer or investment manager to obtain instructions. The outstanding action is maintained on a "tickler file" within the CAS. As the deadline for the action approaches, the customer or investment manager is contacted at specified and increasingly shorter intervals. If no instructions are received by the day before the action is due, the matter is referred to the account administrator for resolution.

Client Accounting

Periodic accounting statements are prepared for each account by the TAS.

The TAS receives information on income and corporate actions affecting accounts from interfaces with the SMAC, the AIS, and the CAS. Holdings of exchange-traded securities are recorded at market value in the accounting statements based on prices transmitted from independent pricing service organizations. If prices are received from more than one pricing service organization, the prices are compared and any significant deviations are investigated. Nonexchange traded securities or other types of investments are valued. . . .

Subservice Organizations

Example Trust Organization uses industry recognized subservice organizations to achieve operating efficiency and to obtain specific expertise. The organization periodically reviews the quality of the subservice organizations' performance and reviews and monitors the subservice organizations' reports on management's description of a service organization's system and the suitability of the design and operating effectiveness of controls (type 2 reports).

The following are the principal subservice organizations used by Example Trust Organization:

- *Depositories and Subcustodians—In addition to the organization's vaults, Example Trust Organization uses the DTC, the FED, and XYZ Bank, as depositories, and uses DEF Bank and JKL Bank as custodians to settle and safe-keep customer assets.*

- *Pricing Services—RTR Example Trust Organization uses, ABC Pricing Service Organization, BLB Inc., xTRA, and to obtain market data and to price securities. Information from these organizations is primarily received electronically and interfaces with SMAC.*

- *Corporate Actions Services—Example Trust Organization uses BRD Inc., NR Trust, and DEF Bank to obtain corporate action events and dividend data. Corporate action information is obtained both automatically and manually.*

Complementary User Entity Controls

Example Trust Organization's processing of transactions and the controls over the processing were designed with the assumption that certain controls would be placed in operation by user entities. This section describes some of the controls that should be in operation at user entities to complement the controls at Example Trust Organization. User auditors should determine whether user entities have established controls to provide reasonable assurance that

- Instructions and information provided to Example Trust Organization from institutional trust users are in accordance with the provisions of the servicing agreement, trust agreement, or other applicable governing agreements or documents between Example Trust Organization and the user.
- Physical and logical access to Example Trust Organization's systems via terminals at user locations are restricted to authorized individuals.
- Timely written notification of changes to the plan, its objectives, participants, and investment managers is adequately communicated to Example Trust Organization.
- Timely written notification of changes in the designation of individuals authorized to instruct Example Trust Organization regarding activities, on behalf of the institutional trust user, is adequately communicated to the organization.
- Timely review of reports provided by Example Trust Organization of institutional trust account balances and related activities is performed by the institutional trust user, and written notice of discrepancies is provided to the organization.
- Timely written notification of changes in related parties for purposes of identifying parties-in-interest transactions is adequately communicated to Example Trust Organization.

4

Example Trust Organization's Control Objectives and Related Controls and Independent Service Auditor's Tests of Controls and Results of Tests

This section presents the following information provided by Example Trust Organization:

- The control objectives specified by the management of Example Trust Organization
- The controls established and specified by Example Trust Organization to achieve the specified control objectives

Also included in this section is the following information provided by the service auditor:

- A description of the tests performed by the service auditor to determine whether the service organization's controls were operating

Illustrative Type 2 Reports

with sufficient effectiveness to achieve specified control objectives. The service auditor determined the nature, timing, and extent of the testing performed.

- The results of the service auditor's tests of controls.

Transaction Processing Control Objectives and Related Controls

Control Objective 1

Controls provide reasonable assurance that investment purchases and sales are authorized.

Example Trust Organization's Controls[8]	*Service Auditor's Tests*	*Results of Tests*
Only authorized users are able to input trades into the institutional delivery system (IDS).	Tested the logical access controls, as described in control objective 24.	No exceptions noted.
	Tested the program change controls, as described in control objective 20.	No exceptions noted.
Trades that are initiated via fax or telephone are authenticated by signature verification or callback.	Inspected a sample of fax source documentation for evidence of signature verification. Compared the input documentation with the IDS output.	No exceptions noted.
	For a sample of transactions, observed the performance of the callback procedure over five days.	No exceptions noted.
	Observed personnel in the securities processing group input transactions.	No exceptions noted.

Control Objective 2

Controls provide reasonable assurance that investment purchases and sales are entered into the system in a complete, accurate, and timely manner.

---

[8] An alternative to the 3-column presentation shown in example 4 is a 2-column format, such as "Example Trust Organizations's Controls" and "Results of Tests" in column 1 and "Service Auditor's Tests" in column 2.

Example Trust Organization's Controls	Service Auditor's Tests	Results of Tests
The institutional delivery system (IDS) compares the trade information from the investment adviser with the trade notifications from the broker or dealer. Differences are identified by IDS and resolved on a timely basis. Items that are unresolved on a timely basis require review and approval by management.	Processed a sample of test purchase and sale transactions through the IDS to determine whether differences were properly identified by the system. The sample included matched and unmatched items.	No exceptions noted.
	Inspected a sample of IDS trade difference reports noting the number and age of differences reported.	No exceptions noted.
	Observed personnel in the execution of follow-up procedures to resolve trade differences.	No exceptions noted.
	To corroborate written evidential matter, made inquiries of the trade settlement personnel regarding the procedures followed to resolve differences.	No exceptions noted.
	Made inquiries of the trade-settlement personnel regarding the operation of the procedures through November 30, 20X1.	No exceptions noted.
	Tested the program change controls, as described in control objective 20.	No exceptions noted.
The IDS compares the trade affirmations received from outside depositories with the trade input information received from the investment adviser. Differences are identified by the IDS and resolved on a timely basis.	Processed a sample of test purchase and sale transactions through the IDS to determine whether exceptions are properly identified and reported by the IDS. The sample included matched and unmatched items.	No exceptions noted.

Example Trust Organization's Controls	Service Auditor's Tests	Results of Tests
	Inspected a sample of IDS trade difference reports noting the number and age of the differences reported.	No exceptions noted.
	Observed personnel in the execution of follow-up procedures to resolve trade differences.	No exceptions noted.
	Made inquiries of the trade settlement personnel regarding the operation of the procedures through November 30, 20X1.	No exceptions noted.
	Tested the program change controls, as described in control objective 20.	No exceptions noted.
Security positions with the DTC and the Federal Reserve Bank (FED) are reconciled on a daily basis, and security positions with XYZ Bank are reconciled monthly. The reconciliations are performed through an automated matching process (SMAC versus IDS). A report listing balancing positions and out-of-balance positions is produced for review and follow-up (as subsequently described).	Reperformed the daily reconciliation for the DTC and the FED to determine whether the reconciliation was performed completely and accurately.	No exceptions noted.
	Reperformed the monthly reconciliation for XYZ Bank to determine whether the reconciliation was performed completely and accurately.	No exceptions noted.
	Inspected evidence of management review of the reconciliations to determine whether it was performed on a timely basis and to determine whether identified out of balance items were resolved on a timely basis.	No exceptions noted.

(continued)

Example Trust Organization's Controls	Service Auditor's Tests	Results of Tests
	Tested the program change controls, as described in control objective 20.	No exceptions noted.
Corporate actions are monitored and identified on a timely basis and are recorded in the corporation action system (CAS). The CAS properly values and records corporate actions.	Observed the daily processing and made inquiries of the corporate-actions unit personnel regarding the CAS's ability to identify and process corporate actions and the third-party sources for corporate actions that are interfaced directly to CAS.	No exceptions noted.
	Used online testing to determine whether corporate action data feeds are received completely and accurately.	No exceptions noted.
	Tested the proper recording for a sample of corporate actions per the CAS and the trust accounting system and the validity of the reported corporate actions.	No exceptions noted.
	Selected corporate actions occurring on a sample of days during the test period that had been recorded in business publications to ascertain whether they were properly recorded by the CAS.	No exceptions noted.
	Tested the program-change controls as described in control objective 20.	No exceptions noted.
Fixed-Income Securities. Assets with regular or fixed payments, such as corporate and government bonds, are set up on the SMAC at the time of acquisition. The SMAC automatically passes information about such assets to the automated income system (AIS).	For a sample of fixed-income security positions, compared the details of the security holdings (for example, coupon rate, maturity date, payment frequency and dates) per the SMAC to the AIS.	No exceptions noted.

Example Trust Organization's Controls	Service Auditor's Tests	Results of Tests
Only authorized personnel can set up securities on the SMAC at the time of acquisition.	For a sample of securities set up on the SMAC during the test period, compared the details of the security holding per the SMAC with the offering prospectus or comparable external documentation noting agreement.	No exceptions noted.
	Tested the logical access controls as described in control objective 24.	No exceptions noted.

Control Objective 3

Controls provide reasonable assurance that investment income is recorded accurately and timely.

Example Trust Organization's Controls	Service Auditor's Tests	Results of Tests
The security movement and control system (SMAC) and the automated income system (AIS) security holdings are automatically compared daily and, if necessary, reconciled by authorized individuals.	Made inquiries of management regarding the reconciliation procedures and the exception-resolution process.	No exceptions noted.
	Observed the performance of the daily reconciliation procedures.	No exceptions noted.
	Inspected a sample of reconciliations to assess the reasonableness, number, and age of the reconciling items.	No exceptions noted.
	Made inquiries of the income-collection personnel regarding the operation of the procedure through November 30, 20X1.	No exceptions noted.

(continued)

Example Trust Organization's Controls	Service Auditor's Tests	Results of Tests
The AIS accrues uncollected investment income and automatically passes the accrual information to the trust accounting system (TAS).	For a sample of various types of securities, recalculated the income accruals at September 30, 20X1, and compared the accrual per the AIS to the accrual per the TAS.	No exceptions noted.
	Tested the program change controls as described in control objective 20.	No exceptions noted.
Equity Securities. To properly record income on equity securities, a computer tape of dividends declared is prepared and transmitted to the AIS by an outside service on a daily basis. The computer tape of securities reporting dividends for the day is compared with asset holdings on the SMAC, and anticipated dividend maps are created by the AIS.	Made inquiries of the income-collection personnel regarding the source of daily dividend tapes and the procedures followed to interface with the SMAC and the AIS.	No exceptions noted.
	Observed the daily processing.	No exceptions noted.
	For a sample of equity securities, determined whether dividends declared were properly reflected in the AIS.	No exceptions noted.
	Tested the controls over data transmission, as described in control objective 26.	No exceptions noted.
Dividend income is credited to the customer on the ex-dividend date.	Selected a sample of dividends per the AIS and verified that they were recorded in the TAS on the ex-date.	No exceptions noted.

Note to Readers: The control objectives and controls included in this type 2 report are presented for illustrative purposes only and are not intended to represent a complete set of control objectives. Control objectives 1 through 3 and the related controls presented on the preceding pages cover certain aspects of transaction processing. This report would also contain other control objectives, for example, 4 through 19 related to transaction processing and the following control objectives related to CIS. The controls for control objectives 20–27 are not included in this illustrative report.

Control Objective 20

Controls provide reasonable assurance that changes to applications are authorized, tested, documented, approved and implemented in a complete, accurate, and timely manner.

Control Objective 21

Controls provide reasonable assurance that new applications being developed are authorized, tested, documented, approved, and implemented in a complete, accurate, and timely manner.

Control Objective 22

Controls provide reasonable assurance that changes to the existing system software and implementation of new system software are authorized, tested, documented, approved, implemented in a complete, accurate, and timely manner.

Control Objective 23

Controls provide reasonable assurance that physical access to computer resources is restricted to properly authorized and appropriate individuals.

Control Objective 24

Controls provide reasonable assurance that logical access to system resources (for example, programs, data, tables, and parameters) is restricted to properly authorized and appropriate individuals.

Control Objective 25

Controls provide reasonable assurance that job schedules are appropriately authorized and executed, and deviations, problems, and errors are identified, tracked, recorded, and resolved in a complete, accurate, and timely manner.

Control Objective 26

Controls provide reasonable assurance that data transmissions between Example Trust Organization and its users and other entities are from authorized sources and are complete, accurate, secure, and timely.

Control Objective 27

Controls provide reasonable assurance that data is backed up regularly and available for restoration in the event of processing errors and/or unexpected processing interruptions.

Appendix C

Illustrative Management Representation Letters

Illustrative Management Representation Letter for a Type 2 Engagement

[*Service Organization's Letterhead*]

[*Date*][1]

[*Service Auditor's Name*]

[*Address*]

In connection with your engagement to report on [*name of service organization*]'s (service organization) description of its [*type or name of*] system for processing user entities' transactions [*or identification of the function performed by the system*] throughout the period [*date*] to [*date*] (description) and the suitability of the design and operating effectiveness of controls to achieve the related control objectives stated in the description, we recognize that obtaining representations from us concerning the information contained in this letter is a significant procedure in enabling you to form an opinion on whether the description fairly presents the system that was designed and implemented throughout the period [*date*] to [*date*] and whether the controls related to the control objectives stated in the description were suitably designed and operating effectively throughout the period [*date*] to [*date*] to achieve those control objectives, based on the criteria described in our assertion.

We confirm, to the best of our knowledge and belief, as of [*date*], the date of your report, the following representations made to you during your examination.[2]

1. We reaffirm our assertion attached to [*or included in*] the description.
2. We have provided you with all relevant information and access to all information such as records and documentation, including service level agreements, of which the service organization is aware and that is relevant to the description and our assertion.
3. We have responded fully to all inquiries made to us by you during the examination.
4. We have disclosed to you any of the following of which we are aware:
    a. Instances of noncompliance with laws and regulations or uncorrected errors attributable to the service organization's management or employees that may affect one or more user entities
    b. Knowledge of any actual, suspected, or alleged intentional acts by the service organization's management or employees that could adversely affect the fairness of the

---

[1] This representation letter should be dated as of the date of the service auditor's report.

[2] If management does not provide one or more of the written representations requested by the service auditor, the service auditor should discuss the matter with management, evaluate the effect of such exclusions, and take appropriate action, which may include disclaiming the opinion or withdrawing from the engagement.

presentation of the description or the completeness or achievement of the control objectives stated in the description

c. Design deficiencies in controls

d. Instances in which controls have not operated as described

e. Any events subsequent to the period covered by the service organization's description of its system up to the date of your report that could have a significant effect on our assertion

5. We understand that your examination was conducted in accordance with attestation standards established by the American Institute of Certified Public Accountants and was designed for the purpose of expressing an opinion on the fairness of the presentation of the description and on the suitability of the design and operating effectiveness of the controls to achieve the related control objectives stated in the description, based on your examination, and that your procedures were limited to those that you considered necessary for that purpose.

[Add any other representations that may be required in the letter because of special circumstances, such as industry specific matters.]

To the best of our knowledge and belief, no changes in the [name of service organization]'s controls that are likely to be relevant to user entities' internal control over financial reporting or other factors that might significantly affect those controls have occurred subsequent to [date of the end of the period being reported on] and through the date of this letter.

———————————————————————
[Name and title of appropriate member of management]

———————————————————————
[Name and title of appropriate member of management]

———————————————————————
[Name and title of appropriate member of management]

Illustrative Management Representation Letter for a Type 1 Engagement

[Service Organization's Letterhead]

[Date][3]

[Service Auditor's Name]

[Address]

In connection with your engagement to report on [name of service organization]'s (service organization) description of its [type or name of] system for processing user entities' transactions [or identification of the function performed by the system] as of [date] (description) and the suitability of the design of controls to achieve the related control objectives stated in the description, we recognize that obtaining representations from us concerning the information contained

———————————————————————

[3] See footnote 1.

Illustrative Management Representation Letters 245

in this letter is a significant procedure in enabling you to form an opinion on whether the description fairly presents the system that was designed and implemented as of [date] and whether the controls related to the control objectives stated in the description were suitably designed to provide reasonable assurance that those control objectives would be achieved if the controls operated effectively as of [date], based on the criteria described in our assertion.

We confirm, to the best of our knowledge and belief, as of [date], the date of your report, the following representations made to you during your examination.[4]

1. We reaffirm our assertion attached to [or *included in*] the description.
2. We have provided you with all relevant information and access to all information such as records and documentation, including service level agreements, of which the service organization is aware and that is relevant to the description and our assertion.
3. We have responded fully to all inquiries made to us by you during the examination.
4. We have disclosed to you any of the following of which we are aware:
    a. Instances of noncompliance with laws and regulations or uncorrected errors attributable to the service organization's management or employees that may affect one or more user entities
    b. Knowledge of any actual, suspected, or alleged intentional acts by the service organization's management or employees that could adversely affect the fairness of the presentation of the description or the completeness or achievement of the control objectives stated in the description
    c. Design deficiencies in controls
    d. Instances in which controls have not operated as described
    e. Any events subsequent to the period covered by the service organization's description up to the date of your report that could have a significant effect on our assertion
5. We understand that your examination was conducted in accordance with attestation standards established by the American Institute of Certified Public Accountants and was designed for the purpose of expressing an opinion on the fairness of the presentation of the description and on the suitability of the design of the controls to achieve the related control objectives stated in the description, based on your examination, and that your procedures were limited to those that you considered necessary for that purpose.

[*Add any other representations that may be required in the letter because of special circumstances, such as industry specific matters.*]

To the best of our knowledge and belief, no changes in the service organization's controls that are likely to be relevant to user entities' internal control over financial reporting or other factors that might significantly affect those controls

---

[4] See footnote 2.

have occurred subsequent to [*date of the end of the period being reported on*] and through the date of this letter.

[*Name and title of appropriate member of management*]

[*Name and title of appropriate member of management*]

[*Name and title of appropriate member of management*]

Illustrative Management Representation Letter for a Type 2 Engagement in Which the Inclusive Method Is Used to Present the Subservice Organization

[*Subservice Organization's Letterhead*]

[*Date*][5]

[*Service Auditor's Name*]

[*Address*]

In connection with your engagement to report on [*name of service organization*]'s (service organization) and [*name of subservice organization*]'s (subservice organization) description of its [*type or name of*] system for processing user entities' transactions [*or identification of the function performed by the system*] throughout the period [*date*] to [*date*] (description) and on the suitability of the design and operating effectiveness of controls to achieve the related control objectives stated in the description, we recognize that obtaining representations from us concerning the information contained in this letter is a significant procedure in enabling you to form an opinion on whether the description fairly presents the system that was designed and implemented throughout the period [*date*] to [*date*] and whether the controls related to the control objectives stated in the description were suitably designed and operating effectively throughout the period [*date*] to [*date*] to achieve those control objectives, based on the criteria described in our assertion.

We confirm, to the best of our knowledge and belief, as of [*date*], the date of your report, the following representations made to you during your examination.[6]

1. We reaffirm our assertion attached to [*or included in*] the description.
2. We have provided you with all relevant information and access to all information such as records and documentation, including service level agreements, of which the service organization or subservice organization is aware and that is relevant to the description of the service organization's and subservice organization's system and our assertion.
3. We have responded fully to all inquiries made to us by you during the examination.
4. We have disclosed to you any of the following of which we are aware:

---

[5] See footnote 1.
[6] See footnote 2.

Illustrative Management Representation Letters

        a. Instances of noncompliance with laws and regulations or uncorrected errors attributable to the service organization's or subservice organization's management or employees that may affect one or more user entities

        b. Knowledge of any actual, suspected, or alleged intentional acts by the service organization's or subservice organization's management or employees that could adversely affect the fairness of the presentation of the description or the completeness or achievement of the control objectives stated in the description

        c. Design deficiencies in controls

        d. Instances in which controls have not operated as described

        e. Any events subsequent to the period covered by the service organization's and subservice organization's description up to the date of your report that could have a significant effect on management's assertion

    5. We understand that your examination was conducted in accordance with attestation standards established by the American Institute of Certified Public Accountants and was designed for the purpose of expressing an opinion on the fairness of the presentation of the description and on the suitability of the design of the controls to achieve the related control objectives stated in the description, based on your examination, and that your procedures were limited to those that you considered necessary for that purpose.

[Add any other representations that may be required in the letter because of special circumstances, such as industry specific matters.]

To the best of our knowledge and belief, no changes in the service organization's or subservice organization's controls that are likely to be relevant to user entities' internal control over financial reporting or other factors that might significantly affect those controls have occurred subsequent to [*date of end of period being reported on*] and through the date of this letter.

_____
[*Name and title of appropriate member of management*]

_____
[*Name and title of appropriate member of management*]

_____
[*Name and title of appropriate member of management*]

Appendix D

Illustrative Control Objectives for Various Types of Service Organizations

This appendix illustrates typical control objectives that may be encountered for the following outsourced services:

- General Computer Controls
- Application Service Provider
- Claims Processor
- Credit Card Payment Processor
- Investment Manager
- Payroll Processor
- Transfer Agent

The illustrative control objectives in this appendix are not meant to be all encompassing. Rather, they represent typical control objectives included in descriptions of a service organization's system for service organizations that provide the services listed in the preceding paragraph; these control objectives should be tailored to the particular service organization's business. Additionally, the service organization should review the entire appendix before determining which control objectives best fit its needs. For example, control objectives for transaction processing are presented in a number of ways in this appendix.

To assist the service organization is identifying applicable control objectives, the appendix contains footnotes designed to further explain and clarify the control objectives as written.

Control Objectives Related to General Computer Controls

General computer controls can be used alone or in combination with the business process controls depending on the nature of the outsourced service. The service organization tailors these control objectives to the services provided selecting control objectives that are likely to be relevant to controls over financial reporting at user entities.

Illustrative Control Objectives

Information Security

Controls provide reasonable assurance that

- logical access[1] to programs, data, and computer resources[2] is restricted to authorized and appropriate users.[3]
- physical access to computer and other resources[4] is restricted to authorized and appropriate personnel.

Change Management

Controls provide reasonable assurance that

- changes to application programs and related data management systems[5] are authorized, tested, documented, approved, and implemented to result in the complete, accurate, and timely[6] processing and reporting of transactions and balances.[7]
- network infrastructure[8] is configured as authorized to (1) support the effective functioning of application controls to result in valid, complete, accurate, and timely[9] processing and reporting of

---

[1] In assessing the logical access controls over programs, data, and computer resources, the service organization considers

- logical access controls that may affect the user entities' financial statements. Generally this would begin with the access controls directly over the application. If the effectiveness of application level security is dependent on the effectiveness of network and operating system controls, these are also considered. Controls over direct access to the databases or data files and tables are considered as well.
- the configuration and administration of security tools and techniques and monitoring controls designed to identify and respond to security violations in a timely manner.

[2] Computer resources include, but are not limited to, computer equipment, network equipment, storage media, and other hardware supporting the services provided by the service organization.

[3] Many service organizations have features enabling customers to directly access programs and data. In assessing the logical access controls over programs and data, the service organization considers the controls over security related to service organization personnel, the service organization's customers, and the customers' clients, as applicable, as well as the likely effect of these controls on user entities' financial statements.

[4] Computer resources include, but are not limited to, computer equipment, network equipment, storage media, and other hardware supporting the services provided by the service organization. Other resources include, but are not limited to, buildings, vaults, and negotiable instruments.

[5] Data management systems include database management systems, specialized data transport or communications software (often called middleware), data warehouse software, and data extraction or reporting software. Controls over data management systems may enhance user authentication or authorization, the availability of system privileges, data access privileges, application processing hosted within the data management systems, and segregation of duties.

[6] Timeliness may be relevant in particular situations, for example, when emergency changes are needed or when changes that would likely affect the user entities' information systems are being implemented to meet contractual requirements. Controls for emergency changes typically will be different from those for planned changes.

[7] This control objective is quite broad and should be tailored to the service organization's environment. For example, if the service organization has different controls for developing new applications or for making changes to applications or databases, it might be clearer to have separate control objectives for each of these.

[8] Network infrastructure includes all of the hardware, software, operating systems, and communication components within which the applications and related data management systems operate.

[9] Timeliness may be relevant in particular situations, for example, when emergency changes are needed or when changes are being implemented to meet contractual requirements.

transactions and balances and (2) protect data from unauthorized changes.[10]

Computer Operations

Controls provide reasonable assurance that

- application and system processing[11] are authorized and executed in a complete, accurate, and timely manner, and deviations, problems, and errors are identified, tracked, recorded, and resolved in a complete, accurate, and timely manner.

- data transmissions between the service organization and its user entities and other outside entities are from authorized sources and are complete, accurate, secure, and timely.[12]

Illustrative Control Objectives for an Application Service Provider[13]

In addition to the illustrative control objectives in this section, the control objectives in the preceding section, "Control Objectives Related to General Computer Controls," may be appropriate for an application service provider (ASP). An ASP may perform some or all of the following services for user entities:

- Providing a commonly used application that is accessed using an Internet protocol such as HTTPS or a Web browser

- Maintaining and operating the application software on behalf of its clients

- Owning, operating, and maintaining the servers that support the software

- Billing the ASP's clients on a "per use" basis

---

[10] Program change controls over network infrastructure include, as appropriate, the authorization, testing, documentation, approval, and implementation of changes to network infrastructure In assessing change management, the service organization considers the configuration and administration of the security tools and techniques, and monitoring controls designed to identify exceptions to authorized network infrastructure applications and data management systems (for example, database structures) and act upon them in a timely manner. If the service organization has different controls for new implementations or for making changes to either the infrastructure, applications, or data management systems, it might be clearer to have separate control objectives that address the controls over each type of infrastructure. There also may be separate control objectives for controls over new implementations and controls over changes to existing resources.

[11] The processing in this control objective refers to the batch processing of data. It typically does not include scheduling of file backups. Should the service organization have significant online, real-time processing, it may tailor this control objective or add a new control objective to address controls over the identification, tracking, recording, and resolution of problems and errors in a complete, accurate, and timely manner.

[12] This control objective also may be presented as part of logical access security or as part of the business operations related to data input or reporting.

[13] An application service provider (ASP) may provide software for functions, such as credit card payment processing or timesheet services, or may provide a particular financial application or solution package for a specific type of customer, such as a dental practice.

Illustrative Control Objectives

New Customer Setup and Maintenance

Controls provide reasonable assurance that

- new customers are established on the system in accordance with the applicable contracts and requirements.[14]
- maintenance instructions[15] are properly authorized, recorded completely and accurately, and processed timely.

Transaction Processing

Controls provide reasonable assurance that

- client transactions are initially recorded completely, accurately, and in a timely manner.
- invalid transactions and errors are identified, rejected, and correctly reentered into the system in a timely manner.
- client transactions are processed in a timely manner and reported in accordance with client specific business rules.
- the contents of data files remain complete and accurate, and the correct versions of all data files are used in processing.[16]

Customer Support

Controls provide reasonable assurance that

- production and business problems[17] are identified, recorded, analyzed, and resolved completely and in a timely manner.
- system availability is monitored, and issues are identified and resolved on a timely basis.

Illustrative Control Objectives for a Claims Processor

The illustrative control objectives in this section may be appropriate for a service organization that processes claims for user entities such as health insurers. The claims processor may perform some or all of the following services for user entities:

- Maintaining eligibility and enrollment information for customers

---

[14] Because most ASPs provide a service that is flexible and can be tailored to a particular customer, it is important that a new customer's business rules be properly established on the system to ensure that processing of its data is in accordance with expectations and requirements.

[15] Maintenance instructions are required to make changes to customer information.

[16] This control objective includes controls in place to ensure that the correct versions of the files are used to validate and update transactions entered for processing. This control objective can be used as a control objective related to any transaction processing. The service organization determines the nature and extent of the control objective and whether the control objective belongs with the business process controls or with the general computer controls, based on the services provided and the relevance of these controls to the preparation of financial statements.

[17] *Production and business problems* refer to the issues encountered by user entities the computer systems that support the services or the general business questions user entities may have regarding the services rendered.

AAG-ASO APP D

Illustrative Control Objectives for Various Types of Service Organizations

- Processing claims, such as insurance or medical benefit claims, on behalf of customers of the user entities based on contractual arrangements
- Adjudicating claims on behalf of their customers
- Processing bills to customers

Illustrative Control Objectives

Groups or Customers[18]

Controls provide reasonable assurance that group and benefits contracts[19] are authorized and that contract terms are established[20] and maintained in a complete, accurate, and timely manner.

Providers

Controls provide reasonable assurance that provider contracts are authorized and provider data is established[21] and maintained in a complete, accurate, and timely manner.

Enrollments[22]

Controls provide reasonable assurance that enrollment and eligibility information received from customers is authorized and processed in a complete, accurate, and timely manner.

Claims Receipts and Adjudication[23]

Controls provide reasonable assurance that

- claims are received only from authorized sources.
- claims received are entered in a complete, accurate, and timely manner.
- claims are validated and adjudicated in a complete, accurate, and timely manner.
- claim adjustments are authorized and processed in a complete, accurate, and timely manner.
- claim actions for subrogation, coordination of benefits, and other recoveries for submitted claims are processed in a complete, accurate, and timely manner.[24]

---

[18] Group or customer information would include information such as member benefits, global pricing, and reimbursement schedules.

[19] Group and benefits contracts may refer to physician, dental, and other health care provider agreements.

[20] Establishing this information in the application software may also be referred to as installation of the group and customer information.

[21] Establishing this information in the application software may also be referred to as installation of the provider information.

[22] Enrollment information may be received through various channels either electronically via fax, Internet, or specific feeds or as a hard copy. If the controls for each channel are different, the service organization should consider establishing individual control objectives for each channel.

[23] Claims may be received in paper or electronic format. The service organization may establish separate control objectives for each method of receipt, depending on the control activities and the needs of the user entities.

[24] This control objective should include controls over the collection and payment to the appropriate parties of any funds recovered. In such cases, the service organization may consider a separate control objective for these controls.

Claim Payments and Billing Operations

Controls provide reasonable assurance that

- adjudicated claims are paid in a complete, accurate, and timely manner.
- customer invoices and funding requests are authorized and processed in a complete, accurate, and timely manner.
- reports provided to customers are complete, accurate, and timely.

Illustrative Control Objectives for a Credit Card Payment Processor

The illustrative control objectives in this section may be appropriate for a service organization that processes credit card payments. The credit card payment processor may perform some or all of the following services for user entities:

- Processing transactions initiated by credit card holders at authorized merchants
- Paying merchants for authorized credit card transactions
- Preparing and managing cardholder invoices and payments
- Managing and reporting potential fraudulent transactions
- Managing blank cards and personal identification numbers
- Reporting to the merchants and credit bureaus
- Managing rewards programs

Illustrative Control Objectives

Merchant and Sales Partner Setup

Controls provide reasonable assurance that

- new merchant accounts are authorized and set up accurately and completely, according to the contractual agreement.
- new sales partners are authorized and set up accurately and completely, according to the contracted agreement.
- changes to merchant and sales partner data are authorized and processed accurately, completely, and in a timely manner.

Authorization Processing

Controls provide reasonable assurance that authorization requests are received, transmitted to the processing system, properly evaluated based on the cardholder's available credit and current account status, and that the authorization or denial message received from the processor is transmitted back to the originating merchant.

Transaction Processing

Controls provide reasonable assurance that

- all and only authorized transactions are processed and settled completely, accurately, timely, and only once.
- all data is validated and errors are rejected and reported for user entity follow up and correction.

Illustrative Control Objectives for Various Types of Service Organizations   255

- transmissions to and from clearinghouses are accurate, complete, and valid.
- the contents of data files remain complete and accurate, and the correct versions of all data files are used in processing.[25]

Chargebacks and Refunds

Controls provide reasonable assurance that all and only authorized chargeback or refund data received is processed and settled accurately, completely, and in a timely manner.

Merchant Payments

Controls provide reasonable assurance that

- amounts payable to merchants are computed completely and accurately, and amounts due are transferred to the merchant using the appropriate remittance option.
- sales partner residual amounts are calculated completely, accurately, and in a timely manner.

Client Settlement

Controls provide reasonable assurance that

- the system is in balance prior to settlement with the interchange clearinghouses and the client's processing, and net settlement amounts are properly computed.
- all outgoing wire transfers are properly authorized and all incoming wire transfers are received accurately and on a timely basis.

Cardholder Accounting

Controls provide reasonable assurance that

- transactions are processed in accordance with system descriptions and posted completely and accurately to the correct cardholder accounts in a timely manner.
- problem accounts (for example, accounts that exceed limits or are delinquent) are identified by the system and reported to the client for follow up.

Cardholder Inquiry Management

Controls provide reasonable assurance that cardholder inquiries are logged and processed to permit a timely response to the inquiry or resolution of the problem.

Cardholder Statements and Communication

Controls provide reasonable assurance that cardholder statements are generated on a timely basis and distributed no more than 10 days after statement generation.

---

[25] This control objective includes controls in place to ensure that the correct versions of the files are used to validate and update transactions entered for processing. This can be used as a control objective related to any transaction processing. The service organization determines the nature and extent of the control objective and whether the control objective belongs with the business process controls or the IT general controls, based on the services provided and the relevance of these controls to the preparation of financial statements.

AAG-ASO APP D

Risk Management

Controls provide reasonable assurance that periodic credit reviews, fraud investigations, and collections are routinely performed, monitored, and reported for follow up on a timely basis.

Rewards

Controls provide reasonable assurance that cardholder rewards processing functions and calculations are performed in accordance with system descriptions and all and only authorized transactions are posted to the correct cardholder account in the proper accounting period.

Blank Cards

Controls provide reasonable assurance that

- blank cards are safeguarded and protected from unauthorized use.
- blank cards are not lost or duplicated during the personalization process.
- adjustments to inventory levels are authorized by appropriate individuals.

Personal Identification Numbers

Controls provide reasonable assurance that

- personal identification numbers (PINs) used to authenticate cash advance transactions are protected from unauthorized disclosure.
- cardholder PINs generated and mailed during the card issuance process are protected from unauthorized disclosure.
- access to the information used to produce the PIN mailer, as well as the printed mailers, is restricted to authorized and appropriate individuals.
- client-defined encryption keys are protected from unauthorized disclosure.

Report Statement Generation and Distribution

Controls provide reasonable assurance that client reports are complete, accurate, and distributed on a timely basis.

Credit Bureau Reporting

Controls provide reasonable assurance that month-end credit bureau reporting files are complete, accurate, and transmitted to the appropriate credit bureaus in the agreed-upon timeframes and in accordance with client specifications.

Illustrative Control Objectives for an Investment Manager

The illustrative control objectives in this section may be relevant to asset management service organizations. They also can be adapted and used, as appropriate, for investment management organizations, trust organizations, hedge fund advisers, or hedge fund of fund advisers.

The control objectives included in this section would be appropriate for an investment manager that performs some or all of the following functions:

- Initiating and executing purchase and sale transactions, either by specific direction from the client or under discretionary authority granted by the client
- Determining whether transactions comply with guidelines and restrictions
- Reconciling records of security transactions and portfolio holdings, for each client, to statements received from the custodian
- Reporting to the customer on portfolio performance and activities

Illustrative Control Objectives

New Account Setup and Administration

Controls provide reasonable assurance that

- new accounts are authorized and set up in accordance with client instructions and guidelines in a complete, accurate, and timely manner.
- account modifications are authorized and implemented in a complete, accurate, and timely manner.
- new account holdings and cash are reconciled to custodian bank statements in a complete, accurate, and timely manner.[26]

Security Setup

Controls provide reasonable assurance that new securities and changes to existing securities are authorized and entered in the security master file in a complete, accurate, and timely manner.

Investment Transaction Processing

Controls provide reasonable assurance that

- investment transaction instructions are authorized and entered into the system in a complete, accurate, and timely manner.
- portfolio guidelines are monitored and exceptions are identified and resolved in a complete, accurate, and timely manner.[27]
- allocations are approved by a portfolio manager.
- block orders are allocated to clients on a pro-rata basis for equity trades and a predetermined allocation for fixed income trades.

---

[26] The service organization may consider establishing a separate control objective that covers the applicable controls related to account conversions or new account set up or including these controls as part of the reconciliation control objective listed subsequently.

[27] This control objective may also be combined with the first control objective in this section by including the additional wording "investment transactions are authorized and executed in accordance with the portfolio policies."

Confirmation, Affirmation, or Settlement

Controls provide reasonable assurance that

- investments are settled in a complete, accurate, and timely manner.
- custodians are informed of transactions in a complete, accurate, and timely manner.

Loans

Controls provide reasonable assurance that

- loans and collateral are authorized and processed and recorded in a complete, accurate, and timely manner.
- collateral on loans is invested in accordance with the lender agreement and recorded and monitored in a complete, accurate, and timely manner.
- loan repayments are processed and recorded completely, accurately, and in a timely manner.

Pricing

Controls provide reasonable assurance that

- security prices are received from an authorized source and updated in a complete, accurate, and timely manner.
- price overrides are authorized and processed in a complete, accurate, and timely manner.

Corporate Actions

Controls provide reasonable assurance that corporate action notices are identified and received from an authorized source and are updated in the system in a complete, accurate, and timely manner.

Investment Income

Controls provide reasonable assurance that

- interest, dividend, and other income information is received from an authorized source and recorded in a complete, accurate, and timely manner.
- cash received for interest and dividends is processed in a complete, accurate, and timely manner.

Money Movement

Controls provide reasonable assurance that money movement (receipts and disbursements) is authorized and processed in a complete, accurate, and timely manner.[28]

Custodian Reconciliation

Controls provide reasonable assurance that security positions and cash balances reflected in the portfolio accounting system are reconciled in a complete,

---

[28] The service organization may consider establishing separate control objectives for receipts and disbursements.

accurate, and timely manner to actual positions and balances held by custodians.[29]

Fees
Controls provide reasonable assurance that investment management fees and other expenses are authorized, calculated, and recorded in a complete, accurate, and timely manner.[30]

Net Asset Valuation
Controls provide reasonable assurance that net asset values are authorized and calculated in a complete, accurate, and timely manner.

Account Statements and Client Reports
Controls provide reasonable assurance that account statements and client reports detailing client account holdings and market values are complete, accurate, and provided to clients in a timely manner.

Illustrative Control Objectives for a Payroll Processor

The illustrative control objectives included in this section may be appropriate for a service organization that performs some or all of the following functions:

- Processing various types of payroll
- Calculating payroll tax liabilities for federal, state, and local jurisdictions
- Preparing and submitting payroll tax returns and compliance reports
- Printing and distributing payroll checks
- Calculating workers' compensation, state unemployment, and other benefit costs
- Making payments to appropriate agencies and other third parties

Illustrative Control Objectives

Payroll Processing Setup
Controls provide reasonable assurance that

- client requirements are properly authorized and set up in the system completely, accurately, and timely.
- payroll taxes and other deductions are authorized and set up completely, accurately, and timely.
- payroll tax and other deductions tables are updated completely, accurately, and timely, as required.
- changes to client requirements, payroll taxes, and other deductions are updated completely, accurately, and timely.

---

[29] The service organization may consider establishing separate control objectives for security positions and cash balances.

[30] A service organization may establish separate control objectives for the accrual of the expense and the payment of the expense.

AAG-ASO APP D

Payroll Data Authorization and Recording

Controls provide reasonable assurance that

- payroll data is received from authorized sources.
- payroll data is recorded completely, accurately, and timely.
- rejected transactions and errors are identified, reported to user entities for follow up, and properly reentered into the system on a timely basis.
- payroll transactions are processed completely, accurately, and timely.
- payroll adjustments are received from authorized sources and processed completely, accurately, and timely.
- data transmissions to or from clients are authorized, complete, accurate, secure, and processed timely.

Payroll Processing

Controls provide reasonable assurance that

- processing is scheduled and performed appropriately in accordance with client specifications; deviations from the schedule are identified and resolved timely.[31]
- payroll deductions and tax withholdings are calculated by the system in accordance with statutory and client specifications.

Reporting

Controls provide reasonable assurance that

- payroll checks, pay statements, and reports are produced completely, accurately, and timely in accordance with client specifications.
- disbursements of direct deposits are authorized, complete, accurate, and processed timely.
- data transmissions of money movement and files from the system to outside parties and to the clients' banks are authorized, complete, accurate, secure, and processed in a timely manner.

Illustrative Control Objectives for a Transfer Agent

The illustrative control objectives in this section may be appropriate for a transfer agent that performs transfer or registrar functions. Transfer agents may also perform securities custodial services or execute trades based on authorized instructions. If this is the case, refer to the control objectives under the heading, "Illustrative Control Objectives for an Investment Manager," for control objectives that may apply to these functions.

---

[31] This control objective includes controls in place to ensure that the correct versions of the files are used to validate and update transactions entered for processing. This can be used as a control objective related to any transaction processing. The service organization determines the nature and extent of the control objective and whether the control objective belongs with the business process controls or the IT general controls, based on the services provided and the relevance of these controls to the preparation of financial statements.

The transfer function may include any of the following tasks:

- Processing old certificates that are properly presented and endorsed in good deliverable form
- Reviewing legal documents to ensure that they are complete and appropriate, before transferring the securities
- Notifying the presenter if the documents are incomplete, or returning rejected documents that are incorrect, insufficient, or otherwise unexecutable
- Issuing new certificates in the name of the new owner
- Making appropriate adjustments to the issuer's shareholder records

The registrar function may include any of the following tasks:

- Monitoring the issuance of authorized securities
- Ensuring that the issuance of the new securities will not cause the authorized number of shares in an issue to exceed the total permitted to be issued
- Ensuring that the number of shares transferred corresponds to the number of shares canceled

As part of the transfer and registrar functions previously noted, a transfer agent's functions may also include

- maintaining records of the name and address of each security holder, the number of securities owned by each security holder, the certificate numbers corresponding to a security holder's position, the issue date of the security certificate, and the cancellation date of the security certificate, if applicable.
- logging and tracking shareholder and issuer correspondence, and resolving inquiries in the correspondence in a timely manner.
- acting as paying agent for cash dividends, dividend reinvestments, and distributions of stock dividends and stock splits.
- monitoring and controlling the proxy voting process.

Illustrative Control Objectives

Issuer and Shareholder Setup and Maintenance

Controls provide reasonable assurance that

- new clients are authorized and established in the system in a complete, accurate, and timely manner in accordance with client instructions.
- changes to client data are authorized and updated in the system in a complete, accurate, and timely manner.
- shareholder account information and maintenance instructions are authorized and recorded in a complete, accurate, and timely manner.

Securities Transfers

Controls provide reasonable assurance that

- only eligible securities can be transferred, and stock transfers are processed accurately, completely, and on a timely basis.
- subscriptions are authorized and processed in a complete, accurate, and timely manner.
- exchanges are authorized and processed in a complete, accurate, and timely manner.
- redemptions are authorized and processed in a complete, accurate, and timely manner.
- total outstanding share balances are accurately maintained and reconciled in a timely manner.

Dividends

Controls provide reasonable assurance that

- dividend rates are authorized and payments are calculated and distributed to shareholders of record in a complete, accurate, and timely manner.
- dividend reinvestments are processed only for authorized individuals and the processing is complete, accurate, and timely.
- dividend check replacement requests are processed completely, accurately, and in a timely manner.

Safeguarding Assets

Controls provide reasonable assurance that securities and checks in the custody or possession of the transfer agent are protected from loss, misappropriation, or other unauthorized use.

Certificate Replacements

Controls provide reasonable assurance that

- notifications of lost or stolen certificates are authorized and recorded in a complete, accurate, and timely manner.
- certificate replacement requests are authorized and processed completely, accurately, and in a timely manner.

Appendix E

Comparison of SOC 1, SOC 2, and SOC 3 Engagements and Related Reports

Statement on Standards for Attestation Engagements (SSAE) No. 16, *Reporting on Controls at a Service Organization* (AICPA, *Professional Standards*, AT sec. 801), provides guidance to practitioners engaged to report on controls at a service organization that are likely to be relevant to user entities' internal control over financial reporting. A practitioner may be engaged to examine and report on controls at a service organization relevant to subject matter other than user entities' internal control over financial reporting, for example, controls that affect the privacy of information processed for user entities' customers. The applicable attestation standard for such engagements may vary, depending on the subject matter. To make practitioners aware of the various professional standards and guides available to them for examining and reporting on controls at a service organization and to help practitioners select the appropriate standard or guide for a particular engagement, the AICPA has introduced the term *service organization controls (SOC) reports*. The following are designations for three such engagements and the source of the guidance for performing and reporting on them:

- SOC 1: SSAE No. 16 and the AICPA Guide *Service Organizations: Applying SSAE No. 16*, Reporting on Controls at a Service Organization
- SOC 2: The AICPA Guide *Reporting on Controls at a Service Organization Relevant to Security, Availability, Processing Integrity, Confidentiality, or Privacy*
- SOC 3: TSP section 100, *Trust Services Principles, Criteria, and Illustrations for Security, Availability, Processing Integrity, Confidentiality, and Privacy* (AICPA, *Technical Practice Aids*)

The following table identifies differences between SOC 1, SOC 2, and SOC 3 engagements and related reports:

	SOC 1 Reports	SOC 2 Reports	SOC 3 Reports
Under what professional standard is the engagement performed?	Statement on Standards for Attestation Engagements No. 16, *Reporting on Controls at a Service Organization* (AICPA, *Professional Standards*, AT sec. 801). The AICPA Guide *Service Organizations:*	AT section 101, *Attest Engagements* (AICPA, *Professional Standards*). The AICPA Guide *Reporting on Controls at a Service Organization Relevant to Security, Availability, Processing Integrity, Confidentiality, or Privacy*.	AT section 101. TSP section 100, *Trust Services Principles, Criteria, and Illustrations for Security, Availability, Processing Integrity, Confidentiality, and Privacy* (AICPA, *Technical Practice Aids*), provides the

(continued)

	SOC 1 Reports	SOC 2 Reports	SOC 3 Reports
	Applying SSAE No. 16, Reporting on Controls at a Service Organization.		criteria for evaluating the design and operating effectiveness of controls in these engagements, as well as the criteria for the content of a privacy notice.
What is the subject matter of the engagement?	Controls at a service organization relevant to user entities' internal control over financial reporting.	Controls at a service organization relevant to security, availability, processing integrity, confidentiality, or privacy. If the report addresses the privacy principle, the service organization's compliance with the commitments in its statement of privacy practices.	Controls at a service organization relevant to security, availability, processing integrity, confidentiality, or privacy. If the report addresses the privacy principle, the service organization's compliance with the commitments in its privacy notice.[1]
What is the purpose of the report?	To provide the auditor of a user entity's financial statements with information and a CPA's opinion	To provide management of a service organization, user entities, and other specified parties with information and a CPA's opinion about controls at	To provide interested parties with a CPA's opinion about controls at the service

---

[1] Entities that collect personal information generally establish and document their policies regarding the nature of the information they collect and how that information will be used, retained, disclosed, and disposed of or anonymized. These policies and the entity's commitment to adhere to them when included in a written communication to individuals about whom personal information is collected (sometimes referred to as *data subjects*) are referred to as a *privacy notice*. A privacy notice also includes information about such matters as the purpose of collecting the information; the choices individuals have related to their personal information; the security of such information; and how individuals can contact the entity with inquiries, complaints, and disputes related to their personal information. When a user entity collects personal information from individuals, it typically provides a privacy notice to those individuals.

When a service organization is involved in any of the phases of the personal information life cycle, it may or may not be responsible for providing a privacy notice to the individuals about whom information is collected. If the user entity is responsible for providing the privacy notice, the service organization provides a statement of privacy practices to the user entities that includes the same types of policies and commitments as would be included in a privacy notice, but the statement is written from the perspective of the service organization communicating its privacy-related policies and commitments to the user entities. The statement of privacy practices provides a basis for the user entities to prepare a privacy notice to be sent to individuals or for ensuring that the service organization has appropriate practices for meeting the existing privacy commitments of user entities.

Comparison of SOC 1, SOC 2, and SOC 3 Engagements and Related Reports

	SOC 1 Reports	SOC 2 Reports	SOC 3 Reports
	about controls at a service organization that may be relevant to a user entity's internal control over financial reporting. It enables the user auditor to perform risk assessment procedures and, if a type 2 report is provided, to use the report as audit evidence that controls at the service organization are operating effectively.	the service organization relevant to security, availability, processing integrity, confidentiality, or privacy. A type 2 report that addresses the privacy principle also provides information and a CPA's opinion about the service organization's compliance with the commitments in its statement of privacy practices.	organization relevant to security, availability, processing integrity, confidentiality, or privacy. A report that addresses the privacy principle also provides a CPA's opinion about the service organization's compliance with the commitments in its privacy notice.
What are the components of the report?	A description of the service organization's system. A written assertion by management of the service organization regarding the description of the service organization's system; the suitability of the design of the controls; and in a type 2 report, the operating effectiveness of the controls in achieving the specified control objectives. A service auditor's report that contains an opinion on the fairness of the presentation of the description of the service	A description of the service organization's system. A written assertion by management of the service organization regarding the description of the service organization's system; the suitability of the design of the controls; and in a type 2 report, the operating effectiveness of the controls in meeting the applicable trust services criteria. If the report addresses the privacy principle, the assertion also covers the service organization's compliance with the commitments in its statement of privacy practices. A service auditor's report that contains an opinion on the fairness of the presentation of the description of the service design of the controls to meet the applicable trust	A description of the system and its boundaries[2] or, in the case of a report that addresses the privacy principle, a copy of the service organization's privacy notice. A written assertion by management of the service organization regarding the effectiveness of controls in meeting the applicable trust services criteria and, if the report addresses the privacy principle, compliance with the commitments in the service organization's privacy notice. A service auditor's report on whether the entity maintained

(continued)

---

[2] These descriptions are typically less detailed than the descriptions in service organization controls (SOC) 1 or SOC 2 reports and are not covered by the practitioner's opinion.

	SOC 1 Reports	SOC 2 Reports	SOC 3 Reports
	organization's system; the suitability of the design of the controls to achieve specified control objectives; and in a type 2 report, the operating effectiveness of those controls. In a type 2 report, a description of the service auditor's tests of the controls and the results of the tests.	services criteria; and in a type 2 report, the operating effectiveness of those controls. If the report addresses the privacy principle, the service auditor's opinion on whether the service organization complied with the commitments in its statement of privacy practices. In a type 2 report, a description of the service auditor's tests of controls and the results of the tests. In a type 2 report that addresses the privacy principle, a description of the service auditor's tests of the service organization's compliance with the commitments in its statement of privacy practices and the results of those tests.	effective controls over its system as it relates to the principle being reported on (that is, security, availability, processing integrity, confidentiality, or privacy), based on the applicable trust services criteria. If the report addresses the privacy principle, the service auditor's opinion on whether the service organization complied with the commitments in its privacy notice.
Who are the intended users of the report?	Management of the service organization; user entities during some or all of the period covered by the report (for type 2 reports) and user entities as of a specified date (for type 1 reports); and auditors of the user entities' financial statements.	Management of the service organization and other specified parties who have sufficient knowledge and understanding of the following: • The nature of the service provided by the service organization • How the service organization's system interacts with user entities, subservice organizations, and other parties • Internal control and its limitations • Complementary user-entity controls and how they interact with related controls at the service organization to meet the applicable trust services criteria	Anyone.

AAG-ASO APP E

Comparison of SOC 1, SOC 2, and SOC 3 Engagements and Related Reports

	SOC 1 Reports	SOC 2 Reports	SOC 3 Reports
		• The applicable trust services criteria • The risks that may threaten the achievement of the applicable trust services criteria and how controls address those risks	
Who are the intended users of the report?	Management of the service organization; user entities during some or all of the period covered by the report (for type 2 reports) and user entities as of a specified date (for type 1 reports); and auditors of the user entities' financial statements.	Management of the service organization and other specified parties who have sufficient knowledge and understanding of the following: • The nature of the service provided by the service organization • How the service organization's system interacts with user entities, subservice organizations, and other parties • Internal control and its limitations • Complementary user-entity controls and how they interact with related controls at the service organization to meet the applicable trust services criteria • The applicable trust services criteria • The risks that may threaten the achievement of the applicable trust services criteria and how controls address those risks	Anyone.

AAG-ASO APP E

Appendix F

Other Referenced Authoritative Standards

Standards Referenced in Statement on Standards for Attestation Engagements (SSAE) No. 16, *Reporting on Controls at a Service Organization*

Section Number	Title of Standard	Paragraph Reference in SSAE No. 16
AT 101	Attest Engagements	2, 4, 10, 13, 41, A2–A3, A6, A22, A61–A62
AT 201	Agreed-Upon Procedures Engagements	A4
AT 601	Compliance Attestation	2
AU 314	Understanding the Entity and Its Environment and Assessing the Risks of Material Misstatement	A24, A29, A32
AU 322	The Auditor's Consideration of the Internal Audit Function in an Audit of Financial Statements	35
AU 324	Service Organizations	1
AU 350	Audit Sampling	25
AU 561	Subsequent Discovery of Facts Existing at the Date of the Auditor's Report	43
SQCS 7	A Firm's System of Quality Control	A58

Professional Standards Referenced in the AICPA Guide Service Organizations—Applying SSAE No. 16, Reporting on Controls at a Service Organization (SOC 1)

Section Number	Title of Standard	Chapter in the Guide					
		Preface	1	2	3	4	5
AT 101	Attest Engagements	X	X		X	X	X
AT 201	Agreed-Upon Procedures Engagements		X		X		
AT 501	An Examination of an Entity's Internal Control Over Financial Reporting That Is Integrated With an Audit of Its Financial Statements			X			
AT 601	Compliance Attestation		X				
AU 314	Understanding the Entity and Its Environment and Assessing the Risks of Material Misstatement	X	X	X	X	X	
AU 318	Performing Audit Procedures in Response to Assessed Risks and Evaluating the Audit Evidence Obtained			X			
AU 322	The Auditor's Consideration of the Internal Audit Function in an Audit of Financial Statements				X	X	
AU 324	Service Organizations	X	X	X	X		
AU 325	Communicating Internal Control Related Matters Identified in an Audit			X			
AU 326	Audit Evidence					X	
AU 339	Audit Documentation					X	
AU 350	Audit Sampling					X	
AU 561	Subsequent Discovery of Facts Existing at the Date of the Auditor's Report						X
SQCS 7	A Firm's System of Quality Control					X	